MOON HANDBOOKS

MONTEREY & CARMEL

outer bay exhibit at Monterey Bay Aquarium

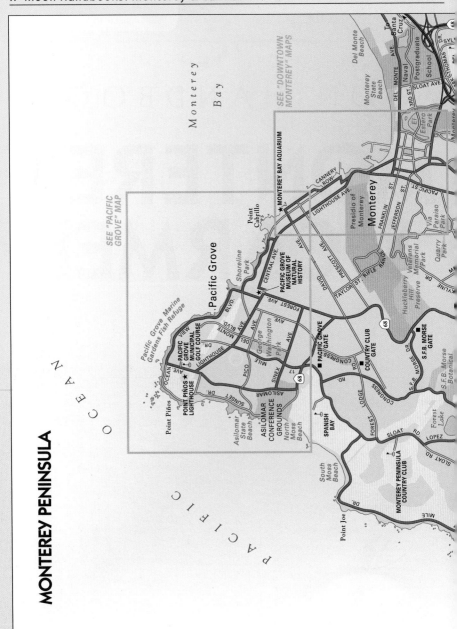

MONTEREY PENINSULA

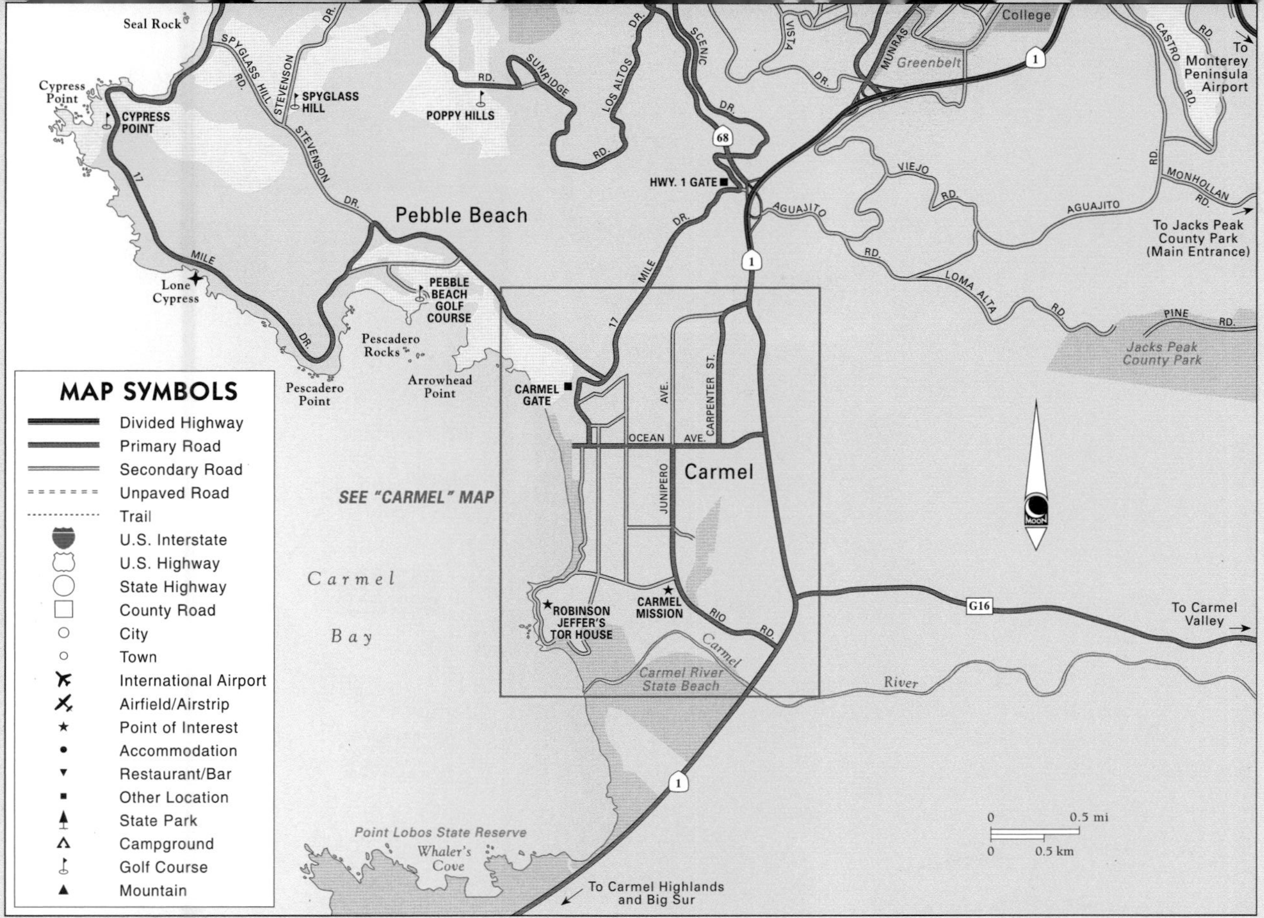

MAP SYMBOLS

▬▬	Divided Highway
▬▬	Primary Road
▬▬	Secondary Road
▬▬	Unpaved Road
········	Trail
◖	U.S. Interstate
◯	U.S. Highway
▢	State Highway
◯	County Road
●	City
○	Town
✈	International Airport
✈	Airfield/Airstrip
★	Point of Interest
●	Accommodation
◄	Restaurant/Bar
■	Other Location
▲	State Park
Λ	Campground
⌖	Golf Course
▲	Mountain

SEE "CARMEL" MAP

Carmel Bay

Point Lobos State Reserve

Whaler's Cove

Cypress Point

Lone Cypress

CYPRESS POINT

Seal Rock

17 MILE DR.

SPYGLASS HILL RD.

STEVENSON DR.

SPYGLASS HILL

STEVENSON

Pebble Beach

POPPY HILLS

POPPY HILLS RD.

SUNRIDGE RD.

LOS ALTOS DR.

SCENIC RD.

68

HWY. 1 GATE

Pescadero Point

Pescadero Rocks

Arrowhead Point

PEBBLE BEACH GOLF COURSE

CARMEL GATE

17 MILE DR.

OCEAN AVE.

JUNIPERO AVE.

CARPENTER ST.

Carmel

CARMEL MISSION

ROBINSON JEFFER'S TOR HOUSE

Carmel River State Beach

RIO RD.

To Carmel Highlands and Big Sur

1

River

G16

To Carmel Valley

0   0.5 mi
0   0.5 km

AGUAJITO RD.

LOMA ALTA RD.

VIEJO RD.

AGUAJITO RD.

PINE RD.

MONHOLAN

VISTA DR.

MUNRAS

Greenbelt

College

1

CASTRO RD.

Jacks Peak County Park

To Jacks Peak County Park (Main Entrance)

To Monterey Peninsula Airport

Colton Hall, Monterey

MOON HANDBOOKS

MONTEREY
& CARMEL

FIRST EDITION

KIM WEIR

AVALON
TRAVEL

Moon Handbooks: Monterey & Carmel
First Edition

Kim Weir

Published by
Avalon Travel Publishing
1400 65th Street, Suite 250
Emeryville, CA 94608, USA

Please send all comments, corrections,
additions, amendments, and critiques to:

Moon Handbooks: Monterey & Carmel
AVALON TRAVEL PUBLISHING
1400 65TH SREET, SUITE 250
EMERYVILLE, CA 94608, USA
email: atpfeedback@avalonpub.com
www.moon.com

Text © 2002 by Kim Weir.
Illustrations and maps © 2002 by Avalon Travel Publishing, Inc.
All rights reserved.
Photos, some illustrations, and some text are used by permission
and are the property of their original copyright owners.

Printing History
1st edition—October 2002
5 4 3 2 1

ISBN: 1-56691-445-0
ISSN: 1539-9656

Editor: Ellen Cavalli
Series Manager: Erin Van Rheenen
Copy Editors: Valerie Blanton Sellers, Peg Goldstein
Graphics Coordinators: Melissa Sherowski, Erika Howsare
Production Coordinator: Alvaro Villanueva
Cover Designer: Kari Gim
Interior Designers: Amber Pirker, Alvaro Villanueva, Kelly Pendragon
Map Editors: Naomi Adler Dancis, Olivia Solís, Mike Ferguson
Cartographers: Annette Olson, Bart Wright, Mike Morgenfeld
Proofreader: Erika Howsare
Indexer: Rachel Kuhn

Front cover photo: © John Elk III

Distributed by Publishers Group West

Printed in China through Colorcraft Ltd., Hong Kong

ABOUT THE AUTHOR
Kim Weir

Kim Weir was born in Southern California but raised in far Northern California. For a time Kim's father operated a beer distributorship, a weekend job that required rattling around the foothills and mountains of Northern California in a Falstaff delivery van. Some of the author's earliest summer adventures involved washboarding with her dad down back roads, the stench of stale beer rising from flats of empties. Kim Weir has happily explored California byways ever since—typically without the beer.

Since childhood Kim Weir has struggled with herself over the relative merits of travel and books, as well as the challenges of hitching the two together. Take her first trip to the Grand Canyon. Upon arrival her parents insisted that the 11-year-old put away James Michener long enough to at least get out and take a good look at that #!^%#$*&!! hole in the ground. Kim did better than that, though. She walked all the way down into the canyon that day—and back up—toting copies of *The Source, Gone with the Wind,* and other tomes in her knapsack as useful ballast against the wind.

Kim Weir's love of California, travel, and doorstopper-quality books finally came together in 1990 with the publication of the comprehensive and colorful *Moon Handbooks: Northern California*. Other big books soon followed, including Moon's Southern California, Coastal California, and California guides. Smaller books have joined the lineup, too, including the Moon guide to Monterey and Carmel.

Among other worthwhile pursuits Kim has worked as an editor at Scholars Press and as communications director for the Faculty Association of California Community Colleges (FACCC). She holds a degree in environmental studies and analysis from CSU, Chico and is now pursuing her MFA in Creative Writing. She is also an active member of the Society of American Travel Writers (SATW).

Contents

Maps

Keeping Current

This being California, most things change faster than traffic lights. Because of this unfortunate fact of life in the fast lane of travel writing, comments, corrections, inadvertent omissions, and update information are always greatly appreciated. Though every effort was made to keep all current facts corralled and accounted for, it's no doubt true that *something* (most likely, a variety of things) will already be inaccurate by the time the printer's ink squirts onto the paper at press time.

Just remember this: whatever you divulge may indeed end up in print—so think twice before sending too much information about your favorite hole-in-the-wall restaurant, cheap hotel, or "secret" world's-best swimming hole or hot springs. Once such information falls into the hands of a travel writer, it probably won't be a secret for long. Address all correspondence to:

Moon Handbooks: Monterey & Carmel
Avalon Travel Publishing
1400 65th Street, Suite 250
Emeryville, CA 94608, USA
atpfeedback@avalonpub.com

Introduction

One Bay, Many Worlds

The only remembered line of the long-lost Ohlone people's song of world renewal, "dancing on the brink of the world," has a particularly haunting resonance around Monterey Bay. Here, in the unfriendly fog and ghostly cypress along the untamed coast, the native "coast people" once danced. Like the area's vanished dancers, Monterey Bay is a mystery: everything seen, heard, tasted, and touched only hints at what remains hidden.

The first mystery is magnificent Monterey Bay itself, almost 60 miles long and 13 miles wide. Its offshore canyons, grander than Arizona's Grand Canyon, are the area's most impressive (if unseen) feature: the bay's largest submarine valley dips to 10,000 feet, and the adjacent tidal mudflats teem with life.

A second mystery is how cities as different as Carmel, Monterey, and Santa Cruz could take root and thrive near Monterey Bay.

The monied Monterey Peninsula is fringed by shifting sand dunes and some of the state's most ruggedly wild coastline. Carmel, or Carmel-by-the-Sea, is where Clint Eastwood once made everybody's day as mayor. (Inland is Carmel Valley, a tennis pro playground complete with shopping centers. The Carmel Highlands hug the coast on the way south to Big Sur.) Noted for its storybook cottages and spectacular crescent beach, Carmel was first populated by artists, writers, and other assorted bohemians who were shaken out of San Francisco following the 1906 earthquake. Yet the founding of Carmel would have to be credited to Father Junípero Serra and the Carmelite friars of the Carmel Mission, built here in 1771, the second Spanish mission in California.

MELISSA SHEROWSKI

surfers at Spanish Bay,
Pacific Grove

The original version of the Carmel mission was built the previous year, however, near the Spanish presidio in what is now Monterey. The cultured community of Monterey would later boast California's first capital, first government building, first federal court, first newspaper, and—though other towns also claim the honor—first theater. Between Carmel and Monterey is peaceful Pacific Grove, where alcohol has been legal only since the 1960s—and where the annual Monarch butterfly migration is big news.

Just inland from the Monterey Peninsula is the agriculturally rich Salinas Valley, boyhood stomping grounds of John Steinbeck. Steinbeck's focus on Depression-era farm workers unleashed great local wrath—all but forgotten and almost forgiven since his fame has subsequently benefited area tourism. South of Salinas and east of Soledad is Pinnacles National Monument, a fascinating volcanic jumble and almost "the peak" for experienced rock climbers. Not far north, right on the San Andreas Fault, is Mission San Juan Bautista, where Jimmy Stewart and Kim Novak conquered his fear of heights in Alfred Hitchcock's *Vertigo*. Nearby are the headwaters of San Benito Creek, where lucky rockhounds might stumble upon some gem-quality, clear or sapphire-blue samples of the state's official gemstone, benitoite, found only here. Also in the neighborhood is Gilroy, self-proclaimed garlic capital of the world.

Once working-class Santa Cruz has the slightly seedy Boardwalk, sandy beaches, good swimming, surfers, and—helped along by the presence of UC Santa Cruz—an intelligent and open-minded social scene. Nearby are the redwoods, waterfalls, and mountain-to-sea hiking trails of Big Basin, California's first state park, plus the Año Nuevo coastal area, until recently the world's only mainland mating ground for the two-ton northern elephant seal.

CALIFORNIA AS AN ISLAND IN SPACE AND TIME

California's isolated, sometimes isolationist human history has been shaped more by the land itself than by any other fact. That even early European explorers conceived of the territory as an island is a fitting irony, since in many ways—particularly geographically, but also in the evolutionary development of plant and animal life—California was, and still is, an island in both space and time.

The third-largest state in the nation, California spans 10 degrees of latitude. With a meandering 1,264-mile-long coastline, the state's western boundary is formed by the Pacific Ocean. Along most of California's great length, just landward from the sea, are the rumpled and eroded mountains known collectively as the Coast Ranges.

MONTEREY BAY AS FISH HOOK

The Bay of Monterey has been compared by no less a person than General Sherman to a bent fish-hook; and the comparison, if less important than the march through Georgia, still shows the eye of a soldier for topography. Santa Cruz sits exposed at the shank; the mouth of the Salinas River is at the middle of the bend; and Monterey itself is cosily ensconced beside the barb. Thus the ancient capital of California faces across the bay, while the Pacific Ocean, though hidden by low hills and forest, bombards her left flank and rear with never-dying surf. In front of the town, the long line of sea-beach trends north and northwest, and then westward to inclose the bay. The waves which lap so quietly about the jetties of Monterey grow louder and larger in the distance; you can see the breakers leaping high and white by day; at night the outline of the shore is traced in transparent silver by the moonlight and the flying foam; and from all around, even in quiet weather, the low, distant, thrilling roar of the Pacific hangs over the coast and the adjacent country like smoke above a battle.

Excerpted from Robert Louis Stevenson's "The Old Pacific Capital,"
Fraser's Magazine, *1880*

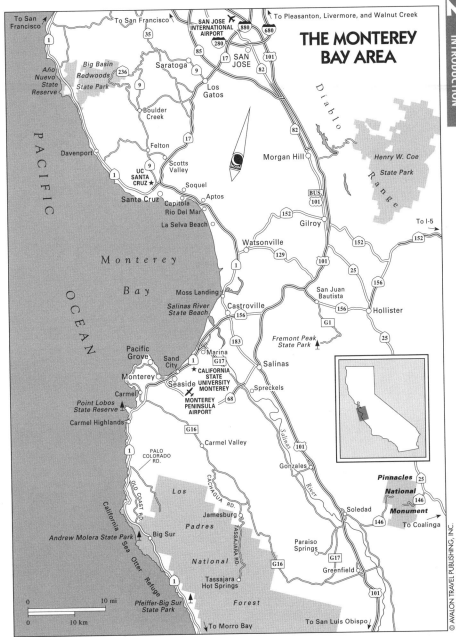

THE MONTEREY BAY AREA

Perched along the Pacific Ring of Fire, California is known for its violent volcanic nature and for its earthquakes. Native peoples have always explained the fiery, earth-shaking temperament of the land quite clearly, in a variety of myths and legends, but the theory of plate tectonics is now the most widely accepted scientific creation story. According to this theory, the earth's crust is divided into 20 or so major solid rock (or lithospheric) "plates" upon which both land and sea ride. The interactions of these plates are ultimately responsible for all earth movement, from continental drift and landform creation to volcanic explosions and earthquakes.

Most of California teeters on the western edge of the vast North American Plate. The adjacent Pacific Plate, which first collided with what is now California about 250 million years ago, grinds slowly but steadily northward along a line more or less defined by the famous San Andreas Fault (responsible for the massive 1906 San Francisco earthquake and fire as well as the more recent shake-up in 1989). Plate movement itself is usually imperceptible: at the rate things are going,

within 10 million years Los Angeles will slide north to become San Francisco's next-door neighbor. But the steady friction and tension generated between the two plates sometimes creates special events. Every so often sudden, jolting slippage occurs between the North American and Pacific Plates in California—either along the San Andreas or some other fault line near the plate border—and one of the state's famous earthquakes occurs. Though most don't amount to much, an average of 15,000 earthquakes occur in California every year.

A still newer theory augments the plate tectonics creation story, suggesting a much more fluid local landscape—that California and the rest of the West literally "go with the flow," in particular the movement of hot, molten rock beneath the earth's crust. "Flow" theory explains the appearance of earthquake faults where they shouldn't be, scientists say, and also explains certain deformations in the continental crust. According to calculations published in the May 1996 edition of the journal *Nature,* the Sierra Nevada currently flows at the rate of one inch every three years.

Monterey Peninsula coastline

MONTEREY BAY BY LAND AND BY SEA

Much of the redwood country from San Francisco to Big Sur resembles the boulder-strewn, rough-and-tumble coast of far Northern California. Here the Pacific Ocean is far from peaceful; posted warnings about dangerous swimming conditions and undertows are no joke. Inland, the San Andreas Fault menaces, veering inland from the eastern side of the Coast Ranges through the Salinas Valley and on to the San Francisco Bay Area.

The Monterey Peninsula

Steinbeck captured the mood of the Monterey Peninsula in *Tortilla Flats*—"The wind. . . drove the fog across the pale moon like a thin wash of watercolor. . . . The treetops in the wind talked huskily, told fortunes and foretold deaths." The peninsula juts into the ocean 115 miles south of San Francisco and forms the southern border of Monterey Bay. The north shore sweeps in a crescent toward Santa Cruz and the Santa Cruz Mountains; east is the oak- and pine-covered Santa Lucia Range, rising in front of the barren Gabilan ("Sparrow Hawk") Mountains beloved by Steinbeck. Northward are the ecologically delicate Monterey Bay Dunes, now threatened by off-road vehicles and development. To the south, the piney hills near Point Pinos and Asilomar overlook rocky crags and coves dotted with wind-sculpted trees; farther south, beyond Carmel and the Pebble Beach golf mecca, is Point Lobos, said to be Robert Louis Stevenson's inspiration for Spyglass Hill in *Treasure Island*.

Monterey "Canyon"

Discovered in 1890 by George Davidson, Monterey Bay's submerged valley teems with sealife: bioluminescent fish glowing vivid blue to red, squid, tiny rare octopi, tentacle-shedding jellyfish, and myriad microscopic plants and animals. This is one of the most biologically prolific spots on the planet. Swaying with the ocean's motion, dense kelp thickets are home to sea lions, seals, sea otters, and giant Garibaldi "goldfish." Opal-eyed perch in schools of hundreds swim by leopard sharks and bottom fish. In the understory near the rocky ocean floor live abalones, anemones, crabs, sea urchins, and starfish.

Students of Monterey Canyon geology quibble over the origins of this unusual underwater valley. Computer-generated models of canyon creation suggest that the land once used to be near Bakersfield and was carved out by the Colorado River; later it shifted westward due to plate tectonics. More conventional speculation focuses on the creative forces of both the Sacramento and San Joaquin Rivers, which perhaps once emptied at Elkhorn Slough, Monterey Canyon's principal "head."

However Monterey Canyon came to be, it is now centerpiece of the 5,312-square-mile

CALIFORNIA COASTAL NATIONAL MONUMENT

The new California Coastal National Monument runs the entire length of the California coast between Oregon and Mexico, extends out from the shoreline 12 nautical miles, and includes thousands of islands, rocks, exposed reefs, and pinnacles. Established by President Bill Clinton on January 11, 2000, for the primary purpose of protecting the coast's important "biological and geological values," the new monument is cooperatively managed by the U.S. Bureau of Land Management (BLM) with other federal, state, and local government agencies as well as universities and private interests.

The monument's incalculable acreage begins just off shore and ends at the boundary between the continental shelf and the continental slope, taking in all land masses above mean high tide not otherwise protected. The sensitive offshore geology provides feeding and nesting habitat for breeding seabirds—gulls, the endangered California least tern, and the brown pelican, among them—and mammal species including the threatened southern sea otter. Offshore vegetation is also protected

For more information about the California Coastal National Monument, contact: Bureau of Land Management, Hollister Field Office, tel. 831/630-5000, www.ca.blm.gov/hollister/coastal_monument.html.

Monterey Bay National Marine Sanctuary which extends some 400 miles along the coast, from San Francisco's Golden Gate in the north to San Simeon in the south. Established in 1992 after a 15-year political struggle, this federally sanctioned preserve is now protected from off-shore oil drilling, dumping of hazardous materials, the killing of marine mammals or birds, jet skis, and aircraft flying lower than 1,000 feet. As an indirect result of its federal protection, Monterey Bay now boasts a total of 18 marine research facilities.

Big Sur: A Contrary Coast

Farther south the land itself is unfriendly, at least from the human perspective. The indomitable, unstable terrain—with its habit of sliding out from under whole hillsides, houses, highways, and hiking trails during winter rains and otherwise at the slightest provocation—has made the area hard to inhabit. But despite its contrariness, the central coast, that unmistakable pivotal point between California's north and south, successfully blends both.

Though the collective Coast Ranges continue south through the region, here the terrain takes on a new look. Northern California's redwoods begin to thin out, limiting themselves to a few large groves in Big Sur country and otherwise straggling south a short distance beyond San Simeon, tucked into hidden folds in the rounded coastal mountains. Where redwood country ends, either the grasslands of the dominant coastal oak woodlands begin or the chaparral takes over, in places almost impenetrable. Even the coastline reflects the transition—the rocky rough-and-tumble shores along the Big Sur coast transform into tamer beaches and bluffs near San Simeon and points south.

Los Padres National Forest inland from the coast is similarly divided into two distinct sections. The northernmost (and largest) Monterey County section includes most of the rugged 100-mile-long Santa Lucia Range and its Ventana Wilderness. The southern stretch of Los Padres, essentially the San Luis Obispo and Santa Barbara backcountry, is often closed to hikers and backpackers during the summer due to high fire danger.

Another clue that the north-south transition occurs here is water or, moving southward, the increasingly obvious lack of it. Though both the North and South Forks of the Little Sur River, the Big Sur River a few miles to the south, and other northern waterways flow to the sea throughout

ON MONTEREY FOG

It is the Pacific that exercises the most direct and obvious power upon the climate. At sunset, for months together, vast, wet, melancholy fogs arise and come shoreward from the ocean. From the hilltop above Monterey the scene is often noble, although it is always sad. The upper air is still bright with sunlight; a glow still rests upon the Gabelano Peak; but the fogs are in possession of the lower levels; they crawl in scarves among the sand-hills; they float, a little higher, in clouds of a gigantic size and often of a wild configuration; to the south, where they have struck the seaward shoulder of the mountains of Santa Lucia, they double back and spire up skyward like smoke. Where their shadow touches, color dies out of the world. The air grows chill and deadly as they advance. The trade-wind freshens, the trees begin to sigh, and all the windmills in Monterey are whirling and creaking and filling their cistern with the brackish water of the sands. It takes but a little while till the invasion is complete. The sea, in its lighter order, has submerged the earth. Monterey is curtained in for the night in thick, wet, salt, and frigid clouds; so to remain till day returns; and before the sun's rays slowly disperse and retreat in broken squadrons to the bosom of the sea. And yet often when the fog is thickest and most chill, a few steps out of town and up the slope the night will be dry and warm and full of inland perfume.

Excerpted from Robert Louis Stevenson's
"The Old Pacific Capital,"
Fraser's Magazine, *1880*

COURTESY MONTEREY COUNTY CONVENTION & VISITORS BUREAU/© JULIE ARMSTRONG

native plant species on the Pacific Grove coast

the year, as does the Cuyama River in the south (known as the Santa Maria River as it nears the ocean), most of the area's streams are seasonal. But off-season hikers, beware: even inland streams with a six-month flow are not to be dismissed during winter and spring, when deceptively dinky creekbeds can become death-dealing torrents overnight.

Major lakes throughout California's central coast region are actually water-capturing reservoirs, including Lake San Antonio, known for its winter bald eagle population, Lake Nacimiento on the other side of the mountains from San Simeon, and Santa Margarita Lake east of San Luis Obispo near the headwaters of the Salinas River.

Monterey Bay Climate

The legendary California beach scene is almost a fantasy here—almost but not quite. Surfers can be seen here year-round, though often in wetsuits. Sunshine warms the sands (between storms) from fall to early spring, but count on fog from late spring well into summer. Throughout the Monterey Bay area it's often foggy and damp, though clear summer afternoons can get hot; the warmest months along the coast are August, September, and October. (Sunglasses, suntan lo-

tion, and hats are prudent, but always bring a sweater.) Inland, expect hotter weather in summer, colder in winter. Rain is possible as early as October, though big storms don't usually roll in until December.

NATURAL MONTEREY BAY
Monterey Bay Flora

California's central coast region, particularly near Monterey, exhibits tremendous botanic diversity. Among the varied vascular plant species found regionally is the unusually fast-growing Monterey pine, an endemic tree surviving in native groves only on hills and slopes near Monterey, Cambria, and Año Nuevo, as well as on Guadalupe and Cedros Islands off the coast of Baja, Mexico. It's now a common landscaping tree—and the world's most widely cultivated tree, grown commercially for its wood and pulp throughout the world. The unusual Monterey cypress is a relict, a specialized tree that can't survive beyond the Monterey Peninsula. The soft green Sargent cypress is more common, ranging south to Santa Barbara along the coast and inland. The Macnab cypress is found only on poor serpentine soil, as are Bishop pines, which favor swamps

THE CURSE OF MONTEREY PINE PITCH CANKER

Eons ago, Monterey pines blanketed much of California's coastline. Today, only a few native stands remain in California—and within a decade at least 80 percent of these trees will be gone, done in by a fungus. That fungus, known as pine pitch canker, was first discovered in Alameda and Santa Cruz Counties in the mid-1980s. Since then, it has spread throughout California, via contaminated lumber and firewood, Christmas trees, infected seedlings, pruning tools, insects, birds, and wind; there is no known cure. Afflicted trees first turn brown at the tips of their branches, then erupt in pitchy spots; within the tree, water and nutrients are choked off. The open infections attract bark beetles, which bore into tree trunks and lay eggs, an invasion that hastens tree death. Usually within four years, an infected tree is completely brown and lifeless. The United Nations has declared the Monterey pine an endangered species.

Enjoy the majestic groves of Monterey pine near Monterey while they still stand, endangered as they are both by disease and further development plans. Also take care to avoid being an unwitting "carrier" for the disease; don't cart home any forest products as souvenirs. Pine pitch canker has been found in at least eight other species, including the Ponderosa pine, sugar pine, and Douglas fir, though it appears the Monterey pine is most susceptible. The California Department of Forestry is justifiably concerned that the disease will soon spread—or is already spreading—into the Sierra Nevada and California's far northern mountains.

knobcone pine, with its tenaciously closed "fire-climax" cones. Other regional trees include the California wax myrtle, the aromatic California laurel or "bay" tree, the California nutmeg, the tan oak (and many other oaks), plus alders, big-leaf maples, and occasional madrones. Eucalyptus trees thrive in the coastal locales where they've been introduced.

Whales and Sharks

The annual migration of the California gray whale, the state's official mammal, is big news all along the coast. From late October to January, these magnificent 20- to 40-ton creatures head south from Arctic seas toward Baja (pregnant females first). Once the mating season ends, males, newly pregnant females, and juveniles start their northward journey from February to June. Females with calves, often traveling close to shore, return later in the year, between March and July. Once in a blue moon, when the krill population mushrooms in winter, rare blue whales will feed in and around Monterey Bay and north to the Farallon Islands.

A wide variety of harmless sharks are common in Monterey Bay. Occasionally, 20-foot-long great white sharks congregate here to feed on sea otters, seals, and sea lions. Unprovoked attacks on humans do occur (to surfers more often than scuba divers) but are very rare. The best protection is avoiding ocean areas where great whites are common, such as Año Nuevo Island at the north end of the bay; don't go into the water alone and never where these sharks have been recently sighted.

Seals and Sea Lions

Common in these parts is the California sea lion; the females are the barking "seals" popular in aquatic amusement parks. True seals don't have external ears, and the gregarious, fearless creatures swimming in shallow ocean waters or lolling on rocky jetties and docks usually do. Also here are northern or Steller's sea lions—which roar instead of bark and are usually lighter in color. Chunky harbor seals (no ear flaps, usually with spotted coats) more commonly haul out on sandy beaches, since they're awkward on land. Less common but rapidly increasing in numbers along

and the slopes from "Huckleberry Hill" near Monterey south to the San Luis Range near Point Buchon and Santa Barbara County.

Coastal redwoods thrive near Santa Cruz and south through Big Sur. Not as lusty as those on the north coast, these redwoods often keep company with Douglas fir, pines, and a dense understory of shade-loving shrubs. Other central coast trees include the Sitka spruce and beach pines. A fairly common inland tree is the chaparral-loving the California coast—viewable at the Año Nuevo rookery during the winter mating and birthing season—are the massive northern elephant seals, the largest pinnipeds (fin-footed mammals) in the Western Hemisphere. One look at the two- or three-ton, 18-foot-long males explains the creatures' common name: their long, trunklike noses serve no real purpose beyond sexual identification, as far as humans can tell.

Sea Otters: Declining Again?

The California sea otter population, listed as a threatened species under the federal Endangered Species Act, is dwindling again—and scientists aren't quite sure why. Infectious disease, coastal pollution (which also contaminates food supplies), and entrapment in wire fishing pots are all suspected reasons.

In centuries past, an estimated one-time population of almost 16,000 sea otters along the California coast was decimated by eager fur hunters. A single otter pelt was worth upward of $1,700 in 1910, when it was generally believed that sea otters were extinct here. But a small pod survived off the coast near Carmel, a secret well guarded by biologists until the Big Sur Highway opened in 1938. Until recently, the sea otters seemed to be making a comeback; their range had expanded widely up and down the coast. Much to the chagrin of the south coast commercial shellfish industry, sea otters had even started moving south past Point Concepcion into shellfish waters. Even so, the number of sea otters is declining. In 1995, the U.S. Fish and Wildlife Service counted 2,377. By 1998, the population had dropped to 1,937—and some 200 dead otters washed ashore on area beaches, for reasons unknown.

Sea otters frolic north along the coast to Jenner in Sonoma County, and south to Cambria (and beyond). Watching otters eat is quite entertaining; to really see the show, binoculars are

WATCHING THE CALIFORNIA GRAYS

A close-up view of the California gray whale, the state's official (and largest) mammal, is a life-changing experience. As those dark, massive, white-barnacled heads shoot up out of the ocean to suck air, spray with the force of a firehose blasts skyward from blowholes. Watch the annual migration of the gray whale all along the California coast—from "whale vistas" on land or by boat.

Despite the fascination they hold for Californians, little is yet known about the gray whale. Once endangered by whaling—as so many whale species still are—the grays are now swimming steadily along the comeback trail. Categorized as baleen whales—which dine on plankton and other small aquatic animals sifted through hundreds of fringed, hornlike baleen plates—gray whales were once land mammals that went back to sea. In the process of evolution, they traded their fore and hind legs for fins and tail flukes. Despite their fishlike appearance, these are true mammals: warm-blooded, air-breathing creatures who nourish their young with milk.

Adult gray whales weigh 20–40 tons, not counting a few hundred pounds of parasitic barnacles. Calves weigh in at a hefty 1,500 pounds at birth and can expect to live for 30–60 years. They feed almost endlessly from April to October in the arctic seas between Alaska and Siberia, sucking up sediment and edible creatures on the bottom of shallow seas, then squeezing the excess water and silt out their baleen filters. Fat and sassy with an extra 6–12 inches of blubber on board, early in October they head south on their 6,000-mile journey to the warmer waters of Baja in Mexico.

Pregnant females leave first, traveling alone or in small groups. Larger groups make up the rear guard, with the older males and nonpregnant females engaging in highly competitive courtship and mating rituals along the way—quite a show for human voyeurs. The rear guard becomes the frontline on the way home: males, newly pregnant females, and young gray whales head north from February to June. Cows and calves migrate later, between March and July.

BEACHCOMBING BY THE BAY

Beachcombing is finest in February and March after winter storms—especially if searching for driftwood, agates, jasper, and jade—and best near the mouths of creeks and rivers. While exploring tidepools, refrain from taking or turning over rocks, which provide protective habitat for sea critters (the animals don't like being molested, either). Since low tide is the time to "do" the coast, coastwalkers, beachcombers, and clammers need a current tide table (useful for a range of about 100 coastal miles), available at local sporting goods stores and dive shops. Also buy a California fishing license, since a permit is necessary for taking mussels, clams, and other sea life. But know the rules: many regulations are enforced to protect threatened species, and others are for *human* well-being. There's an annual quarantine on mussels, for example, usually from May through October, to protect omnivores from nerve paralysis caused by the seasonal "red tide."

usually necessary. Carrying softball-sized rocks in their paws, sea otters dive deep to dislodge abalone, mussels, and other shellfish, then return to the surface and leisurely smash the shells and dine while floating on their backs, "rafting" at anchor in forests of seaweed. The playful sea creatures feed heartily, each otter consuming about two and a half tons of seafood per year—much to the dismay of commercial shellfish interests.

Brown Pelicans

The ungainly looking, web-footed brown pelicans—most noticeable perched on pilings or near piers in and around harbors—are actually incredibly graceful when diving for their dinners. A squadron of 25 or more pelicans "gone fishin'" first glide above the water then, one by one, plunge dramatically to the sea. Brown pelicans are another back-from-the-brink success story, their numbers increasing dramatically since DDT (highly concentrated in fish) was banned. California's pelican platoons are often accompanied by greedy gulls, somehow convinced they can snatch fish from the fleshy pelican pouches if they just try harder.

Other Seabirds

Seabirds are the most obvious seashore fauna; besides brown pelicans you'll see long-billed curlews, ashy petrels nesting on cliffs, surf divers like grebes and scooters, and various gulls. Pure white California gulls are seen only in winter here (they nest inland), but yellow-billed western gulls and the scarlet-billed, white-headed Heermann's gulls are common seaside scavengers. Look for the hyperactive, self-important sandpipers along the shore, along with dowitchers, plovers, godwits, and avocets. Killdeers—so named for their "ki-dee" cry—lure people and other potential predators away from their clutches of eggs by feigning serious injury.

Tidepool Life

The twice-daily ebb of ocean tides reveals an otherwise hidden world. Tidepools below rocky headlands are nature's aquariums, sheltering abalone, anemones, barnacles, mussels, hermit crabs, starfish, sea snails, sea slugs, and tiny fish. Distinct zones of marine life are defined by the tides. The highest, or "splash," zone is friendly to creatures naturally protected by shells from desiccation, including black turban snails and hermit crabs. The intertidal zones

BOB RACE

brown pelican

(high and low) protect spiny sea urchins and the harmless sea anemone. The "minus tide" or surf zone—farthest from shore and almost always underwater—is home to hazardous-to-human-health stingrays (particularly in late summer, watch where you step) and jellyfish.

The History of the Golden Dream

FOREIGNERS PLANT THEIR FLAGS

The first of California's official explorers were the Spanish. Though Hernán Cortés discovered a land he called California in 1535, Juan Rodríguez Cabrillo—actually a Portuguese, João Rodrigues Cabrilho—first sailed the coast of Alta California ("upper," as opposed to "lower" or Baja California, which then included all of Mexico) and rode at anchor off its shores.

But the first European to actually set foot on California soil was the English pirate Sir Francis Drake, who in 1579 came ashore somewhere along the coast (exactly where is still disputed, though popular opinion suggests Point Reyes) and whose maps—like others of the day—reflected his belief that the territory was indeed an island. Upon his return to England, Drake's story of discovery served primarily to stimulate Spain's territorial appetites. Though Sebastián Vizcaíno entered Monterey Bay in 1602 (18 years before the Pilgrims arrived at Plymouth), it wasn't until 1746 that even the Spanish realized California wasn't an island. San Francisco Bay was discovered by Gaspar de Portolá in 1769 and the settlements of San Diego and Monterey were founded in 1770.

Though the Spanish failed to find California's mythical gold, between 1769 and 1823 they did manage to establish 21 missions (sometimes with associated presidios) along El Camino Real or "The Royal Road" from San Diego to Sonoma. And from these busy mission ranch outposts, maintained by the free labor of "heathen" natives, Spain grew and manufactured great wealth.

But even at its zenith, Spain's supremacy in California was tenuous. The territory was vast and relatively unpopulated. Even massive land grants—a practice continued under later Mexican rule—did little to allay colonial fears of success-ful outside incursions. Russian imperialism, spreading east into Siberia and Central Asia, and then to Alaska and an 1812 outpost at Fort Ross on the north coast, seemed a clear and present danger—and perhaps actually would have been, if the Russians' agricultural and other enterprises hadn't failed. And enterprising Americans, at first just a few fur trappers and traders, were soon in the neighborhood.

As things happened, the challenge to Spain's authority came from its own transplanted population. Inspired by the news in 1822 that an independent government had been formed in Mexico City, young California-born Spanish ("Californios") and independence-seeking resident Spaniards declared Alta California part of the new Mexican empire. By March 1825, when California proper officially became a territory of the Republic of Mexico, the new leadership had already achieved several goals, including secularizing the missions and "freeing" the associated native neophytes (not officially achieved until 1833), which in practice meant that most became servants elsewhere. The Californios also established an independent military and judiciary, opened the territory's ports to trade, and levied taxes.

During the short period of Mexican rule, the American presence was already prominent. Since even Spain regularly failed to send supply ships, Yankee traders were always welcome in California. In no time at all, Americans had organized and dominated the territory's business sector, established successful ranches and farms, married into local families, and become prominent citizens. California, as a possible political conquest, was becoming increasingly attractive to the United States.

Gen. John C. Frémont, officially on a scientific expedition but perhaps acting under secret orders from Washington (Frémont would never say),

MONTEREY BAY IN 1786

Monterey Bay, bounded by Point Año Nuevo to the north and Cypress Point [Point of Pines] to the south, presents an opening of eight leagues in this direction, and nearly six in depth to the eastward, where the land is low and sandy. The sea rolls to the foot of the sand dunes which border the coast and produces a noise which we heard when more than a league distant. The lands to the north and south are elevated and covered with trees. Vessels intending to stop here must follow the southern shore. When they have doubled the Point of Pines, which projects to the north, the presidio appears in view, and they may drop anchor in ten fathoms of water, within and rather near to the point, which shelters them from the winds of the sea. The Spanish vessels which make a long stay at Monterey usually approach within one or two cable lengths of the shore and moor in six fathoms of water by making fast to an anchor, which they bury in the sand on the beach. They have then nothing to fear from the south winds, which are sometimes strong, but not at all dangerous, as they blow from the coast. . . .

It is impossible to describe either the number of whales with which we were surrounded, or their familiarity. They spouted within every half minute within half a pistol shot of our frigates, and cause a most annoying stench. We were unacquainted with this property in the whale, but the inhabitants informed us that the water thrown out by them is impregnated with this offensive smell, which is perceived at a considerable distance. . . .

The sea was covered with pelicans. It appears that these birds never fly more than five or six leagues from the land, and navigators who encounter them during a fog may be certain of being no further distant from it. We saw them for the first time in Monterey Bay, and I have since been informed that they are common over the whole coast of California. The Spaniards call them *alcatraz*. . . .

We found at Monterey a Spanish commissary, Mr. Vicente Vasadre y Vega, who had brought orders to the governor enjoining him to collect all the sea otter skins of his four presidios and the ten missions, all of which the government itself reserves to itself the exclusive commerce. Mr. Fages assured me that twenty thousand might be collected annually. . . .The sea otter is an amphibious animal as common along the whole coast of America, from the 28th to the 60th degree of north latitude, as the seal on the coast of Labrador and in Hudson's Bay.

Excerpted from Monterey in 1786:
The Journals of Jean François de La Pèrouse.

had been stirring things up in California since 1844—engaging in a few skirmishes with the locals or provoking conflicts between Californios and American citizens in California. Though the U.S. declared war on Mexico on May 13, 1846, Frémont and his men apparently were unaware of that turn of events and took over the town of Sonoma for a short time in mid-June, raising the secessionist flag of the independent—but very short-lived—Bear Flag Republic.

With Californios never mustering much resistance to the American warriors, Commodore John C. Sloat sailed unchallenged into Monterey Bay on July 7, 1848, raised the Stars and Stripes above the Custom House in town, and claimed California for the United States. Within two days, the flag flew in both San Francisco and Sonoma, but it took some time to end the statewide skirmishes. It took even longer for official Americanization—and statehood—to proceed. The state constitution established, among other things, California as a "free" state (but only to prevent the unfair use of slave labor in the mines). This upset the balance of congressional power in the nation's anti-slavery conflict and indirectly precipitated the Civil War. Written in Monterey, the new state's constitution was adopted in October 1849 and ratified by voters in November.

GOLD IN THEM THAR HILLS

California's legendary gold was real, as it turned out. And the Americans found it—but quite by accident. The day James Marshall, who was building a lumber mill on the American River for John Sutter, discovered flecks of shiny yellow metal in the mill's tailrace seemed otherwise quite ordinary. But that day, January 24, 1848, changed everything—in California and in the world.

As fortune seekers worldwide succumbed to gold fever and swarmed into the Sierra Nevada foothills in 1849, modern-day California began creating itself. In the no-holds-barred search for personal freedom and material satisfaction (better yet, unlimited wealth), something even then recognizable as California's human character was also taking shape: the belief that anything is possible, for anyone, no matter what one's previous circumstances would suggest. Almost everyone wanted to entertain that belief. (Karl Marx was of the opinion that the California gold rush was directly responsible for delaying the Russian revolution.) New gold dreamers—all colors and creeds—came to California, by land and by sea, to take a chance on themselves and their luck. The luckiest ones, though, were the merchants and businesspeople who cashed in on California's dream by mining the miners.

Because of the discovery of gold, California skipped the economically exploitive U.S. territorial phase typical of other western states. With almost endless, indisputable capital at hand, Californians thumbed their noses at the Eastern financial establishment almost from the start: they could exploit the wealth of the far West themselves. And exploit it they did—mining not only the earth, but also the state's forests, fields, and water wealth. Wild California would never again be the same.

Almost overnight, "civilized" California became an economic sensation. The state was essentially admitted to the union on its own terms—because California was quite willing to go its own way and remain an independent entity otherwise. The city of San Francisco grew from a sleepy enclave of 500 souls to a hectic, hell-bent business and financial center of more than 25,000 within two years. Other cities built on a foundation of prosperous trade included the inland supply port of Sacramento. Agriculture, at first important for feeding the state's mushrooming population of fortune hunters, soon became a de facto gold mine in its own right. Commerce expanded even more rapidly with the completion of the California-initiated transcontinental railroad and with the advent of other early communications breakthroughs such as the telegraph. California's dreams of prosperity became self-fulfilling prophecies. And as California went, so went the nation.

THE MONTEREY BAY STORY: CALIFORNIA FIRSTS

Cabrillo spotted Point Piños and Monterey Bay in 1542. Sixty years later, Vizcaíno sailed into the bay and named it for the viceroy of Mexico, the count of Monte-Rey. A century later came Portolá and Father Crespi, who, later joined by Father Junípero Serra, founded both Monterey's presidio and the mission at Carmel.

The quiet redwood groves near Santa Cruz remained undisturbed by civilization until the arrival of Portolá's expedition in 1769. The sickly Spaniards made camp in the Rancho de Osos section of what is now Big Basin, experiencing an almost miraculous recovery in the valley they called Cañada de Salud (Canyon of Health). A Spanish garrison and mission were soon established on the north end of Monterey Bay.

Father Junípero Serra

By the end of the 1700s, the entire central California coast was solidly Spanish, with missions, pueblos, and military bases or presidios holding the territory for the king of Spain. With the Mexican revolution, Californio loyalty went with the new administration closer to home. But the people here carried on their Spanish cultural heritage despite the secularization of the missions, the increasing influence of cattle ranches, and the foreign flood (primarily American) that threatened existing California tradition. Along the rugged central coast just south of the boisterous and booming gold rush port of San Francisco, the influence of this new wave of "outsiders" was felt only later and locally, primarily near Monterey and Salinas.

Monterey: Capital of Alta California

In addition to being the main port city for both Alta and Baja California, from 1775 to 1845 Monterey was the capital of Alta California—and naturally enough, the center of much political intrigue and scheming. Spared the devastating earthquakes that plagued other areas, Monterey had its own bad times, which included being burned and ransacked by the Argentinean revolutionary privateer Hippolyte Bouchard in 1818. In 1822, Spanish rule ended in California, and Mexico took over. In 1845, Monterey lost part of its political prestige when Los Angeles temporarily became the territory's capital city. When the rancheros surrendered to Commodore Sloat in July 1846, the area became officially American, though the town's distinctive Spanish tranquility remained relatively undisturbed until the arrival of farmers, fishing fleets, fish canneries, and whalers. California's first constitution was drawn up in Monterey, at Colton Hall, in 1849, during the state's constitutional convention.

Santa Cruz and the Bad Boys of Branciforte

Santa Cruz, the site of Misión Exaltación de la Santa Cruz and a military garrison on the north end of Monterey Bay, got its start in 1791. But the 1797 establishment of Branciforte—a "model colony" financed by the Spanish government just across the San Lorenzo River—made life hard for the mission fathers. The rowdy, quasi-criminal culture of Branciforte so intrigued the native peoples that Santa Cruz men of the cloth had to use leg irons to keep the Ohlone home. And things just got worse. In 1818, the threat of pirates at nearby Monterey sent the mission folk into the hills, with the understanding that Branciforte's bad boys would pack up the mission's valuables and cart them inland for safekeeping. Instead, they looted the place and drank all the sacramental wine. The mission was eventually abandoned, then demolished by an earthquake in 1857. A small port city grew up around the plaza and borrowed the mission's name—Santa Cruz—while Branciforte, a smuggler's haven, continued to flourish until the late 1800s.

Carmel: Art, Artists, and the Tourist Trade

Carmel-by-the-Sea was established in 1903 by real estate developers who vowed to create a cultured community along the sandy beaches of Carmel Bay. To do this they offered to "creative people" such incentives as building lots for as little as $50. As the result of such irresistible inducements Carmel was soon alive with an assortment of tents and shacks, these eventually giving way to cottages and mansions.

Tourism grew right along with the art colony; the public had a passion for travel during those early days of automobile adventuring. Quaint Carmel, home to "real Bohemians," also offered tourists the chance to view (and buy) artworks—a prospect cheered by the artists themselves. Carmel's commitment to the arts and artists was formalized with the establishment of the Carmel Art Association in 1927. Still going strong, with strict jury selection, this artists' cooperative is a cultural focal point in contemporary Carmel.

California Travel Basics

California is crowded—both with people trying to live the dream on a permanent basis and with those who come to visit, to re-create themselves on the standard two-week vacation plan. Summer, when school's out, is generally when the Golden State is most crowded, though this pattern is changing rapidly now that year-round schools and off-season travel are becoming common. Another trend: "mini-vacations," with workaholic Californians and other Westerners opting for one- to several-day respites spread throughout the year rather than traditional once-a-year holidays. It was once a truism that great bargains, in accom-modations and transport particularly, were wide-ly available during California's nonsummer trav-el season. Given changing travel patterns, this is no longer entirely true, though expect some deals during cold rainy winters.

Spontaneous travel, or following one's whims wherever they may lead, was once feasible in the Monterey area. Unfortunately, given the immense popularity of the destination, those days are long gone. Particularly for those traveling on the cheap and for travelers with special needs or specific de-sires, some of the surprises encountered during im-pulsive adventuring may be unpleasant. If the

Pacific Grove bike trail, Monterey Peninsula

© ROBERT HOLMES/CALTOUR

availability of specific types of lodgings (including campgrounds and hostels) or eateries, or if transport details, prices, hours, and other factors are important for a pleasant trip, the best bet is calling ahead to check details and/or to make reservations. (Everything changes rapidly here.) For a good overview of what to see and do in advance of a planned trip, including practical suggestions beyond those in this guide, also contact the chambers of commerce and/or visitors centers listed. Other good sources for local and regional information are bookstores, libraries, sporting goods and outdoor supply stores, and local, state, and federal government offices.

Being Here: Basic Truths

CONDUCT AND CUSTOMS: SMOKING, DRINKING, AND GENERAL TRUTHS

Smoking is a major social sin in California, against the law in public buildings and on public transport, with regulations particularly stringent in urban areas. People sometimes get violent over other people's smoking, so smokers need to be respectful of others' "space" and smoke outdoors when possible. Smoking has been banned outright in California restaurants and bars, and smoking is not allowed on public airplane flights, though nervous fliers can usually smoke somewhere inside—or outside—airline terminals. Many bed and breakfasts in California are either entirely nonsmoking or restrict smoking to decks, porches, or dens; if this is an issue, inquire by calling ahead. Hotels and motels, most commonly in major urban areas or popular tourist destinations, increasingly offer nonsmoking rooms (or entire floors). Ask in advance.

The legal age for buying and drinking alcohol in California is 21. Though Californians tend to (as they say) "party hearty," public drunkenness is not well tolerated. Drunken driving—which means operating an automobile (even a bicycle, technically) while under the influence—is definitely against the law. California is increasingly no-nonsense about the use of illegal drugs, too, from marijuana to cocaine, crack, and heroin. Doing time in local jails is not the best way to do the Monterey Bay area.

English is the official language in California, and English-speaking visitors from other countries have little trouble understanding Califor-

nia's "dialect" once they acclimate to the accents and slang expressions. (Californians tend to be very creative in their language.) When unsure what someone means by some peculiar phrase, ask for a translation into standard English. Particularly in urban areas, many languages are commonly spoken, and—even in English—the accents are many. You can usually obtain at least some foreign-language brochures, maps, and other information from city visitors centers and popular tourist destinations. (If this is a major concern, inquire in advance.)

Californians are generally casual, in dress as well as etiquette. If any standard applies in most situations, it's common courtesy—still in style, generally speaking, even in California. Though "anything goes" just about anywhere, elegant restaurants usually require appropriately dressy attire for women, jacket and tie for men. (Shirts and shoes—pants or skirt too, usually—are required in any restaurant.)

By law, public buildings in California are wheelchair-accessible, or at least partially so. The same is true of most major hotels and tourist attractions, which may offer both rooms and restrooms with complete wheelchair accessibility; some also have wheelchairs, walkers, and other mobility aids available for temporary use. Even national and state parks, increasingly, are attempting to make some sights and campgrounds more accessible for those with physical disabilities; to make special arrangements, inquire in advance. But private buildings, from restaurants to bed and breakfasts, may not be so accommodating. Those with special needs should definitely ask specific questions in advance.

ENTERTAINMENT, EVENTS, HOLIDAYS

Not even the sky's the limit on entertainment in California. From air shows to harvest fairs and rodeos, from symphony to opera, from rock 'n' roll to avant-garde clubs and theater, from strip shows (male and female) to ringside seats at ladies' mud-wrestling contests, from high-stakes bingo games to horse racing—anything goes in the Golden State. Most communities offer a wide variety of special, often quite unusual, annual events; many of these are listed by city elsewhere in this guide.

Official holidays, especially during the warm-weather travel season and the Thanksgiving-Christmas-New Year holiday season, are often the most congested and popular (read: more expensive) times to travel or stay in the Monterey Bay area. Yet this is not always true; great holiday-season bargains in accommodations are sometimes available at swank hotels that primarily cater to businesspeople. Though most tourist destinations are usually jumping, banks and many businesses close on the following major holidays: New Year's Day (January 1); Martin Luther King Day (the third Monday in January); Presidents' Day (the third Monday in February); Memorial Day (the last Monday in May); Independence Day (July 4); Labor Day (the first Monday in September); Veterans Day (November 11); Thanksgiving (the fourth Thursday in November); and Christmas (December 25). California's newest state holiday is César E. Chávez Day, in honor of the late leader of the United Farm Workers (UFW), signed into law in August 2000 and celebrated each year on the Friday or Monday closest to March 31, Chávez's birthday. In honor of the nation's most famous Latino civil rights leader, all state offices close but banks and other businesses may not.

SHOPPING STANDARDS

Most stores are open during standard business hours (weekdays 8 A.M.–5 P.M. or 9 A.M.–5 P.M.) and often longer, sometimes seven days a week, because of the trend toward two-income families and ever-reduced leisure time. This trend is particularly noticeable in cities, where shops and department stores are often open until 9 P.M. or later, and where many grocery stores are open 24 hours.

Shopping malls—almost self-sustaining cities, with everything from clothing and major appliances to restaurants and entertainment—are the standard California trend, but cities large and small with viable downtown shopping districts often offer greater variety and uniqueness in goods and services. Also popular are flea markets and arts-and-crafts fairs, the former usually held on weekends, the latter best for handcrafted items and often associated with the Thanksgiving-through-Christmas shopping season and/or festivals and special events. California assesses a 7.25 percent state sales tax—sometimes 7 percent, depending on the state of the state's economy—on all nonfood items sold in the state, and many municipalities levy additional sales tax.

Playing Here: Outdoor Recreation

With its tremendous natural diversity, recreationally the Monterey Bay area offers something for just about everyone. Popular spring-summer-fall activities include hiking and backpacking; all water sports, from pleasure boating and water-skiing to sailing, windsurfing, and swimming; whitewater rafting, canoeing, and kayaking; mountain and rock-climbing; even hang gliding and hunting. Also high on the "most popular" list of outdoor California sports: bicycling, walking and running, and coastal diversions from beachcombing to surfing. The most likely places to enjoy these and other outdoor activities are mentioned throughout this book.

And where do people go to re-create themselves in the great outdoors? To California's vast public playgrounds—to the rugged coast and almost endless local, regional, and state parks as well as national parks and forest lands. For more information on the national parks, national forests, and other state- and federally owned lands (including Bureau of Land Management wilderness areas) mentioned in this book, contact each directly.

NATIONAL PARKS INFORMATION AND FEES

For those planning to travel extensively in national parks in California and elsewhere in the U.S., a one-year Golden Eagle Passport provides unlimited park access (not counting camping fees) for the holder and family, for the new price of $50. Those age 62 or older qualify for the $10 Golden Age Passport, which provides free access to national parks, monuments, and recreation areas, and a 50 percent discount on RV fees. Disabled travelers are eligible for the $10 Golden Access Passport, with the same privileges. You can buy all three special passes at individual national parks or obtain them in advance, along with visitor information, from: **U.S. National Park Service,** National Public Inquiries Office, U.S. Department of the Interior, 1849 C St., P.O. Box 37127, Washington, DC 20013, website: www.nps.gov. For regional national parks information covering California, Nevada, and Arizona, contact: **Western Region Information Office,** U.S. National Park Service, Fort Mason, Bldg. 201, San Francisco, CA 94123, 415/556-0560 (recorded) or 415/556-0561.

To support the protection of U.S. national parks and their natural heritage, contact the nonprofit **National Parks and Conservation Association** (NPCA), 1776 Massachusetts Ave. NW, Washington, DC 20036, 202/223-6722, fax 202/659-0650, website: www.npca.org/home /npca. Both as a public service and fundraiser, the NPCA publishes a number of comprehensive regional "overview" guides to U.S. national parks—Alaska, the Pacific, the Pacific Northwest, the Southwest included—that cost less than $10 each, plus shipping and handling. To order one or more titles, call toll-free 800/395-7275.

the Monterey marina

NATIONAL FORESTS AND OTHER FEDERAL LANDS

For general information about U.S. national forests, including wilderness areas and campgrounds, contact: **U.S. Forest Service,** U.S. Department of Agriculture, Publications, P.O. Box 96090, Washington, DC 20090, 202/205-1760. For a wealth of information via the Internet, try www.fs.fed.us. For information specifically concerning national forests and wilderness areas in California, and for maps, contact: **U.S. Forest Service, Pacific Southwest Region,** 630 Sansome St., San Francisco, CA 94111, 415/705-2870. Additional California regional offices are mentioned elsewhere in this guide.

Some U.S. Forest Service and Army Corps of Engineers campgrounds in California can be reserved through ReserveAmerica's **National Recreation Reservation Service** (with MasterCard or Visa) at www.reserveusa.com, or call toll-free 877/444-6777 (TDD: 877/833-6777), a service available 5 A.M.–9 P.M. (8 A.M.–midnight Eastern time) from April 1 through Labor Day and otherwise 7 A.M.–4 P.M. (10 A.M.–7 P.M. Eastern time). From outside the U.S., call 518/885-3639. Reservations for individual campsites can be made up to eight months in advance, and for group camps up to 360 days in advance. Along with the actual costs of camping, expect to pay a per-reservation service fee of $8–9 for individual campsites (more for group sites). In addition to its first-come, first-camped campgrounds, in some areas the U.S. Forest Service offers the opportunity for "dispersed camping," meaning that you can set up minimal-impact campsites in various undeveloped areas. For detailed current recreation, camping, and other information, contact specific national forests mentioned elsewhere in this book.

Anyone planning to camp extensively in national forest campgrounds should consider buying U.S. Forest Service "camp stamps" (at national forest headquarters or at ranger district stations) in denominations of 50 cents, $1, $2, $3, $5, and $10. These prepaid camping coupons amount to a 15 percent discount on the going rate. (Many national forest campgrounds are first-come, first-camped; without a reserved campsite, even camp stamps won't guarantee one.) Senior adults, disabled people, and those with national Golden Age and Golden Access recreation passports pay only half the standard fee at any campground and can buy camp stamps at half the regular rate as well.

For information on national wildlife reserves and other protected federal lands, contact: **U.S. Fish and Wildlife Service,** Division of Refuges, 4401 N. Fairfax Dr., Room 640, Arlington, VA 22203, toll-free 800/344-9453, website: www.fws.gov.

CALIFORNIA STATE PARKS

California's 275 beloved state parks, which include beaches, wilderness areas, and historic homes, have seen bad times recently—the unfortunate result of increasing public use combined with budget cuts. That trend was dramatically reversed in 2000, as Governor Gray Davis decided to share with the state parks—and, indirectly, the public—some of the revenue wealth generated by booming economic times. State park support has increased, park day-use fees cut in half, and camping fees reduced. (Whether or not this largess can last, given the state's economic slide in 2001, is anyone's guess.)

Day-use fees for admission to California state parks now range from free (rare) to $2 or $3 per vehicle. In highly congested areas, state parks charge no day-use fee but do charge a parking fee—making it more attractive to park elsewhere and walk or take a bus. For information on special assistance available for individuals with disabilities or other special needs, contact individual parks—which make every effort to be accommodating, in most cases.

Annual passes (nontransferable), which you can buy at most state parks and at the State Parks Store in Sacramento (see below), are $35 for day use. Golden Bear passes, for seniors age 62 and older with limited incomes and for certain others who receive public assistance, are $5 per year and allow day-use access to all state parks and off-road vehicle areas except Hearst/San Simeon, Sutter's Fort, and the California State Railroad Museum. For details on income eligibility and other requirements, call

916/653-4000. "Limited use" Golden Bear passes, for seniors age 62 and older, allow free parking at state parks during the nonpeak park season (usually Labor Day through Memorial Day) and are $20 per year; they can be purchased in person at most state parks. Senior discounts for state park day use ($1 off) and camping ($2 off, but only if the discount is requested while making reservations) are also offered. Special state park discounts and passes are also offered for the disabled and disabled veterans/POWs (prisoners of war). For more information, contact state park headquarters (see below).

Detailed information about area state parks, beaches, and recreation areas is scattered throughout this guide. To obtain a complete parks listing, including available facilities, campground reservation forms, and other information, contact: **California State Parks,** Public Information, P.O. Box 942896, Sacramento, CA 94296, 916/653-6995 (recorded, with an endless multiple-choice menu), website: www.cal-parks.ca.gov.

State park publications include the *Official Guide to California State Parks* map and facilities listing, which includes all campgrounds, available free with admission to most state parks but available by mail, at last report, for $2; send check or money order to the attention of the Publications Section. Also available, and free: a complete parks and recreation publications list (which includes a mail order form). Other publications include the annual magazines *Events and Programs at California State Parks,* chockfull of educational and entertaining things to do, and *California Escapes,* a reasonably detailed regional rundown on all state parks.

For information about the state parks' Junior Ranger Program—many parks offer individual programs emphasizing both the state's natural and cultural heritage—call individual state parks. For general information, call 916/653-8959.

California state parks offer excellent campgrounds. In addition to developed "family" campsites, which usually include a table, fire ring or outdoor stove, plus running water, flush toilets, and hot showers (RV hookups, if available, are extra), some state campgrounds also offer more primitive "walk-in" or environmental campgrounds and very simple hiker-biker campsites. Group campgrounds are also available (and reservable) at many state parks. If you plan to camp over the Memorial or Labor Day weekends, or the July 4th holiday, be sure to make reservations as early as possible.

MELISSA SHEROWSKI

Año Nuevo State Reserve

COASTWALKING: THE CALIFORNIA COASTAL TRAIL

Californians love their Pacific Ocean coastline. Love of the coast has inspired fierce battles over the years concerning just what does, and what does not, belong there. Among the things most Californians would agree belong along the coast are hiking trails—the reason for the existence of the nonprofit educational group **Coastwalk,** which sponsors group walks along the California Coastal Trail to introduce people to the wonders of the coast.

The California Coastal Trail seems to be an idea whose time has come. It is now a Millennium Legacy Trail, honored at a special White House ceremony in October 1999 recognizing 50 unique trails in the U.S., Washington, D.C., Puerto Rico, and the Virgin Islands. In March 2000 the California Coastal Trail also received a special $10,000 Millennium Trails Grant from American Express.

Yet in some places, the trail is still just an idea. It doesn't yet exist everywhere along the California coastline—and changing that fact is the other primary purpose of this unique organization. Since 1983, Coastwalk's mission has been to establish a border-to-border California Coastal Trail as well as preserve the coastal environment.

Guided four- to six-day coastwalking trips offered in 1999, typically covering 5-10 miles each day, included in the far north the Del Norte coastline, Redwood National Park in Humboldt County, the rugged Mendocino shoreline, the "Lost Coast" of Sonoma County, and Marin County. In central California, coastwalks were offered near San Francisco Bay, along the San Mateo and Santa Cruz coasts, in Monterey and San Luis Obispo Counties, and along the Santa Barbara and Ventura coasts. Southern California coastwalks in 1999 covered Los Angeles (the Santa Monica Mountains) and Catalina Island, Orange County, and San Diego County. Always popular, too, is the eight-day Lost Coast Backpack in Humboldt and Mendocino Counties.

Accommodations, arranged as part of the trip by Coastwalk, include state park campgrounds and hostels with hot showers. "Chuckwagon" dinners, prepared by volunteers, are also provided; bring your own supplies for breakfast and lunch. All gear—you'll be encouraged to travel light—is shuttled from site to site each night, so you need carry only the essentials as you walk: water bottle, lunch, camera, and jacket.

At last report daily coastwalk fees were $45 adults, $20 full-time students, and $15 children ages 12 and under—all in all a very reasonable price for a unique vacation.

For more information and to join Coastwalk—volunteers are always needed—contact Coastwalk, 7207 Bodega Ave. (across from the Sebastopol Library at Bodega Ave. and High St.), Sebastopol, CA 95472, tel. 707/829-6689, www.coastwalk.org or www.californiacoastaltrail.org.

Make campground reservations at California state parks (with MasterCard or Visa) through **ReserveAmerica,** website: www.reserveamerica.com, or call toll-free 800/444-7275 (444-PARK) weekdays 8 A.M.–5 P.M. For TDD reservations, call toll-free 800/274-7275 (274-PARK). And to cancel state park campground reservations, from the U.S. call toll-free 800/695-2269. To make reservations from Canada or elsewhere outside the U.S., call 619/638-5883. As in other camping situations, before calling to make reservations, know the park and campground name, how you'll be camping (tent or RV), how many nights, and how many people and vehicles. In addition to the actual camping fee, which can vary from $7 for more primitive campsites (without showers and/or flush toilets) to $8–12 for developed campsites, there is an $8–9 reservations fee. Sites with hookups cost $6 more. You can make camping reservations up to seven months in advance. Certain campsites, including some primitive environmental and hiker/biker sites (now just $1) can be reserved only through the relevant state park.

To support the state's park system, contact the nonprofit **California State Parks Foundation,** 800 College Ave., P.O. Box 548, Kentfield, CA 94914, 415/258-9975, fax 415/258-9930, website: www.calparks.org. Through memberships and contributions, the foundation has financed about $100 million in park preservation and improvement projects in the past several decades. Volunteers are welcome to contribute sweat equity, too.

OTHER RECREATION RESOURCES

For general information and fishing and hunting regulations, usually also available at sporting goods stores and bait shops where licenses and permits are sold, call the **California Department of Fish and Game** in Sacramento at 916/653-7664; for license information, call 916/227-2244, website: www.dfg.ca.gov. For additional sportfishing information, call toll-free 800/275-3474 (800-ASK-FISH).

For environmental and recreational netheads, the California Resources Agency's CERES website, a.k.a. the California Environmental Resources Evaluation System at ceres.ca.gov, offers an immense amount of additional information, from reports and updates on rare and endangered species to current boating regulations. The database is composed of federal, state, regional, and local agency information as well as a multitude of data and details from state and national environmental organizations—from REINAS, or the Real-time Environmental Information Network and Analysis System at the University of California at Santa Cruz, The Nature Conservancy, and NASA's Imaging Radar Home Page. Check it out.

Worth it for inveterate wildlife voyeurs is the recently revised *California Wildlife Viewing Guide* (Falcon Press, 1997), produced in conjunction with 15 state, federal, and local agencies in addition to Ducks Unlimited and the Wetlands Action Alliance. About 200 wildlife viewing sites are listed—most of these in Northern California. Look for the *California Wildlife Viewing Guide* at local bookstores, or order a copy by calling toll-free 800/582-2665. With the sale of each book, $1 is contributed to California Watchable Wildlife Project nature tourism programs.

To support California's beleaguered native plantlife, join, volunteer with, and otherwise contribute to the **California Native Plant Society** (CNPS), 1722 J St., Ste. 17, Sacramento, CA 95814, 916/447-2677, fax 916/447-2727, website: www.cnps.org. In various areas of the state, local CNPS chapters sponsor plant and habitat restoration projects. The organization also publishes some excellent books. Groups including the **Sierra Club, Audubon Society,** and **The Nature Conservancy** also sponsor hikes, backpack trips, birdwatching treks, backcountry excursions, and volunteer "working weekends" in all areas of California; call local or regional contact numbers (in the telephone book) or watch local newspapers for activity announcements.

Staying and Eating

CAMPING OUT

Because of many recent years of drought, and painful lessons learned about extreme fire danger near suburban and urban areas, all California national forests, most national parks, and many state parks now ban all backcountry fires—with the exception of controlled burns (under park supervision), increasingly used to thin understory vegetation to prevent uncontrollable wildfires. Some areas even prohibit portable campstoves, so be sure to check current conditions and all camping and hiking or backpacking regulations before setting out.

To increase your odds of landing a campsite where and when you want one, make reservations (if reservations are accepted). For details on reserving campsites at both national and state parks in California, see relevant listings under Playing Here: Outdoor Recreation, immediately above, and listings for specific parks elsewhere in this book. Without reservations, seek out "low-profile" campgrounds during the peak camping season—summer as well as spring and fall weekends in most places—or plan for off-season camping. Some areas also offer undeveloped, environmental, or dispersed "open camping" not requiring reservations;

contact relevant jurisdictions above for information and regulations.

Private campgrounds are also available throughout the Monterey Bay area, some of these included in the current *Campbook for California and Nevada,* available at no charge to members of the American Automobile Association (AAA), which lists (by city or locale) a wide variety of private, state, and federal campgrounds. Far more comprehensive is Tom Stienstra's *Foghorn Outdoors: California Camping* (Avalon Travel Publishing), available in most local bookstores.

BARGAIN ROOM RATES AND BED-AND-BREAKFASTS

Even if you don't belong to a special group or association, you can benefit from "bulk-buying" power, particularly in large cities—which is a special boon if you're making last-minute plans or are otherwise having little luck on your own. Various room brokers or "consolidators" buy up blocks of rooms from hoteliers at greatly discounted rates and then broker them through their own reservations services. In many cases, brokers still have bargain-priced rooms available—at rates 40–65 percent below standard rack rates—when popular hotels are otherwise sold out. For sometimes great hotel deals, though regions can be quite broadly defined, try **Hotel Discounts,** toll-free 800/715-7666, website: www.hoteldiscount.com. Particularly helpful for online reservations is the discounted **USA Hotel Guide,** toll-free 888/729-7705, website: www.usahotelguide.com.

Another hot trend is the bed-and-breakfast phenomenon. Many bed-and-breakfast guides and listings are available in bookstores, and some recommended B&Bs are listed in this book. Unlike the European tradition, with bed and breakfasts a low-cost yet comfortable lodging alternative, in California these inns are actually burgeoning small-businesses—rates are usually quite pricey, in the $100–150+ range (occasionally less expensive)—and often more of a "special weekend getaway" for exhausted city people than a mainstream accommodations option. In some

areas, though, where motel and hotel rooms are on the high end, bed and breakfasts can be quite competitive.

For more information on what's available the area, including private home stays, contact **Bed and Breakfast California,** P.O. Box 282910, San Francisco, CA 94128, 650/696-1690 or toll-free 800/872-4500, fax 650/696-1699, website: www.bbintl.com, affiliated with Bed and Breakfast International, the longest-running bed-and-breakfast reservation service in the United States. Or contact the **California Association of Bed and Breakfast Inns,** 2715 Porter St., Soquel, CA 95073, 831/462-9191, fax 831/462-0402, website: www.cabbi.com.

LAND OF FRUITS AND NUTS AND CALIFORNIA CUISINE

One of the best things about traveling in California is the food: they don't call the Golden State the land of fruits and nuts for nothing. In agricultural and rural areas, local "farm trails" or winery guides are often available—ask at local chambers of commerce and visitors centers—and following the seasonal produce trails offers visitors the unique pleasure of gathering (sometimes picking their own) fresh fruits, nuts, and vegetables direct from the growers.

This fresher, direct-to-you produce phenomenon is also quite common in most urban areas, where regular farmers' markets are *the* place to go for fresh, organic, often exotic local produce and farm products. Many of the most popular Monterey area farmers' markets are listed elsewhere in this book—but ask around wherever you are, since new ones pop up constantly. For a reasonably comprehensive current listing of California Certified Farmers' Markets (meaning certified as locally grown), contact: **California Federation of Certified Farmers' Markets,** P.O. Box 1813, Davis, CA 95617, 707/753-9999, fax 707/756-1853, farmersmarket.ucdavis.edu.

Threaded with freeways and accessible on-ramp, off-ramp commercial strips, particularly in urban areas, California has more than its fair share of fast-food eateries and all-night quick-stop outlets. (Since they're so easy to find, few are listed in this guide.) Most cities and communities also have locally popular cafés and fairly inexpensive restaurants worth seeking out; many are listed here, but also ask around. Genuinely inexpensive eateries often refuse to take credit cards, so always bring some cash along just in case.

The northstate is also famous for its "California cuisine," which once typically meant consuming tastebud-tantalizing, very expensive food in very small portions—almost a cliché—while oohing and aahing over the presentation throughout the meal. But the fiscally frugal early 1990s restrained most of California's excesses, and even the best restaurants offer less-pretentious menus and slimmed-down prices. The region's culinary creativity is quite real, and worth pursuing (sans pretense) in many areas. Talented chefs, who have migrated throughout the region from Los Angeles and San Francisco as well as from France and Italy, usually prefer locally grown produce, dairy products, meats, and herbs and spices as basic ingredients. To really "do" the cuisine scene, wash it all down with some fine California wine.

In the Know: Services and Information

BASIC SERVICES

Except for some very lonely areas, even backwater areas of California aren't particularly primitive. Gasoline, at least basic groceries, laundries of some sort, even video rentals are available just about anywhere. Outback areas are not likely to have parts for exotic sports cars, however, or 24-hour pharmacies, hospitals, and garages, or natural foods stores or full-service supermarkets, so you should take care of any special needs or problems before leaving the cities. It's often cheaper, too, to stock up on most supplies, including outdoor equipment and groceries, in urban areas.

GENERAL INFORMATION

Visitors can receive free California travel-planning information by writing the **California Division of Tourism,** P.O. Box 1499, Dept. 61, Sacramento, CA 95812-1499, or by calling toll-free 800/462-2543, extension 61. Or try the Internet site, www.visitcalifornia.com, which also includes an accommodations reservation service. California's tourism office publishes a veritable gold rush of useful travel information, including the annual *California Official State Visitors Guide* and *California Celebrations*. Particularly useful for outdoor enthusiasts is the new 16-page *California Outdoor Recreation* guide. The quarterly *California Travel Ideas* magazine is distributed free at agricultural inspection stations at the state's borders. For travel industry professionals, the *California Travel and Incentive Planner's Guide* is also available.

Most of these California tourism publications, in addition to regional and local publications, are also available at the various roadside volunteer-staffed **California Welcome Centers,** a burgeoning trend. The first official welcome center was unveiled in 1995 in Kingsburg, in the San Joaquin Valley, and the next four—in Rohnert Park, just south of Santa Rosa; in Anderson, just south of Redding; in Oakhurst in the gold country, on the way to Yosemite National Park; and at Pier 39 on San Francisco's Fisherman's Wharf—were also in Northern California. There are others in Northern California, too, including the fairly new one in Arcata, and several in Southern California. Eventually the network will include virtually all areas of California; watch for signs announcing new welcome centers along major highways and freeways.

Most destinations in the Monterey Bay area also have very good visitor information bureaus and visitors centers, listed elsewhere in this book. Many offer accommodations reservations and other services; some offer information and maps in foreign languages. Chambers of commerce can be useful, too. In less populated areas, chambers of commerce are something of a hit-or-miss proposition, since office hours may be minimal; the best bet is calling ahead for information. Asking locals—people at gas stations, cafés, grocery stores, and official government outposts—is often the best way to get information about where to go, why, when, and how. Slick city magazines, good daily newspapers, and weekly news and entertainment tabloids are other good sources of information.

Special Information for the Disabled

Twin Peaks Press, P.O. Box 129, Vancouver, WA 98666, 360/694-2462, or toll-free 800/637-2256 for orders only, publishes particularly helpful books, including *Wheelchair Vagabond, Travel for the Disabled,* and *Directory of Travel Agencies for the Disabled.* Also useful is the *Travelin' Talk Directory* put out by **Travelin' Talk,** P.O. Box 3534, Clarksville, TN 37043, 615/552-6670, a network of disabled people available "to help travelers in any way they can." Membership is only $10, a bargain by any standard, since by joining up you suddenly have a vast network of allies in otherwise strange places who are all too happy to tell you what's what. Also helpful: **Mobility International USA,** P.O. Box 10767, Eugene, OR 97440, tel. and TDD 541/343-1284, fax 541/343-6812, website: www.miusa.org, which provides two-way international leadership exchanges. Disabled people who want to go to Europe to study theater, for example, or British citizens who want to come to the Monterey Bay area for Elderhostel programs—anything beyond traditional leisure travel—should call here first. The individual annual membership fee is $25 for individuals, $35 for organizations.

Special Information for Seniors

Senior adults can benefit from a great many bargains and discounts. A good source of information is the *Travel Tips for Older Americans* pamphlet published by the U.S. Government Printing Office, 202/275-3648, website: www.gpo.gov, available for $1.25. (Order it online at www.pueblo.gsa.gov/travel.) The federal government's Golden Age Passport offers free admission to national parks and monuments and half-price discounts for federal campsites and other recreational services; state parks also offer senior discounts. (For detailed information, see appropriate recreation listings under Playing Here: Outdoor Recreation, above.) Discounts are also frequently offered to seniors at major tourist attractions and sights as well as for many arts, cultural, and entertainment destinations and events in the Monterey Bay area. Another benefit of experience is eligibility for the international **Elderhostel** program, 75 Federal St., Boston, MA 02110, 617/426-7788 or toll-free 877/426-8056, website: www.elderhostel.org, which offers a variety of fairly reasonable one-week residential programs in California.

For information on travel discounts, trip planning, tours, and other membership benefits of the U.S.'s largest senior citizen organization, contact the **American Association of Retired Persons** (AARP), 601 E St. NW, Washington, DC 20049, 202/434-2277 or toll-free 800/227-7737, website: www.aarp.org. Despite the name, anyone age 50 and older—retired or not—is eligible for membership. Other membership-benefit programs for seniors include the **National Council of Senior Citizens,** 8403 Colesville Rd., Ste. 1200, Silver Springs, MD 20910, 301/578-8800, fax 301/578-8999, website: www.ncscinc.org.

NOT GETTING LOST: GOOD MAPS

The best all-around maps for the Monterey Bay area, either in the city or out in the countryside, are those produced by the **American Automobile Association,** which is regionally organized as the California State Automobile Association (CSAA) in Northern and Central California, and as the Automobile Club of Southern California in the southstate. The AAA maps are available at any local AAA office, and the price is right (free, but for members only). In addition to its California state map, AAA provides urban maps for most major cities, plus regional maps with at least some backcountry routes marked (these latter maps don't necessarily show the entire picture, however; when in doubt about unusual routes, ask locally before setting out). For more information about AAA membership and services in Northern California, contact the **California State Automobile Association;** the main office address is 150 Van Ness Ave., P.O. Box 1860, San Francisco, CA 94101-1860, 415/565-2012 or 415/565-2468, website: www.csaa.org, but there are also regional offices throughout the northstate. Members can also order maps, tour books, and other services online. If you'll also be visiting Southern California, the AAA affiliate there is the **Automobile Club of Southern California,** 2601 S. Figueroa St., Los Angeles, CA 90007, 213/741-3686, website: www.aaa-calif.com. For AAA membership information, from anywhere in the U.S. call toll-free 800/222-4357, or try website: www.aaa.com.

The best maps money can buy, excellent for general and very detailed travel in California, are the **Thomas Bros. Maps,** typically referred to as "Thomas guides." For the big picture, particularly useful is the *California Road Atlas & Driver's Guide,* but various other, very detailed spiral-bound book-style maps in the Thomas guide street atlas series—San Francisco and Monterey County, for example—are the standard block-by-block references, continually updated since 1915. Thomas guides are available at any decent travel-oriented bookstore, or contact the company directly. In Northern California, stop by Thomas Bros. Maps, 550 Jackson St., San Francisco, CA 94133, 415/981-7520. Or order any map by calling, from anywhere in California, toll-free 800/899-6277—or, from anywhere in the world, website: www.thomas.com.

When it comes to backcountry travel—where maps quickly become either your best friend or archenemy—the going isn't nearly as easy. U.S. Geological Survey quadrangle maps in most cases

are reliable for showing the contours of the terrain, but U.S. Forest Service and wilderness maps—supposedly the maps of record for finding one's way through the woods and the wilds—are often woefully out of date, with new and old logging roads (as well as disappearing or changed trail routes) confusing the situation considerably. In California, losing oneself in the wilderness is a very real, literal possibility. In addition to topographical maps (carry a compass to orient yourself by landforms if all else fails) and official U.S. maps, backcountry travelers would be wise to invest in privately published guidebooks and current route or trail guides for wilderness areas; the Sierra Club and Wilderness Press publish both. Before setting out, compare all available maps and other information to spot any possible route discrepancies, then ask national forest or parks personnel for clarification. If you're lucky, you'll find someone who knows what's going on where you want to go.

Aside from well-stocked outdoor stores, the primary California source for quad maps is: **U.S. Geological Survey,** 345 Middlefield Rd., Menlo Park, CA 94025, 650/853-8300 (ask for the mapping division); an index and catalog of published California maps is available upon request. Or try the USGS website, info.er .usgs.gov, or call toll-free 888/275-8747. Also contact the U.S. Forest Service and U.S. National Park Service (see Playing Here: Outdoor Recreation, above). The best bet for wilderness maps and guides is **Wilderness Press,** 1200 Fifth St., Berkeley, CA 94710, 510/558-1666 or toll-free 800/443-7227 (for orders), fax 510/558-1696, website: www.wilderness press.com. Most Wilderness Press titles are available in California bookstores.

Surviving: Health and Safety

EMERGENCIES, MEDICAL CARE, AND GENERAL HEALTH

In most places in the Monterey Bay area, call 911 in any emergency; in medical emergencies, life support personnel and ambulances will be dispatched. To make sure health care services will be readily provided, health insurance coverage is almost mandatory; carry proof of coverage while traveling. In urban areas and in many rural areas, 24-hour walk-in health care services are readily available, though hospital emergency rooms are the place to go in case of life-threatening circumstances.

To avoid most health and medical problems, use common sense. Eat sensibly, avoid unsafe drinking water, bring along any necessary prescription pills—and pack an extra pair of glasses or contacts, just in case. Sunglasses, especially for those unaccustomed to sunshine, as well as sunscreen and a broad-brimmed hat can help prevent sunburn, sunstroke, and heat prostration. Drink plenty of liquids, too, especially when exercising and/or in hot weather.

No vaccinations are usually necessary for traveling in California, though here as elsewhere very young children and seniors should obtain vaccinations against annually variable forms of the flu virus; exposure, especially in crowded urban areas and during the winter disease season, is a likelihood.

As in other areas of the United States and the world, the AIDS (Acquired Immune Deficiency Syndrome) virus and other sexually transmitted diseases are a concern. In mythic "anything goes" California, avoiding promiscuous or unprotected sex is the best way to avoid the danger of contracting the AIDS virus and venereal disease—though AIDS is also transmitted via shared drug needles and contaminated blood transfusions. (All medical blood supplies in California are screened for evidence of the virus.) Sexually speaking, "safe sex" is the preventive key phrase, under any circumstances beyond the strictly monogamous. This means always using condoms in sexual intercourse; oral sex only with some sort of barrier precaution; and no sharing sex toys.

CITY SAFETY

Though California's wilderness once posed a major threat to human survival, in most respects the backcountry is safer than the urban jungle of modern cities. Tourism officials don't talk about it much, but crimes against persons and property are a reality in the Monterey Bay area (though the state's overall crime rate has dropped sharply in recent years). To avoid harm, bring along your street-smarts. The best overall personal crime prevention includes carrying only small amounts of cash (inconspicuously, in a money belt or against-the-body money pouch); labeling (and locking) all luggage; keeping valuables under lock and key (and, in automobiles, out of sight); being aware of people and events, and knowing where you are, at all times; and avoiding dangerous, lonely, and unlighted areas after daylight, particularly late at night and when traveling alone. If you're not sure what neighborhoods are considered dangerous or unsafe, ask locals or hotel or motel personnel—or at the police station, if necessary.

Women traveling alone—not generally advisable, because of the unfortunate fact of misogyny in the modern world—need to take special care to avoid harm. For any independent traveler, self-defense classes (and/or a training course for carrying and using Mace) might be a worthwhile investment, if only to increase one's sense of personal power in case of a confrontation with criminals. Being assertive and confident, and acting as if you know where you are going (even when you don't) are also among the best deterrents to predators. Carry enough money for a phone call—or bus or taxi ride—and a whistle. When in doubt, don't hesitate to use it, and yell and scream for help.

GENERAL OUTDOOR SAFETY

The most basic rule is, know what you're doing and where you're going. Next most basic: whatever you do—from swimming or surfing to hiking and backpacking—don't do it alone. For any outdoor activity, be prepared. Check with local park or national forest service officials on weather, trail, and general conditions before setting out. Correct, properly functioning equipment is as important in backpacking as it is in hang gliding, mountain climbing, mountain biking, and sailing. (When in doubt, check it out.)

Among the basics to bring along for almost any outdoor activity: a hat, sunscreen, and lip balm (to protect against the sun in summer, against heat loss, reflective sun, and the elements in winter); a whistle, compass, and mylar "space blanket" in case you become lost or stranded; insect repellent; a butane lighter or waterproof matches; a multipurpose Swiss Army–type knife; nylon rope; a flashlight; and a basic first-aid kit (including bandages, ointments and salves, antiseptics, pain relievers such as aspirin, and any necessary prescription medicines). Hikers, backpackers, and other outdoor adventurers should bring plenty of water—or water purification tablets or pump-style water purifiers for long trips—at least minimal fishing gear, good hiking shoes or boots, extra socks and shoelaces, layered clothing adequate for all temperatures, and a waterproof poncho or large plastic garbage bag. (Even if thunderstorms are unlikely, any sort of packable and wearable plastic bag can keep you dry until you reach shelter.) The necessity of other outdoor equipment, from campstoves to sleeping bags and tents, depends on where you'll be going and what you'll be doing.

Poison Oak

Poison oak (actually a shrublike sumac) is a perennial trailside hazard, especially in lowland foothill areas and mixed forests; it exudes oily chemicals that cause a strong allergic reaction in many people, even with only brief contact. (Always be careful what you're burning around the campfire, too: smoke from poison oak, when inhaled, can in-

flame the lungs and create a life-threatening situation in no time flat.) The best way to avoid the painful, itchy, often long-lasting rashes associated with poison oak is to avoid contact with the plant—in all seasons—and to immediately wash one's skin or clothes if you even suspect a brush with it. (Its leaves are a bright, glossy green in spring and summer, and red or yellow in fall, but poison oak can be a problem even in winter—when this mean-spirited deciduous shrub loses its leaves.) Learn to identify it during any time of year.

Once afflicted with poison oak, never scratch, because the oozing sores just spread the rash. Very good new products on the market include Tecnu's **Poison Oak-n-Ivy Armor** "pre-exposure lotion," produced by Tec Laboratories, Inc., of Albany, Oregon, toll-free 800/482-4464 (800-ITCHING). Apply it before potential exposure to protect yourself. Another excellent product, quite helpful if you do tangle with poison oak, is Tecnu's **Poison Oak-n-Ivy Cleanser,** the idea being to get the toxic oils off your skin as soon as possible, within

poison oak

BOB RACE

hours of initial exposure or just after the rash appears. The cleanser—which smells suspiciously like kerosene—also helps eliminate the itching, remarkably well. (But do *not* apply after oozing begins.) Various drying, cortisone-based lotions, oatmeal baths, and other treatments can help control discomfort if the rash progresses to the oozing stage, but the rash itself goes away only in its own good time.

Lyme Disease and Ticks

Even if you favor shorts for summer hiking, you had better plan on long pants, long-sleeved shirts, even insect repellent. The weather may be mild, but there's an increasing risk—particularly in California coastal and foothill areas—that you'll contract Lyme disease, transmitted by ticks that thrive in moist lowland climates.

A new ailment on the West Coast, Lyme disease is named after the place of its 1975 discovery in Old Lyme, Connecticut. Already the most common vector-transmitted disease in the nation, Lyme is caused by spirochetes transmitted through blood, urine, and other body fluids. Research indicates it has often been wrongly diagnosed; sufferers were thought to have afflictions such as rheumatoid arthritis. Temporary paralysis, arthritic pains in the hands or arm and leg joints, swollen hands, fever, fatigue, nausea, headaches, swollen glands, and heart palpitations are among the typical symptoms. Sometimes a circular red rash appears first, between three and 30 days after the tick bite. Untreated, Lyme disease can mean a lifetime of suffering, even danger to unborn children. Treatment, once Lyme disease is discovered, is simple and 100 percent effective if recognized early: tetracycline and other drugs halt the arthritic degeneration and most symptoms. Long-delayed treatment, even with extremely high doses of antibiotics, is only about 50 percent effective.

Outdoor prudence, coupled with an awareness of possible Lyme symptoms even months later, are the watchwords when it comes to Lyme disease. Take precautions against tick bite: the sooner ticks are found and removed, the better your chances of avoiding the disease. Tuck your pants into your boots, wear long-sleeved shirts, and use insect repellent around all clothing openings as well as on your neck and all exposed skin. Run a full-body "tick check" daily, especially checking hidden areas such as the hair and scalp. Consider leaving dogs at home if heading for Lyme country; ticks they pick up can spread the disease through your human family.

Use gloves and tweezers to remove ticks from yourself or your animals—never crush the critters with your fingers!—and wash your hands and the bitten area afterward. Better yet, smother imbedded ticks with petroleum jelly first; deprived of oxygen, they start to pull out of the skin in about a half hour, making it easy to pluck them off without tearing them or leaving the head imbedded.

Getting Here, Getting Around

By Bicycle

Many parts of California are not much fun for cyclists. Let's face it: cities are car country. Cycling on public roadways here usually means frightening car traffic; brightly colored bicycle clothing and accessories, reflective tape, good lights, and other safety precautions are mandatory. And always wear a helmet. Only the brave would pick this part of the world—or at least the urban part of this world—for bicycle touring, though some do, most wisely with help from books such as *Bicycling the Pacific Coast* (The Mountaineers) by Tom Kirkendall and Vicky Spring. Yet there are less congested areas, and good local bike paths here and there, for more timid recreational bikers; rental bike shops abound, particularly in beach areas. For those who hanker after a little two-wheel backroads sightseeing, many areas along the central and north coasts, throughout the Sonoma and Napa County "wine countries," and in the Sierra Nevada foothills are still sublime.

Various good regional cycling guides are available, though serious local bike shops—those frequented by cycling enthusiasts, not just sales outlets—and bike clubs are probably the best local information sources for local and regional rides as well as special cycling events. For upcoming events, other germane information, and referrals on good publications, contact: **California Association of Bicycling Organizations** (CABO), P.O. Box 26864, Dublin, CA 94568, website: www.cabobike.org. The **Adventure Cycling Association,** P.O. Box 8308, Missoula, MT 59807, 406/721-1776 or toll-free 800/755-2453, fax 406/721-8754, website: www.adv-cycling.org, is a nonprofit national organization that researches long-distance bike routes and organizes tours for members. Its maps, guidebooks, route suggestions, and *Cyclist's Yellow Pages* can be helpful. For mountain biking information via the Internet, also try the **International Mountain Bicycling Association** at website: www.imba.com.

By Bus

Most destinations in the Monterey Bay area are reachable by bus, either by major carrier, by "alternative" carrier, or in various combinations of long-distance and local bus lines. And if you can't get *exactly* where you want to go by bus, you can usually get close.

Greyhound is the universal bus service. Call to obtain a current U.S. route map by mail, but check with local Greyhound offices for more detailed local route information and local specials. Greyhound offers discounts for senior adults and disabled travelers, and children under age 12 ride free when accompanied by a fare-paying adult (one child per adult, half fare for additional children). The **Ameripass** offers unlimited travel with on-off stops for various periods of time, but it is usually more economical for long-distance trips with few stopovers. International travelers should inquire about the **International Ameripass.** For more information, in the U.S. contact Greyhound Bus Lines, Inc., at toll-free 800/232-2222, website: www.greyhound.com.

Then there are alternative bus options, most notably **Green Tortoise,** the hippest trip on wheels for budget travelers, combining long-distance travel with communal sightseeing. Sign on for a westbound cross-country tour to get to California, an eastbound trip to get away— seeing some of the most spectacular sights in the U.S. along the languid, looping way. As the motto emblazoned on the back of the bus says: "Arrive inspired, not dog tired." Unlike your typical bus ride, on Green Tortoise trips you bring your sleeping bag—the buses are con-

"bicycle" built for many

verted sleeping coaches, and the booths and couches convert into beds come nightfall. And you won't need to stop for meals, since healthy gourmet fare (at a cost of about $10 a day) is usually included in the freight; sometimes the food charge is optional, meaning you can bring your own. But Green Tortoise also offers a weekly three-day **California Coast Tour,** with departures from both Los Angeles and San Francisco, making it easy—and fairly entertaining—to get from one end of the state to the other. From San Francisco, you can also get to Southern California on the Green Tortoise **Death Valley National Park** tour; dropoffs can be arranged in either Bakersfield or Mojave, and Greyhound can get you to Los Angeles. For more information, contact: Green Tortoise Adventure Travel, 494 Broadway, San Francisco, CA 94133, 415/956-7500 or, from anywhere in the U.S. and Canada, toll-free 800/867-8647, website: www.greentortoise.com.

By Train

An unusually enjoyable way to travel the length of the West Coast to California, or to arrive here after a trip west over the Sierra Nevada or across the great desert, is by train. Within Northern California, travel along the coast on Amtrak's immensely popular and recently spiffed up **Coast Starlight,** which now features more comfortable tilt-back seats, a parlor car with library and games, and California-style fare in its dining cars. (From the south, the two-way route continues north to Oakland, across the bay from San Francisco, and eventually continues all the way to Seattle.) Regional trains operated by Amtrak within California include the **Pacific Surfliner** (formerly the San Diegans) along the state's central and south coasts, and the **San Joaquins** connecting Sacramento with the greater San Francisco Bay Area.

For **Amtrak** train travel routes (including some jogs between cities in California by Amtrak bus), current price information, and reservations, contact a travel agent or call Amtrak at toll-free 800/872-7245 (USA RAIL), website: www.amtrak.com or amtrakwest.com. For the hearing impaired, Amtrak's toll-free TTY numbers are 800/523-6590 or 800/523-6591.

By Automobile

This being California, almost everyone gets around by car. Urban freeway driving in California, because of congestion and Californians' no-nonsense, get-on-with-it driving styles, can inspire panic in nonlocal native drivers. If this is a problem, plan your trip to skirt the worst congestion—by taking back roads and older highways, if possible, or by trying neighborhood routes—but only if you know something about the neighborhoods. Alternatively, plan to arrive in San Francisco, other Bay Area destinations, and Sacramento well after the day's peak freeway commute traffic, usually any time after 7 or 8 P.M.

A good investment for anyone traveling for any length of time in California is a membership in the American Automobile Association (see above) since—among many other benefits, including excellent maps and trip-planning assistance—a AAA card entitles the bearer to no-cost emergency roadside service, including five gallons of free gas and limited towing, if necessary.

Gasoline in California is typically more expensive than elsewhere in the U.S., up to 40 cents per gallon more, only in part because of California's new cleaner-burning "reformulated" fuels, the world's cleanest gasoline. The effect of using the new gasoline is roughly equivalent to the effect of taking 3.5 million cars off the road on any given day—or sucking about three million pounds of toxins and particulate matter out of the air. The clean fuels are designed to reduce vehicle emissions and improve air quality, which seems to be working, but a new concern is that clean fuel residues (particularly from the additive MTBE) are polluting the water. Though MTBE will soon be banned, the Golden State's pollution solutions are, clearly, ideas that still need work.

To check on current **road conditions** before setting out—always a good idea in a state with so much ongoing road construction and such variable regional weather—call **Caltrans** (California Department of Transportation) from anywhere in California at toll-free 800/427-7623, and from outside California at 916/445-7623. The road-condition phone numbers are accessible from touch-tone and pay phones as well as cellular phones. Or check road conditions for your entire trip route on the regularly updated Caltrans website, www.dot.ca.gov.

Though every municipality has its own peculiar laws about everything from parking to skateboarding or roller skating on sidewalks, there are basic rules everyone is expected to know and follow—especially drivers. Get a complete set of regulations from the state motor vehicles department, which has an office in all major cities and many medium-sized ones. Or contact **California Department of Motor Vehicles,** 2415 First Ave., P.O. Box 942869, Sacramento, CA 94269, website: www.dmv.ca.gov. Foreign visitors planning to drive should obtain an **International Driver's License** before leaving home (they're not available here); licensed U.S. drivers from other states can legally drive in California for 30 consecutive days without having to obtain a California driver's license. Disabled travelers heading for California can get special handicapped-space parking permits, good for 90 days, by requesting applications in advance from the DMV and having them signed by their doctors (there is an application fee). If you'll be renting a car, ask the rental car agency to send you a form when you make reservations.

Among driving rules, the most basic is observing the posted speed limit. Though many Bay Area drivers ignore any and all speed limits, it's at their own peril should the California Highway Patrol be anywhere in the vicinity. The statewide speed limit for open highway driving varies, typically posted as somewhere between 55 and 70 miles per hour; freeway speeds can vary at different points along the same route. Speed limits for cities and residential neighborhoods are substantially slower. Another common traffic ticket can be avoided by *not* indulging in what is colloquially known as the "California stop," slowing down and then rolling right through intersections without first making a complete stop.

Once arrived at your destination, pay attention to parking notices, tow-away warnings, and curb color: red means no parking under any circumstances; yellow means limited stops only (usually for freight delivery); green means very limited

parking; and blue means parking for the disabled only. In hilly areas—and most necessarily in San Francisco—always turn your front wheels into the curb (to keep your car from becoming a rollaway runaway) and set the emergency brake.

Driving while under the influence of alcohol or drugs is a very serious offense in California—aside from being a danger to one's own health and safety, not to mention those of innocent fellow drivers and pedestrians. Don't drink (or do drugs) and drive.

By Rental Car

Renting a car—or a recreational vehicle—in California usually won't come cheap. Rates have been accelerating, so to speak, in recent years, especially when consumers put the kibosh on mileage caps. Turns out people really liked the idea of unlimited "free" mileage. So now the average car rental price is just above $50 a day (lower for subcompacts, higher for roadhogs). Still, bargains are sometimes available through small local agencies. Among national agencies, National and Alamo often offer the lowest prices. But in many cases, with weekly rentals and various group-association (AAA, AARP, etc.) and credit-card discounts ranging from 10–40 percent, you'll do just as well with other major rental car agencies.

Beware the increasingly intense pressure, once you arrive to pick up your rental car, to buy additional insurance coverage. In some companies, rental car agents receive a commission for every insurance policy they sell, needed or not, which is why the person on the other side of the counter is so motivated (sometimes pushy and downright intimidating). Feel free to complain to management if you dislike such treatment—and to take your business elsewhere. This highly touted insurance coverage is coverage you probably don't need, from collision damage waivers—now outlawed in some states, but not in California—to liability insurance, which you probably don't need unless you have no car insurance at all (in which case it's illegal to drive in California). Some people do carry additional rental-car collision or liability insurance on their personal insurance policies—talk to your agent about this—but even that is already covered, at least domestically, if you pay for your rental car with a gold or platinum MasterCard or Visa. The same is true for American Express for domestic travelers, though American Express recently rescinded such coverage on overseas car rentals; it's possible that Visa and MasterCard will soon follow suit. (Check your personal insurance and credit-card coverage before dealing with the rental car agencies.) And bring personal proof of car insurance, though you'll rarely be asked for it. In short—buyer beware.

For current information on options and prices for rental cars in Northern California, Southern California, and elsewhere in the U.S., contact **Alamo,** toll-free 800/327-9633, website: www.alamo.com.; **Avis,** toll-free 800/831-2847, website: www.avis.com; **Budget,** toll-free worldwide 800/527-0700, website: www.budget.com; **Dollar,** toll-free 800/800-4000, website: www.dollar.com; **Enterprise,** toll-free 800/736-8222, website: www.enterprise.com; **Hertz,** toll-free worldwide 800/654-3131, website: www.hertz.com; **National,** toll-free 800/227-7368, website: www.nationalcar.com; and **Thrifty,** toll-free 800/847-4389, website: www.thrifty.com. You can also make rental car arrangements online, either directly through individual home pages or through virtual travel agencies and reservations systems such as **Travelocity,** website: www.travelocity.com, and **Trip,** website: www.trip.com.

Though some rental agencies also handle recreational vehicle (RV) rentals, travelers may be able to get better deals by renting directly from local RV dealers. For suggestions, contact area visitor bureaus—and consult the local telephone book.

By Airplane

Airfares change and bargains come and go so quickly in competitive California that the best way to keep abreast of the situation is through a travel agent. Or via the Internet, where major U.S. airlines regularly offer great deals—discounts of up to 90 percent (typically not *quite* that good). Popular home pages include **American Airlines,** website: www.aa.com; **Continental,** website: www.flycontinental.com; **Delta,**

website: www.delta-air.com; **Northwest,** website: www.nwa.com; **TWA,** website: www.twa.com; **United,** website: www.ual.com; and **US Airways,** website: www.usairways.com. Also look up the people's favorite, **Southwest,** at website: www.iflyswa.com. Have your credit card handy. To find additional websites, know your computer—or call any airline's toll-free "800" number and ask. Fueling travel agents' fears that online airline ticket sales will doom them (and independent online agencies) is the news that five airlines—American, Continental, Delta, Northwest, and United—launched their own "independent" online travel service, **Orbitz,** website: www. orbitz.com.

But the online agencies may be able to fight back: **Travelzoo,** website: www.travelzoo.com, searches the 20 major airline websites for the deep-discounted fares and posts them, so you don't have to spend hours looking for the best deals. Relative newcomer **Hotwire,** website: www.hotwire.com, offers airline tickets at a 40 percent discount (though with limited consumer routing control), with hotel rooms and rental car discounts added to the mix too.

Another good information source for domestic and international flight fares: the travel advertisements in the weekend travel sections of major urban newspapers. Super Saver fares (booked well in advance) can save fliers up to 30–70 percent and more. Peak travel times in and out of California being the summer and the midwinter holiday season, book flights well in advance for June–August and December travel. The best bargains in airfares are usually available from January to early May.

Bargain airfares are often available for international travelers, especially in spring and autumn. Charter flights are also good bargains, the only disadvantage usually being inflexible departure and return-flight dates. Most flights from Europe to the U.S. arrive in New York; from there, other transcontinental travel options are available. Reduced-fare flights on major airlines from Europe abound.

Nothing about air travel is the same since the September 11 attacks on the World Trade Center in New York and the Pentagon. Security search routines are long; the airlines or your travel agent will tell you when to arrive, though plan to show up two to three hours ahead of your scheduled flight. Even before September 11 airlines were increasingly strict about how much baggage you're allowed to carry on with you. Only two pieces of carry-on luggage are allowed on most carriers—some now allow only one—and each must fit in the "sizer" box. Expect everything you carry on to be searched thoroughly; some travelers have decided to simplify the process—or at least their part in it—by checking all baggage. Most airlines allow three pieces of luggage total per passenger. (Fortunately for parents, diaper bags, fold-up strollers, and—at least sometimes—infant carrier seats don't count.) So if you are philosophically opposed to the concept of traveling light, bring two massive suitcases—and check them through—in addition to your carry-on. Some airlines, including American, charge extra for more than two checked bags per person. Contact each airline directly for current baggage guidelines.

Monterey:
A Nostalgia, a Dream

In his novel by the same name, local boy John Steinbeck described Monterey's Cannery Row as "a poem, a stink, a grating noise, a quality of light, a tune, a habit, a nostalgia, a dream," and also as a corrugated collection of sardine canneries, restaurants, honky-tonks, whorehouses, and waterfront laboratories. The street, he said, groaned under the weight of "silver rivers of fish." People here liked his description so much that they eventually put it on a plaque and planted it in today's touristy Cannery Row, among the few Steinbeck-era buildings still standing.

Local promoters claim that the legendary writer would be proud of what the tourist dollar has wrought here, but this seems unlikely. When Steinbeck returned in 1961 from his self-imposed exile, he noted the clean beaches, "where once they festered with fish guts and flies. The canneries which once put up a sick-ening stench are gone, their places filled with restaurants, antique shops, and the like. They fish for tourists now, not pilchards, and that species they are not likely to wipe out."

A Dream "under Siege"

An early port for California immigrants—California's first pier was built here—and now a bustling tourist mecca, Monterey (literally, "the King's Wood") is trying hard to hang onto its once-cloistered charm. The justifiably popular Monterey Bay Aquarium is often blamed for the hopeless summer traffic snarls, though tourism throughout the Monterey Peninsula is the actual culprit. (The region's population and economy otherwise are in flux, with the closure of Fort Ord and its replacement with a new California State University campus, CSU Monterey Bay, in 1995.) More than a decade ago, *Creative States Quarterly*

MELISSA SHEROWSKI

Monterey Bay

editor Raymond Mungo described Monterey as a city "under siege," asking rhetorically: "How do you describe the difference a tornado makes in a small town, or the arrival of sudden prosperity in a sleepy backwater?" How indeed?

During peak summer months you can avoid feeling under siege yourself—and worrying that you're contributing unduly to the city's siege state—by using Monterey's public WAVE shuttles whenever possible.

Seeing and Doing Monterey

MONTEREY BAY AQUARIUM

The fish are back on Cannery Row, at least at the west end. Doc's Western Biological Laboratory and the canneries immortalized by Steinbeck may be long gone, but Monterey now has an aquarium that the bohemian biologist would love.

Just down the street from Doc's legendary marine lab, the Monterey Bay Aquarium on Cannery Row is a world-class cluster of fish tanks built into the converted Hovden Cannery. Luring 2.35 million visitors in 1984, its first year, Monterey's best attraction is the brainchild of marine biologist Nancy Packard and her sister, aquarium director Julie Packard. Much help came from Hewlett-Packard computer magnate

David Packard and wife, Lucile, who supported this nonprofit, public-education endeavor with a $55 million donation to their daughters' cause. Not coincidentally, Packard also personally designed many of the unique technological features of the major exhibits here. Through the aquarium's foundation, the facility also conducts its own research and environmental education and wildlife rescue programs. The aquarium's trustees, for example, have allocated $10 million for a five-year unmanned underwater exploration and research project in the bay's Monterey Canyon.

The philosophy of the folks at the Monterey Bay Aquarium, most simply summarized as "endorsing human interaction" with the natural

Sea otters are one of the Monterey Bay Aquarium's most popular exhibits.

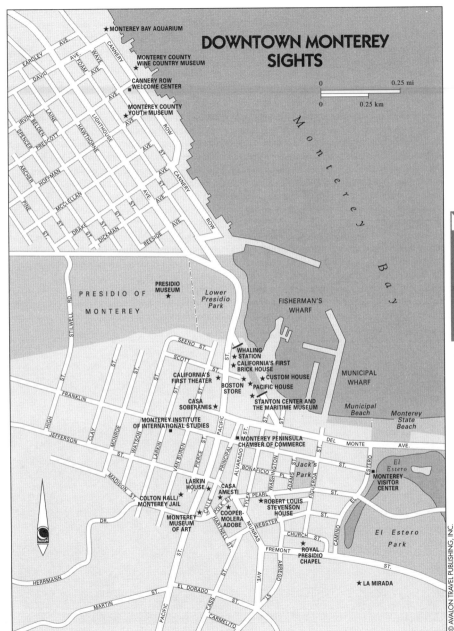

DOWNTOWN MONTEREY
SIGHTS

★ MONTEREY BAY AQUARIUM

MONTEREY COUNTY
WINE COUNTRY MUSEUM

CANNERY ROW
WELCOME CENTER

MONTEREY COUNTY
YOUTH MUSEUM

0   0.25 mi

0   0.25 km

M o n t e r e y   B a y

MONTEREY

PRESIDIO OF
MONTEREY

PRESIDIO
MUSEUM

Lower
Presidio
Park

FISHERMAN'S
WHARF

WHALING
STATION
CALIFORNIA'S FIRST
BRICK HOUSE

CALIFORNIA'S
FIRST THEATER

BOSTON
STORE

CUSTOM HOUSE

PACIFIC HOUSE

MUNICIPAL
WHARF

CASA
SOBERANES

STANTON CENTER AND
THE MARITIME MUSEUM

Municipal
Beach

Monterey
State
Beach

MONTEREY INSTITUTE
OF INTERNATIONAL STUDIES

MONTEREY PENINSULA
CHAMBER OF COMMERCE

Jack's
Park

El
Estero

MONTEREY
VISITOR
CENTER

LARKIN
HOUSE

CASA
AMESTI

COLTON HALL/
MONTEREY JAIL

ROBERT LOUIS
STEVENSON
HOUSE

MONTEREY
MUSEUM
OF ART

COOPER-
MOLERA
ADOBE

El Estero
Park

ROYAL
PRESIDIO
CHAPEL

★ LA MIRADA

© AVALON TRAVEL PUBLISHING, INC.

world, is everywhere apparent. From a multi-level view of kelp forests in perpetual motion to face-to-face encounters with sharks and wolf eels, from petting velvety bat rays and starfish in "touch pools" to watching sea otters feed and frolic, here people can observe the native marine plants and wildlife of Monterey Bay up close and personal. More than 300,000 animals and plants representing 571 species—including fish, invertebrates, mammals, reptiles, birds, and plant life—can be seen here in environments closely approximating their natural communities. Volunteer guides, dressed in rust-colored jackets, are available throughout the aquarium and are only too happy to share their knowledge about the natural history of Monterey Bay.

The engineering feats shoring up the amazingly "natural" exhibits in the 322,000-square-foot Monterey Aquarium are themselves impressive. Most remarkable are the aquatic displays, concrete tanks with unbreakable one-ton acrylic windows more than seven inches thick. The exhibits' "wave action" is simulated by a computer-controlled surge machine and hidden water jets. In the Nearshore Galleries, more than a half-million gallons of fresh seawater are pumped through the various aquarium tanks daily to keep these habitats healthy. During the day, six huge "organic" water filters screen out microorganisms that would otherwise cloud the water. At night, filtration shuts down and raw, unfiltered seawater flows through the exhibits—nourishing filter-feeders and also carrying in plant spores and animal larvae that settle and grow, just as they would in nature. The Outer Bay Galleries operate as a "semi-closed" system, with water from the main intake pipes heated to 68° F and recirculated through the exhibits. Wastes are removed by biological filters and ozone treatment, and a heat-recovery system recaptures energy from the water (cools it) before it is discharged into the bay.

In the event of an oil spill or other oceanic disaster, the aquarium's 16-inch intake pipes can be shut down on a moment's notice and the aquarium can operate as a "closed system" for up to two weeks.

Sea nettles capture the fancy of visitors in the Outer Bay galleries at the Monterey Bay Aquarium.

Seeing and Doing the Aquarium

Just inside the aquarium's entrance, serving as an introduction to the **Nearshore Galleries,** is the 55,000-gallon, split-level **Sea Otter Tank.** These sleek aquatic clowns consume 25 percent of their body weight in seafood daily. If they're not eating or playing with toys, they're grooming themselves—and with 600,000 hairs per square inch on their pelts, it's easy to understand why otters were so prized by furriers (and hunted almost to extinction). To spot an occasional otter or two slipping into the aquarium over the seawall, or to watch for whales, head for the outdoor observation decks, which include telescopes for bay watching. The **Outdoor Tidepool** is surrounded by the aquarium itself on three sides, on the fourth by artificial rock. It is home to sea stars, anemones, small fish—and visiting sea otters and harbor seals that occasionally shimmy up the stairs for a better look at the people. Also here are telescopes for bay watching.

The three-story-tall **Giant Kelp Forest** exhibit, the aquarium's centerpiece and the first underwater forest ever successfully established as a display, offers a diver's-eye view of the undersea world. "Dazzling" is the only word for the nearby **Anchovies** exhibit, a cylindrical tank full of darting silver shapes demonstrating the "safety in numbers" group-mind philosophy. The 90-foot-long hourglass-shaped **Monterey Bay Habitats** display is a simulated underwater slice of sea life. Sharks roam the deep among colorful anemones and sea slugs, bat rays glide under the pier with the salmon and mackerel, accompanied by octopi and wolf eels. The craggy-shored, indoor-outdoor **Coastal Stream** exhibit has a steady rhythm all its own and provides a small spawning ground for salmon and steelhead. In the huge **Marine Mammals Gallery,** you'll see models of a 43-foot-long barnacled gray whale and her calf, plus killer whales, dolphins, sea lions, and seals.

Unusual among the predominantly bay-related exhibits, but popular, is the live chambered nautilus in the **Octopus and Kin** exhibit. Also exciting here, in a spine-tingling way, is watching an octopus suction its way across the window. But to really get "in touch" with native underwater life, visit the **Bat Ray Petting Pool,** the **Touch Tidepool** of

SEAFOOD WATCH

Much of the work done by the Monterey Bay Aquarium is not necessarily visible to visitors. Since the mission of the aquarium is to "inspire conservation of the oceans," public education and scientific research are high priorities.

Particularly useful for seafood fans, and accessible via the aquarium's website, www.mbayaq.org, is its "Seafood Watch—A Guide for Consumers," a regularly updated listing designed to help us all make enlightened choices about the fish and seafood we eat. On the aquarium's "avoid" list at last report, for example, were bluefin tuna from the Atlantic and the Pacific; Chilean seabass; Atlantic cod; lingcod; orange roughy; Pacific red snapper and other rockfish; all sharks; and all farmed salmon, shrimp, and prawns. Consumer guidance in support of sustainable fisheries worldwide is available as a wallet-sized card—to order, call 831/647-6873—which can also be downloaded from the website as a PDF file.

Specific research initiatives sponsored by the Monterey Bay Aquarium include the Sea Otter Research and Conservation Program (SORAC) and the Tuna Research and Conservation Center (TRCC), the latter in conjunction with Stanford University's Hopkins Marine Station. The Monterey Bay Aquarium Research Institute (MBARI) at Moss Landing initiates dozens of bay-related projects each year and is also a full research partner in the Monterey Bay National Marine Sanctuary's Research Program. More information on all of these is available via the website.

starfish and anemones, and the **Kelp Lab.** Visitors can stroll through the **Sandy Shore** outdoor aviary to observe shorebirds.

New exhibits are continually added to the Monterey Bay Aquarium. The stunning and relatively new, $57 million **Outer Bay Galleries** nearly doubled the aquarium's exhibit space when it opened in early 1996. Devoted to marine life "at the edge," where Monterey Bay meets the open ocean, the centerpiece exhibit is a million-gallon "indoor sea," housing a seven-foot sunfish, sharks, barracudas, stingrays, green sea turtles, and schooling bonito—all seen through the largest aquarium window yet built, an acrylic panel some 15 feet high, 54 feet wide, and 78,000 pounds. Quite visually arresting in the **Drifters Gallery** is the orange and deep-blue **Sea Nettles** jellyfish exhibit, where one might stand and watch the show—something like a giant, pulsing lava lamp—for hours. Equally mesmerizing, on the way into the Outer Bay, is the swirling, endlessly circling stream of silvery mackerel directly overhead. The best way to watch—you'll notice that young children, not yet socially self-conscious, figure this out immediately—is by lying flat on your back. The **Mysteries of the Deep** exhibit studies the often-bizarre creatures that inhabit the murky depths. Seldom seen in an aquarium environment, the deep-dwelling species in this exhibit include mushroom soft coral, the predatory tunicate, the spiny king crab, and many others—a total of 40 to 60 species at any one time. In addition, daily video programs present live broadcasts from a remote submersible vehicle exploring the depths of Monterey Bay.

Debuting at the Monterey Bay Aquarium in spring 2000 was the **Splash Zone: Rock and Reef Homes** exhibit, designed particularly for families with small children. On display: some 50 species, from leafy sea dragons to black-footed penguins. An interactive tour leads through two different shoreline habitats. Special activities include crawl-through coral reef structures, "make a wave" water play, dress-up costumes, and sea creature puppets. New exhibits in 2001 included **Saving Seahorses,** exploring the survival challenges of these unique fish that are so popular in traditional Asian medicine, and **Mysteries of the Deep,** an exhibit of more than 40 species of animals collected from the depths of submarine Monterey Canyon just offshore. The 2002 exhibit schedule included **Jellies: Living Art.** Throughout the aquarium, also expect several rotating special exhibits each year.

Aquarium Tickets, Tours, Information, and Practicalities

Advance tickets are highly recommended, especially in summer. Call 831/648-4937 or, from within California, toll-free 800/756-3737. You can also order tickets via Ticketweb at www.mbayaq.org. If you purchase tickets more than 10 days in advance, they can bemailed to you. Otherwise, you can order tickets online as late as 7 A.M. on the day you arrive (assuming

Cannery Row

© ROBERT HOLMES/CALTOUR

they're available); at the aquarium, you won't need to wait in line. Simply present your email confirmation receipt at the will call/group entrance window and walk on in. You also can come on a just-show-up-and-take-your-chances basis—not advisable in summer.

The aquarium is open daily except Christmas, 10 A.M. to 6 P.M. (from 9:30 A.M. in summer). At last report, admission was $15.95 for adults; $13.95 for youths age 13 to 17, students with college ID, seniors, and active-duty military; $7.95 for children ages 3 to 12 and disabled visitors; and free for tots under 3.

Free self-guided tour scripts with maps, also available in Spanish, French, German, and Japanese, are available at the aquarium's information desk, along with current "special event" details, including the exhibit feeding schedule. All aquarium facilities and exhibits are accessible to the disabled; an explanatory brochure is available at the information desk. Taped audio tours are available for rent (for a small fee). Docent-guided aquarium tours and tours of the aquarium's research and operations facilities are also available for a fee. (Guided tours for school groups are free, however.) For group tour information and reservations, call 831/648-4860.

The aquarium's restaurant and gift/bookstores are worthwhile. The **Portola Café and Restaurant** has very good food and an oyster bar—the very idea surely a shock to the aquarium's permanent residents—and is fine for a glass of wine at sunset (open 10 A.M. to 5 P.M.). Along with good books, educational toys, and nature art, the aquarium gift shops have some touristy bric-a-brac and forgettable edibles like chocolate sardines.

For additional information, contact Monterey Bay Aquarium, 886 Cannery Row, Monterey, CA 93940-1085, 831/648-4800 or 831/648-4888 (24-hour recorded information). Or visit the "E-Quarium" anytime for virtual tours and information, website: www.mbayaq.org. For more information about the bay, the **Monterey Bay National Marine Sanctuary** headquarters and information center is near the aquarium at 299 Foam St. (at D St.), 831/647-4201, website: www.mbnms.nos.noaa.gov.

Avoid the worst of the human crush and come in the off-season (weekdays if at all possible). If you do come in summer, avoid the traffic jams by riding Monterey's WAVE shuttle, which operates from late May into September.

CANNERY ROW, FISHERMAN'S WHARF
Searching for Steinbeck on Cannery Row

Today the strip is reminiscent of Steinbeck's Cannery Row only when you consider how tourists are packed in here come summertime: like sardines.

Of all the places the Nobel Prize–winning author immortalized, only "Doc's" marine lab at 800 Cannery Row still stands unchanged—a humble brown shack almost as unassuming as it was in 1948, the year marine biologist Ed Ricketts met his end quite suddenly, his car smashed by the Del Monte Express train just a few blocks away. Today the lab is owned and preserved as a historic site by the city and is open for guided public tours from time to time.

MONTEREY

ABOUT DOC RICKETTS

Marine biologist Edward F. Ricketts (Steinbeck's character "Doc") was, according to Richard Astro, the writer's "closest friend and his collaborator on *Sea of Cortez*—his most important work of nonfiction, a volume which contains the core of Steinbeck's worldview, his philosophy of life, and the essence of a relationship between a novelists and a scientist . . . ." Much of the novelist's success, he says, is due to Ricketts's influence on Steinbeck's thinking.

According to Steinbeck himself: "He was a great teacher and a great lecher—an immortal who loved women. . . . He was gentle but capable of ferocity, small and slight but strong as an ox, loyal and yet untrustworthy, generous but gave little and received much. His thinking was as paradoxical as his life. He thought in mystical terms and hated and mistrusted mysticism."

To explore the world according to both Steinbeck and Ricketts, pick up a copy of *The Log from the Sea of Cortez*, published in a paperback edition by Penguin Books.

Wing Chong Market, Steinbecked as "Lee Chong's Heavenly Flower Grocery," is across the street at 835 Cannery Row and now holds a variety of shops. The fictional "La Ida Cafe" cathouse still survives, too, in actuality the most famous saloon on the Monterey Peninsula, **Kalisa's,** at 851 Cannery Row, 831/644-9316. Billed as "A Cosmopolitan Gourmet Place," Kalisa's, since the 1950s, has really been an eclectic people's eatery. Steinbeck personally preferred the beer milkshake.

Nowadays along Cannery Row, food and wine are becoming attractions in their own right. The new, 10,000-square-foot **Culinary Center of Monterey,** 625 Cannery Row, Ste. #200, 831/333-2133, website: www.culinarycenter ofmonterey.com, bills itself as a "Fantasy Land for Foodies." Here food lovers will find a complete food and wine center offering classes in just about everything—from Artisan Breads, Chocolate Desserts, and Cooking with Beer to Heart Healthy Cuisine and Sushi Party. The latter might be particularly inspiring after a tour through the Monterey Bay Aquarium. (Think about it.) Gourmet takeout is also available, the choices including an in-house bakery, appetizer bar (including local wines and microbrews), and cheese market. Inside the old Monterey Canning Company cannery, 700 Cannery Row, wine enthusiasts can enjoy the **Monterey County Wine Country Museum** and perhaps follow their museum visit with wine tasting, either at **A Taste of Monterey,** 831/646-5446, which offers tastings of regional wines as well as local produce, **Bargetto Winery** downstairs, 831/373-4053, or **Baywood Cellars** across from the Monterey Plaza Hotel, 831/645-9035.

Wine tasting or no, adults might escort the kids to the nearby **Monterey County Youth Museum** (M.Y. Museum), 601 Wave St., 831/649-6444 or 831/649-6446, website: www.mymuseum.org, a hands-on adventure full of interactive exhibits on science, art, and more. The museum is open Monday, Tuesday, Thursday, Friday, and Saturday 10 A.M. to 5 P.M., Sunday noon to 5 P.M. Admission is $5.50.

For more information about Cannery Row, or to seriously trace Steinbeck's steps through the local landscape, check in at the Cannery Row Foundation's **Cannery Row Welcome Center** in the green railroad car at 65 Prescott Ave., 831/372-8512 or 831/373-1902. Guided tours of Cannery Row can also be arranged there. The free and widely available *Official Cannery Row Visitors Guide* is well done, historically, and quite helpful. For other information, see www.canneryrow.com.

Fisherman's Wharf

Tacky and tawdry, built up and beat up, Fisherman's Wharf is no longer a working wharf by any account. Still, a randy ramshackle charm more honest than Cannery Row surrounds this 1846 pier, full of cheap shops, food stalls, decent restaurants, and stand-up bars indiscriminately frosted with gull guano and putrid fish scraps (the latter presumably leftovers from the 50-cent bags tourists buy to feed the sea lions). Built of stone by enslaved natives, convicts, and military deserters when Monterey was Alta California's capital, Fisherman's Wharf was originally a pier for cargo schooners. Later used by whalers and Italian American fishing crews to unload their catches, the wharf today is bright and bustling, full of eateries and eaters. Come early in the morning to beat the crowds, then launch yourself on a summer sightseeing tour of Monterey Bay or a winter whale-watching cruise.

MONTEREY STATE HISTORIC PARK

Monterey State Historic Park, with headquarters at 20 Custom House Plaza, 831/649-7118, website: www.mbay.net/~mshp, protects and preserves some fine historic adobes, most of which were surrounded at one time by enclosed gardens and walls draped with bougainvillea vines. Definitely worth seeing are the Cooper-Molera, Stevenson, and Larkin homes, as well as Casa Soberanes.

The park is open daily 10 A.M. to 4 P.M. (until 5 P.M. in summer) and closed Christmas, Thanksgiving, and New Year's Day. A small all-day admission fee ($5 adults) gets you into all buildings open to visitors. Guided tours of particular buildings are offered, as are general guided walking tours. Schedules vary, so ask about current tour times. You can also design your own tours or organize group tours; call for details. It's also possible to reserve regular guided tours; reservations must be made at least 15 days in advance. To reserve or to change plans, see the park's website or call 831/649-7118 on Monday 9 A.M. to 5 P.M. or on Wednesday or Friday 9 A.M. to 2:30 P.M. Reservations are "confirmed" only when approved by the park office; call to check. Fees must be paid at least 24 hours in advance of the tour. To poke around on your own, pick up the free *Path of History* self-guided walking tour map before setting out. Available at most of the buildings, the brochure details the park's adobes as well as dozens of other historic sights near the bay and downtown. Also stop by the Monterey State Historic Park Visitor Center at the Stanton Center.

Stanton Center and the Maritime Museum

A good place to start any historic exploration is the colossal Stanton Center at 5 Custom House Plaza. Inside you'll find the new **Maritime Museum Visitor Center,** where staff can answer questions about the park. They'll also direct you to the center's **theater,** which screens a 17-minute park-produced film about area history—a good way to quickly grasp the area's cultural context. Most walking tours of the park (led by state park staff) also leave from the Stanton Center. Buy guided walking tour tickets here, as well as tickets for the adjacent maritime museum. The Stanton Visitor Center is open seven days a week, 10 A.M. to 5 P.M. For state historic park information, call 831/649-7118 or try the web at www.mbay.net/~mshp. For visitor information, call 831/649-1770.

Don't miss the Monterey History and Art Association's **Maritime Museum of Monterey,** 831/372-2608, website: www.mntmh.org, which houses an ever-expanding local maritime artifact collection—compasses, bells, ship models, the original Fresnel lens from the Point Sur lighthouse, and much more—as well as the association's maritime research library, an acclaimed ship photography collection, and a scrimshaw collection. The museum's permanent exhibits, many interactive, cover local maritime history, from the first explorers and cannery days to the present. Special exhibits in 2001 included **World War II: The Pacific Theatre** and the **Sites and Citizens** exhibition of 109 black-and-white Robert Lewis photographs from the 1950s. The museum is open Tuesday through Sunday 11 A.M. to 5 P.M., closed Thanksgiving, Christmas, and New Year's Day. Admission is $5 adults, $2.50 seniors and youth, free for children under 12. Guided group tours are available by reservation.

MONTEREY'S DISTINCTIVE ARCHITECTURE

Monterey State Historic Park's **Larkin House,** a two-story redwood frame with low shingled roof, adobe walls, and wooden balconies skirting the second floor, and the **Cooper-Molera Adobe** are both good examples of the "Monterey colonial" architectural style—a marriage of Yankee woodwork and Mexican adobe—that evolved here. Most traditional Monterey adobes have south-facing patios to absorb sun in winter and a northern veranda to catch cool summer breezes. On the first floor were the kitchen, storerooms, dining room, living room, and sometimes even a ballroom. The bedrooms on the second floor were entered from outside stairways, a tradition subsequently abandoned. Also distinctive in Monterey are the "swept gardens"—dirt courtyards surrounded by colorful flowers under pine canopies—which were an adaptation to the originally barren home sites.

That so many fine adobes remain in Monterey today is mostly due to genteel local poverty; until recently, few developers with grandiose plans came knocking on the door. For an even better look at traditional local adobes and their gardens, come to the **Monterey Historic Adobe and Garden Tour** in April, when many private adobes are open for public tours.

Custom House and Pacific House

On July 7, 1846, Commodore John Drake Sloat raised the Stars and Stripes here at Alvarado and Waterfront Streets, commemorating California's passage into American rule. The Custom House Building is the oldest government building on the West Coast—and quite multinational, since it has flown at one time or another the flags of Spain, Mexico, and the United States. Until 1867, customs duties from foreign ships were collected here. Stop by to inspect typical 19th-century cargo, and say hello to Sebastian the parrot.

Once a hotel, then a military supply depot, the building at Scott and Calle Principal was called Pacific House when it housed a public tavern in 1850. Later came law offices, a newspaper, a ballroom for "dashaway" temperance dances, and various small shops. Today the newly renovated Pacific House includes an excellent museum of Native American artifacts (with special attention given to the Ohlone people) upstairs and interactive historical exhibits covering the city's Spanish whaling industry, pioneer/logging periods, California statehood, and more.

Larkin House and Others

Built of adobe and wood in 1835 by Yankee merchant Thomas Oliver Larkin, later the only U.S. consul in the territory during Mexican rule, this home at Jefferson and Calle Principal became the American consulate, then later military headquarters for Kearny, Mason, and Sherman. A fine pink Monterey adobe and the model for the local Colonial style, Larkin House is furnished with more than $6 million in antiques and period furnishings.

The home and headquarters of William Tecumseh Sherman is next door; it's now a museum focusing on both Larkin and Sherman. Around the corner at 540 Calle Principal, another Larkin building, the **House of the Four Winds,** is a small adobe built in the 1830s and named for its weathervane. The **Gutierrez Adobe,** a typical middle-class Monterey "double adobe" home at 580 and 590 Calle Principal, was built in 1841 and later donated to the state by the Monterey Foundation.

Cooper-Molera Adobe

The *casa grande* (big house) at 508 Munras Avenue, a long, two-story, Monterey Colonial adobe, was finished in pinkish plaster when constructed in 1829 by Captain John Bautista Rogers Cooper for his young bride, Encarnación (of California's influential Vallejo clan). The 2.5-acre complex, which includes a neighboring home, two barns, gardens, farm animals, and visitor center, has been restored to its 19th-century authenticity. Stop by the **Cooper Store** here, run by the nonprofit Old Monterey Preservation Society, to sample the wares—unique books, antique reproductions, and other specialty items representing the mid-1800s.

Robert Louis Stevenson House

The sickly Scottish storyteller and poet lived at the French Hotel adobe boardinghouse at 530 Houston Street for several months in 1879 while courting his American love (and later wife) Fanny Osbourne. In a sunny upstairs room is the small portable desk at which he reputedly wrote *Treasure Island.* While in Monterey, Stevenson collected *Treasure* material on his convalescing coast walks and worked on "Amateur Immigrant," "The Old Pacific," "Capital," and "Vendetta of the West." He also worked as a reporter for the local newspaper—a job engineered by his friends, who, in order to keep the flat-broke Stevenson going, secretly paid the paper $2 a week to cover his wages. The restored downstairs is stuffed with period furniture. Several upstairs rooms are dedicated to Stevenson's memorabilia, paintings, and first editions. Local rumor has it that a 19th-century ghost—Stevenson's spirit, according to a previous caretaker—lives upstairs in the children's room.

Casa Soberanes

Also known as the House of the Blue Gate, this is an 1830 Mediterranean-style adobe with a tile roof and cantilevered balcony, hidden by thick hedges at 336 Pacific. Home to the Soberanes family from 1860 to 1922, it was later donated to the state. Take the tour—the furnishings here are an intriguing combination of Mexican folk art and period pieces from China and New Eng-

ON EARLY MONTEREY

The town, when I was there, was a place of two or three streets, economically paved with sea sand, and two or three lanes, which were water-courses in the rainy season, and were, at all times, rent up by fissures four or five feet deep. There were no street lights. Short sections of wooden sidewalk only added to the dangers of the night, for they were often high above the level of the roadway, and no one could tell where they would be likely to begin or end. The houses were, for the most part, built of unbaked adobe brick, many of them old for so new a country, some of very elegant proportions, with low, spacious, shapely rooms, and walls so thick that the heat of summer never dried them to the heart. At the approach of the rainy season a deathly chill and a grave-yard smell began to hang about the lower floors; and diseases of the chest are common and fatal among house-keeping people of either sex.

There was no activity but in and around the saloons, where people sat almost all day long playing cards. The smallest excursion was made on horseback. You would scarcely ever see the main street without a horse or two tied to posts, and making a fine figure with their Mexican housings.

Excerpted from Robert Louis Stevenson's "The Old Pacific Capital," Fraser's Magazine, 1880 **Robert Louis Stevenson**

© CALIFORNIA DEPARTMENT OF PARKS AND RECREATION

MONTEREY

---

land—or just stop to appreciate the garden and its whalebone-and-abalone-bordered flowerbeds, some encircled by century-old wine bottles buried bottoms up.

California's First Theater

First a sailors' saloon and lodging house, this small 1844 weathered wood and adobe building at Scott and Pacific was built by the English sailor Jack Swan. It was commandeered by soldiers in 1848 for a makeshift theater, and it later—with a lookout station added to the roof—became a whaling station. Wander through the place and take a trip into the bawdy past, complete with the requisite painting of a reclining nude over the bar, brass bar rail and cuspidor, oil lamps, ancient booze bottles, and old the-

atrical props and paraphernalia. A modern postscript is the garden out back.

Today, the Troupers of the Gold Coast present melodramas here year-round on Friday and Saturday nights and Wednesday through Saturday in July and August; for information and reservations, call 831/375-4916.

Boston Store

Built by Thomas Larkin at the corner of Scott and Olivier as part of his business empire, this two-story chalk and adobe building once known as Casa del Oro (House of Gold) served a number of purposes. At one time or another it was a barracks for American troops, a general store (Joseph Boston & Co.), a saloon, and a private residence. Rumor has it that this "house of gold" was also once a mint or that (when a saloon) it accepted gold dust in payment for drinks—thus the name. These days it's the Boston Store once more, operated by the nonprofit Historic Garden League and themed as if in the 1850s. Antiques and reproductions, including handcrafted Russian toys and games, are on sale here. The garden league also operates the **Picket Fence** shop. For more information, call 831/649-3364.

Whaling Station

The old two-story adobe Whaling Station at 391 Decatur Street near the Custom House, now maintained and operated by the Junior League of Monterey County, was a flophouse for Portuguese whalers in the 1850s. Tours are sometimes available (call the main state park number for information) and include access to the walled garden. The junior league also makes the house and gardens available for weddings and other special events; call 831/375-5356 for details. Whale lovers, walk softly—the sidewalk in front of the house is made of whalebone.

California's First Brick House

This building nearby at 351 Decatur was started by Gallant Duncan Dickenson in 1847, built with bricks fashioned and fired in Monterey. The builder left for the goldfields before the house was finished, so the home—the first brick house in California—and 60,000 bricks were auctioned off by the sheriff in 1851 for just over $1,000.

OTHER MONTEREY SIGHTS
Colton Hall

The Reverend Walter Colton, Monterey's first American alcalde, or local magistrate, built this impressive, pillared "Carmel Stone" structure at 351 Pacific (between Madison and Jefferson), 831/646-5640, as a schoolhouse and public hall. Colton and Robert Semple published the first American newspaper in California here, cranking up the presses on August 15, 1846. California's constitutional convention took place here during September and October of 1849, and the state constitution was drafted upstairs in Colton Hall. Now a city museum, Colton Hall is open daily 10 A.M. to noon and 1 to 5 P.M. Closed Thanksgiving, Christmas, and New Year's Day.

Next door is the 1854 **Monterey jail** (entrance on Dutra Street), a dreary, slot-windowed prison once home to gentleman-bandit Tiburcio

Colton Hall

MONTEREY

Vasquez and killer Anastacio Garcia, who "went to God on a rope" pulled by his buddies.

Monterey Museum of Art

The fine Monterey Museum of Art at the Civic Center, across the street from Colton Hall at 559 Pacific, 831/372-5477, website: www .montereyart.org, offers an excellent collection of Western art, including bronze cowboy-and-horse statues by Charles M. Russell. The Fine Arts collection includes folk art, high-concept graphics, photography, paintings, sculpture, and other contemporary art in changing exhibits. Open Wednesday through Saturday 11 A.M. to 5 P.M., Sunday 1 to 4 P.M., closed holidays. Admission $5.

An impressive Monterey-style adobe, the amazing **La Mirada,** the onetime Castro Adobe and Frank Work Estate at 720 Via Mirada, 831/372-5477, is now home to the museum's Asian art and artifacts collection. The home itself is exquisite, located in one of Monterey's oldest neighborhoods. The original adobe portion was the residence of Jose Castro, one of the most prominent citizens in California during the Mexican period. Purchased in 1919 by Gouverneur Morris—author/playwright and descendant of the same-named Revolutionary War figure—the adobe was restored and expanded, with the addition of a two-story wing and huge drawing room, to host artists and Hollywood stars. The Dart Wing, added in 1993, was designed by architect Charles Moore.

These days, the 2.5-acre estate overlooking El Estero still reflects the sensibilities of bygone eras. The house itself is furnished in antiques and early California art, and the gardens are perhaps even more elegant, at least in season, with a walled rose garden (old and new varieties), traditional herb garden (medicinal, culinary, fragrant, and "beautifying"), and a rhododendron garden with more than 300 camellias, azaleas, rhododendrons, and other flowering perennials and trees. Changing exhibits are displayed in four contemporary galleries that complement the original estate. La Mirada is open Wednesday through Saturday 11 A.M. to 5 P.M., Sunday 1 to 4 P.M. Admission is $5.

Monterey Institute of International Studies

This prestigious, private, and nonprofit graduate-level college, headquartered at 425 Van Buren, 831/647-4100t, website: www.miis.edu, specializes in foreign-language instruction. Students here prepare for careers in international business and government, and in language translation and interpretation. Fascinating and unique is the school's 200-seat auditorium, set up for simultaneous translations of up to four languages. Visitors are welcome Monday through Friday 8:30 A.M. to 5 P.M., and most of the institute's programs—including guest lectures—are open to the public.

Presidio of Monterey

One of the nation's oldest military posts, the Presidio of Monterey is the physical focal point of most early local history, though the original complex, founded by Portolá in 1770, was located in the area now defined by Webster, Fremont, Abrego, and El Estero Streets. History buffs, note the commemorative monuments to Portolá, Junípero Serra, Vizcaíno, and Commodore Sloat, plus late-in-the-game acknowledgement of native peoples. (When Lighthouse Avenue was widened through here, most of what remained of a 2,000-year-old Rumsen village was destroyed, leaving only a ceremonial rain rock, a rock mortar for grinding acorns, and an ancient burial ground marked by a tall wooden cross.) Also here: incredible panoramic views of Monterey Bay.

The new **Presidio Museum,** in Building 113, Cpl. Ewing Rd., 831/646-3456, once a tack house, is now filled with cavalry artifacts, uniforms, pistols, cannons, photos, posters, and dioramas about local history, beginning with Native Americans and the arrival of the Spanish and continuing into Monterey's Mexican then American periods. The museum is open Thursday through Saturday 10 A.M. to 4 P.M. and Sunday 1 to 4 P.M. Call for driving directions. Pick up a copy of the Presidio's *Walk Through History* brochure at the Command Historian's Archives office, 1759 Lewis Rd., Ste. 209, 831/242-5536, to visit the earthen ruins and cannons of the **Fort Mervine** battlements; they were built by Commodore Sloat and dismantled in 1852. Fort Mervine's log huts were built during the Civil War.

The Presidio's main gate at Pacific and Artillery Streets leads to the **Defense Language Institute,** 831/242-5000, http://pom-www.army.mil.

Royal Presidio Chapel

Originally established as a mission by Father Junípero Serra in June 1770, this building at 555 Church Street near Figueroa became the Royal Presidio Chapel of San Carlos Borromeo when the mission was relocated to Carmel. The chapel was rebuilt from stone in 1791, and after secularization in 1835, it became the San Carlos Cathedral, a parish church. The cathedral's interior walls are decorated with Native American and Mexican folk art. Above, the upper gable facade is the first European art made in California, a chalk-carved Virgin of Guadalupe tucked into a shell niche. To get here, turn onto Church Street just after Camino El Estero ends at Fremont—a district once known as Washerwoman's Gulch.

OUTDOOR MONTEREY

Beaches and Parks

The 18-mile **Monterey Peninsula Recreation Trail** is a spectacular local feature—a walking and cycling path that stretches from Asilomar State Beach in Pacific Grove to Castroville. Scenic bay views are offered all along the way, as the trail saunters past landmarks including Point Pinos Lighthouse, Lovers Point, the Monterey Bay Aquarium, Cannery Row, Fisherman's Wharf, Custom House Plaza, and Del Monte Beach. The 14-acre **Monterey Beach** is not very impressive (day use only), but you can stroll the rocky headlands on the peninsula's north side without interruption, traveling the Monterey Peninsula Recreation Trail past the **Pacific Grove Marine Gardens Fish Refuge** and **Asilomar State Beach,** with tidepools, rugged shorelines, and thick carpets of brightly flowered (but nonnative) ice plants.

For ocean swimming, head south to **Carmel River State Beach,** which includes a lagoon and

bird sanctuary, or to **China Cove** at Point Lobos. **El Estero Park** in town—bounded by Del Monte Avenue, Fremont Boulevard, and Camino El Estero—has a small horseshoe-shaped lagoon with ducks, pedal boat rentals, picnic tables, a par course, hiking and biking trails, and the **Dennis the Menace Playground,** designed by cartoonist Hank Ketcham. (Particularly fun here is the hedge maze.) Also at El Estero is the area's first **French Consulate,** built in 1830, moved here in 1931, and now the local visitor information center. The **Don Dahvee Park** on Munras Avenue (one leg of local motel row) is a secret oasis of picnic tables with a hiking/biking trail.

For information on local parks and beaches, contact the **Monterey Peninsula Regional Park District,** 831/372-3196, website: www.mprpd.org.

Jacks Peak County Park

The highest point on the peninsula (but not *that* high, at only 1,068 feet) and the focal point of a 525-acre regional park, Jacks Peak offers great views, good hiking and horseback trails, and picnicking, plus fascinating flora and wildlife. Named after the land's former owner—Scottish immigrant and entrepreneur David Jacks, best known for his local dairies and their "Monterey Jack" cheese—the park features marked trails, including the self-guided **Skyline Nature Trail.** Almost 8.5 miles of riding and hiking trails wind through Monterey pine forests to breathtaking ridge-top views. From Jacks Peak amid the Monterey pines, you'll have spectacular views of both Monterey Bay and Carmel Valley—and possibly the pleasure of spotting American kestrels or red-shouldered hawks soaring on the currents. The park's first 55 acres were purchased by the Nature Conservancy, and the rest were bought up with county, federal, and private funds. To get here, take Olmstead County Road (from Highway 68 near the Monterey Airport) for two miles.

Other Outdoor Activities

Monterey and vicinity is most famous, of course, as an elite golfing oasis. For information on public access to area courses, which are primarily private, see the Monterey Peninsula Golfing special topic.

MONTEREY PENINSULA GOLFING

Golfers from around the globe make a point of arriving on the Monterey Peninsula, clubs in tow, at some time in their lives. The undisputed golf capital of the world, the Pebble Beach area between Carmel and Pacific Grove is the most famous, largely due to "The Crosby," which is now the AT&T Pebble Beach National Pro Am Golf Tournament. Making headlines in 1999 was news that the Pebble Beach Company and its four world-class courses had been sold to an investor group—Clint Eastwood, Richard Ferris, Arnold Palmer, and Peter Ueberroth—for $820 million.

It may cost a pretty penny—the greens fee at Pebble Beach Golf Links, for example, is more than $350—but the public is welcome at private **Pebble Beach Golf Links**, the **Links at Spanish Bay**, **Spyglass Hill Golf Course**, the **Peter Hay Par 3**, and the **Del Monte Golf Course** (in Monterey), all affiliated with The Lodge at Pebble Beach on 17 Mile Dr., tel. 831/624-3811, 831/624-6611, or toll-free 800/654-9300, www.pebblebeach.com. (Fees at Del Monte are $90 plus cart.) Also open to the public are the **Poppy Hills Golf Course**, 3200 Lopez Rd. (just off 17 Mile Dr.), tel. 831/624-2035, designed by Robert Trent Jones, Jr.; the **Pacific Grove Municipal Golf Links**, 77 Asilomar Ave., tel. 831/648-3177, great for beginners and reasonably priced; the **Bayonet** and **Black Horse Golf Courses** on North-South at former Fort Ord, tel. 831/899-7271; and the Robert Trent Jones (Sr. and Jr.) **Laguna Seca Golf Club** on York Rd. between Monterey and Salinas, tel. 831/373-3701 or toll-free 888/524-8629.

Though Pebble Beach is world-renowned for its golf courses and golf events, Carmel Valley and vicinity has nearly as many courses—most of them private in the country-club model, most recognizing reciprocal access agreements with other clubs. The **Rancho Cañada Golf Club**, about a mile east of Hwy. 1 via Carmel Valley Rd., tel. 831/624-0111 or toll-free 800/536-9459, is open to the public, however. As part of accommodations packages, nonmembers can golf at **Quail Lodge Resort & Golf Club**, 8000 Valley Greens Dr., tel. 831/624-2888, and at **Carmel Valley Ranch**, 1 Old Ranch Rd. in Carmel, tel. 831/625-9500, which features an 18-hole Pete Dye course.

Otherwise, get some fresh air and see the sights by bicycle. Either bring your own or rent one at any of several local outfits. Or tool around on a moped, available for rent through **Monterey Moped Adventures,** 1250 Del Monte Ave., 831/373-2696, which also rents bikes—tandem bikes, bikes with child trailers, and beach cruisers, plus the standards—and offers ample parking and easy access to the bayside bike/hike trail. Bike rentals are also the specialty of **Bay Bikes,** 640 Wave St., 831/646-9090, which has 21-speed, fat-tire bikes. You can rent in-line skates here, too, for around $15 a day. For more on bike rentals, see Monterey Transportation, below.

Another way to "see" Monterey Bay is by getting right in it, by kayak. **Monterey Bay Kayaks,** 693 Del Monte Ave., 831/649-5357, offers tours—bay tours and sunset tours, even trips into Elkhorn Slough and along the Salinas River—as well as classes and rentals of both open and closed kayaks. Wetsuits, paddling jackets, life jackets, water shoes, and a half-hour of on-land instruction are included in the basic all-day rental price of $30 or so. **AB Seas Kayaks,** 32 Cannery Row #5, 831/647-0147 or 888/371-6035, website: www.montereykayak.com, offers similar services at similar prices, including guided wildlife and birding tours. **Adventures by the Sea** also offers kayak rentals and tours—in addition to bike rentals (bikes delivered to your hotel room and picked up again at no charge), bike trips (including a Point Pinos Lighthouse tour), in-line skate rentals, and custom-prepared beach parties. Offices are located at 299 Cannery Row, 831/372-1807 or 831/648-7236.

The 145-foot Tallship **Californian**, the state's official tallship, spends May through August in Northern California waters—some of that time in Monterey Bay. While here, the *Californian* occasionally offers four-hour day sails on Monterey

SUCH A DEAL: SEASIDE AND MARINA

The secret may no longer be much of a secret, but just in case: People who live on the Monterey Peninsula know that prices for both food and lodging can be considerably lower in the "sand dune cities" of Seaside and Marina.

Ethnic eateries abound, most of them quite good. In Seaside, the wonderful **Fishwife Seafood Cafe,** 789 Trinity (at Fremont), tel. 831/394-2027, is everyone's favorite for seafood. The Fishwife offers quick and interesting seafood, pastas, and other California cuisine standards with a Caribbean accent, fresh Salinas Valley produce, and house-made desserts. (There's another Fishwife in Pacific Grove near Asilomar.) For more exceptional seafood, consider the Salvadoran **El Migueleño,** also in Seaside at 1066 Broadway, tel. 831/899-2199. The house specialty, Playa Azul, combines six different kinds of seafood with ranchera sauce, white wine, and mushrooms, served with white rice and beans. Yum.

But there are more nationalities to sample in Seaside. For Chinese food, there's **Chef Lee's Mandarin House,** 2031 N. Fremont St., tel. 831/375-9551. Or head for University Plaza at 1760 N. Fremont, not all that aesthetic but something of a haven for ethnic eateries. Best bets include **Fuji Japanese Restaurant and Sushi Bar,** tel. 831/899-9988, with good lunch specials; **Orient Restaurant,** tel. 831/394-2223, for Chinese and Vietnamese specialties, notably an abundance of soup and noodle dishes; and **Barn Thai,** tel. 831/394-2996, where a great lunch goes for about $5.

Marina offers restaurant possibilities, too, including **Café Pronto! Italian Grill,** 330-H Reservation Rd., tel. 831/883-1207, where pastas, pizzas, and seafood specialties star.

Bay. The trip includes lunch and lectures, and at last report the fee was $75 per person. The *Californian* also offers private charters, five-day Cadet Cruises (for ages 14–19), and three- and four-day hands-on High Sea Adventures for adults. The ship spends part of each year in San Francisco, Long Beach, and Chula Vista; crew positions are sometimes available. The *Californian* is a recreation of the *C.W. Lawrence,* a Revenue Service cutter built in Washington, D.C., in 1848. For current details and advance reservations, contact: **The Nautical Heritage Society,** 1064 Calle Negocio, Unit B, San Clemente, CA 92673, 949/369-6773 or toll-free 800/432-2201 (reservations only); website: www.californian.org.

Carrera Sailing, 66 Fisherman's Wharf (at Randy's Fishing Trips), 831/375-0648, offers the comfortable 30-foot sloop *Carrera* for nature tours, sunset cruises, and chartered sails. **Scenic Bay Sailing School and Yacht Charters,** 831/372-6603 or 831/625-6394, offers sailing lessons and is also willing to sail off into the sunset.

Other boating companies also offer bay tours (including cocktail cruises), winter whale-watching, and fishing trips (discount coupons often available at local visitor information centers). Good choices include **Monterey Sportfishing & Whale Watching Cruises,** 96 Fisherman's Wharf No. 1, 831/372-2203 or toll-free 800/200-2203; **Randy's Fishing Trips,** 66 Fisherman's Wharf #1, 831/372-7440 or 800/251-7440, which also offers Point Sur fishing charters; and **Chris' Fishing Trips,** 48 Fisherman's Wharf #1, 831/375-5951, which offers a fleet of four big boats, including the 70-foot *New Holiday.* **Sanctuary Cruises** at Fisherman's Wharf, 831/917-1042, website: www.sanctuarycruises.com, offers whale-watching aboard the *Princess of Whales,* a double-decked power catamaran that holds up to 149 people.

Another way to see the bay is to get a fish-eye view. An excellent assistant is the **Monterey Dive Center,** 225 Cannery Row, 831/656-0454 or 800/607-2822, website: www.mbdc.to, which offers rentals and lessons, chartered dive trips, guided dives and snorkeling, and night dives. The **Aquarius Dive Shop,** at two Monterey locations—32 Cannery Row, 831/375-6605, and 2040 Del Monte Ave., 831/375-1933, website: www.aquariusdivers.com—is another best bet for rentals, instruction, equipment, and repairs. Aquarius also offers guided underwater tours (specializing in photography and video) and can provide tips on worthwhile dives worldwide. If

In accommodations, less expensive choices in Seaside include the **Thunderbird Motel,** 1933 Fremont Blvd., tel. 831/394-6797, fax 831/394-5568, with some rates under $50. Good rooms are available for $50-100 at the **Best Western Magic Carpet Lodge,** 1875 Fremont Blvd., tel. 831/899-4221, fax 831/899-3377; the **Pacific Best Inn,** 1141 Fremont, tel. 831/899-1881, fax 831/392-1300; the **Seaside Inn,** 1986 Del Monte Blvd., tel. 831/394-4041, fax 831/394-2806; and the **Sandcastle Inn,** 1101 La Salle Ave., tel. 831/394-6556, fax 831/394-1578.

For something more stylish, nestled in next to two fine golf courses, try Seaside's **SunBay Suites,** 5200 Coe Ave., tel. 831/394-0136, fax 831/394-0221, with most apartment-style suites $100-150; weekly and monthly rates are available.

The newest resort on the Monterey Peninsula is in Marina—the plush 30-room **Marina Dunes Resort** in the dunes just west of Hwy. 1 at 3295 Dunes Dr., tel. 831/883-9478 or toll-free 877/944-3863, fax 831/883-9477, www.marinadunes.com. Rooms and suites in these beachfront bungalows feature California King beds, oversized furnishings, gas fireplaces, fully tiled baths with pedestal sinks, and either a private patio or balcony. Extras include heated pool, lap pool, hydrotherapy, and complete spa services—plus the opportunity to stroll on the beach, for miles in either direction. Rates are $150 and up. The lodge building offers meeting facilities and the **A.J. Spurs** restaurant and tapas bar.

For more information about Seaside, Marina, and vicinity, see Sand Dune Cities below.

you primarily need a ride out into the bay, **Monterey Express Diving Charters,** 32 Cannery Row, 831/659-3009 or 888/422-2999, website: www.montereyexpress.com, will take you there.

Adrenaline junkies can get a bird's-eye view of the bay by throwing themselves out of an airplane with **Skydive Monterey Bay,** 3261 Imjin Rd. in Marina, 831/384-3483 or 888/229-5867, website: www.skydivemontereybay.com. No experience is necessary; after a bit of instruction, you'll make a tandem jump harnessed to a veteran skydiver. The cost is $199. The company is open daily, year-round.

SAND DUNE CITIES

The sand-dune city of **Marina** was once the service center supporting Fort Ord. The U.S. Army base is now closed, replaced by the fledgling campus of California State University at Monterey Bay. So Marina, the peninsula's most recently incorporated city (1975), is also being transformed. Marina now boasts a new municipal airport, sports arena, and state beach popular for hang-gliding and surfing. On the ground, explore the nearby dunes; they're serene in a simple, stark way, with fragile shrubs and wildflowers.

Some are quite rare, so don't pick. The new **Fort Ord Dunes State Park,** 831/649-2836, once part of Fort Ord, features a four-mile stretch of beachfront. Head out to the Marina Municipal Airport to visit the two-acre **Sculpture Habitat at Marina,** 711 Neeson Rd., 831/384-2100, a collection of original sculptures by both local and world-renowned artists scattered throughout the grasslands, live oaks, and chaparral shrubs. Handicapped accessible. Check it out at www.sculptureparkatmarina.org.

Seaside and **Sand City,** to Marina's north, share "ownership" of former Fort Ord and the new CSU Monterey campus—and all three cities, the peninsula's traditionally low-rent neighborhoods, are still feuding with more affluent Monterey, Pacific Grove, and Carmel over future development plans. Opponents contend that proposed new hotels, golf courses, conference and shopping centers, and housing developments will adversely affect limited area water supplies, roads and other public infrastructure, and the environment.

But no one seems to object to the new **California State University Monterey** campus—the school's mascot is the sea otter—which has to date taken over some 2,000 acres at Fort Ord (of the 13,065 set aside for it) and is expected to grow to a student population of 13,000 to 15,000 by 2015. The emphasis at California's 21st state university campus is fairly unconventional. The focus here is on mastering subjects, rather than simply amassing course credits. Students are expected to become fluent in a second language as well as fully computer literate and to engage in community service work, along with mastering more than a dozen other essential skills. For information about and reservations (required) for 45-minute individual tours of campus, usually offered Monday through Friday at 10 A.M. and 2 P.M. and Saturday at 10 A.M., call 831/582-3518. Also worth exploring are some 50 miles of trails open to the public—now known as **Fort Ord Public Lands.** The 16,000 acres, administered by the U.S. Bureau of Land Management, are just about the last truly wild areas remaining on the Monterey Peninsula. Two fishable lakes and picnic areas are also available. As fun as it is to be out and about in these wide-open spaces, hikers, bikers, and horseback riders should take care to stick only to authorized trails; military explosives and other hazards are found in still-restricted areas, and habitat restoration is underway. Some 35 rare and endangered species inhabit Fort Ord Public Lands. For current trail information, contact the BLM field office in Hollister, 831/630-5000, website: www.ca.blm.gov/hollister.

Head inland on Canyon del Rey Road to **Work Memorial Park** and the nearby **Frog Pond Natural Area** (entrance in the willows near the Del Rey Oaks City Hall), a seasonal freshwater marsh home to birds and the elusive inch-long Pacific tree frog. Or take Del Monte Avenue off Highway 1 to **Del Monte Beach,** one of the least-bothered beaches of Monterey Bay (no facilities).

Del Monte Avenue also takes you past the **U.S. Naval Post-Graduate School,** 831/656-2441, website: www.nps.navy.mil, a navy preflight training school during World War II and now a military university offering doctorates. It's housed on the grounds of the stately 1880 Spanish-style **Del Monte Hotel.** The state's oldest large resort and queen of American watering holes for California's nouveau riche, the Del Monte was built by Charles Crocker and the rest of the railroading Big Four. You can tour the grounds from 8 A.M. to 4:30 P.M. daily. Downstairs in the old hotel is the school's **museum,** with memorabilia from the Del Monte's heyday (open Monday through Friday 11 A.M. to 2 P.M., closed on major holidays).

MELISSA SHEROWSKI

Marina State Beach

Worth stopping for in Seaside is the tranquil **Monterey Peninsula Buddhist Temple,** 1155 Noche Buena, 831/394-0119, surrounded by beautiful Asian-style gardens and carp-filled ponds. Come in May for the bonsai show.

For the present at least, accommodations are considerably less expensive here than elsewhere on the Monterey Peninsula. For example, RVers can hole up at **Marina Dunes R.V. Park,** 3330 Dunes Dr. in Marina, 831/384-6914, which has sites with full hookups as well as tent sites. It's just nine miles from Monterey, making it a good po-tential base of operations for your visit. And the new **Marina Dunes Resort,** 831/883-9478, website: www.marinadunes.com, is the first new resort hotel built in the greater Monterey area in 20 years. For more information about the sand dune cities, contact the **Marina Chamber of Commerce,** 211 Hillcrest, Wagner Hall, P.O. Box 425, Marina, CA 93933, 831/384-9155, website: www.marinachamber.com, and the **Sea-side/Sand City Chamber of Commerce,** 505 Broadway, Seaside, CA 93955, 831/394-6501, website: www.seaside-sandcity.com.

Practical Monterey

MONTEREY CAMPING AND AREA HOSTELS

Montery Area Camping

Right in downtown Monterey, RV campers can plug in at **Cypress Tree Inn,** 2227 N. Fremont St., 831/372-7586 or toll-free 800/446-8303 (in California), website: www.cypress treeinn.com. This pleasant motel also features amenities for RVers, including water and electric hookups, showers, restrooms, a hot tub, and sauna. Rates are under $50. Also in Monterey, if you're desperate, try pitching a tent in year-round **Veterans Memorial Park** on Via del Rey adjacent to the presidio, 831/646-3865. First-come, first-camped. Hikers and bikers pay a small fee; rates are under $50 for others, including restrooms and hot showers. No hookups. (Arrive before 3 P.M. and get a permit from the attendant.)

Outside town on the way to Salinas is **Lake Laguna Seca,** at the Laguna Seca Raceway just off Highway 68, with 93 tent sites and 87 spots for RVs (under $50). The park is not recommended for light sleepers when the races are on. For information and reservations, contact Laguna Seca County Recreation Area, P.O. Box 367, Salinas, CA 93905, 831/422-6138 (information), 831/647-7799 (reservations), or 888/588-2267, website: www.co.monterey.ca.us/parks.

For other camping options, head south to Carmel.

Hostelling International Monterey/Carpenter's Hall Hostel

It's happened at last: Monterey's onetime Carpenter's Union Hall, now the town's long-awaited 45-bed hostel, is finally open. Thanks to the Monterey Hostel Society, travelers can now bunk in separate women's and men's dorms (shared bathrooms) just four blocks from Cannery Row. Among its other features, the Carpenter's Hall Hostel offers the latest in water conservation technology—token-operated showers, metered faucets, ultra-low-flow half-gallon Microphor toilets, and water-saving appliances. Rates are under $50. The price includes a pillow, sheets, and a blanket; bring your own sleep sack for $1 discount (no sleeping bags allowed). Family and private group rooms (for up to 35) are available. For groups, discounts on overnight fees are available for youths and children. Given the area's popularity, advance reservations are usually essential. Reserve with personal check or Visa/MasterCard. Free on-site parking. To avoid adding to local traffic woes, leave your vehicle here and take public transportation. For more hostel information contact Carpenter's Hall Hostel, 778 Hawthorne St., Monterey, CA 93940, 831/649-0375, website: www.montereyhostel.org. The office is open 8 to 10 A.M. and 5 to 10 P.M.

Now that there is genuinely affordable accommodation available in Monterey, there are debts to be paid. Please express your gratitude by sending an extra contribution to the Monterey Hostel Fund, in care of the hostel.

If you'll be continuing on, excellent HI hostels are available in Santa Cruz, just north, and also farther north along the San Mateo County coastline. If you're heading south, there's also a great hostel in San Luis Obispo. For current details on these and other hostels in California, see http://hostelweb.com/california.htm.

MONTEREY MOTELS AND HOTELS

Current complete listings of accommodations (including prices) and restaurants in Monterey proper are available free from the convention and visitors bureau. Discounts of 50 percent or more are available at many inns, hotels, and motels during off-season promotions.

Monterey has a reasonable supply of decent motels, with most rooms in the $100 to $150 range, but many much higher. Most offer all modern amenities, and many establishments provide complimentary breakfast and other extra services. If you're here for the Jazz Festival, plan to stay at a motel in Marina or Seaside and vicinity, or on Fremont Street (motel and fast-food row) just a block from the fairgrounds. Motels on Munras are generally pricier. Be on the lookout, especially during high season, for "floating" motel rates, wherein the price may double or triple long *after* you've made your reservation. When in doubt, request written reservation and price confirmation.

For assistance in booking midrange to high-end accommodations in and around Monterey, contact **Resort II Me Room Finders,** 800/757-5646, website: www.resort2me.com, a firm with a good track record in matching peninsula visitors with appropriate local lodgings. Or try **Monterey Peninsula Reservations,** 831/655-3487 or 888/655-3424, website: www.monterey-reservations.com.

$50–100

Not many motel choices in Monterey are truly inexpensive. You might try the 15-room **Driftwood Motel,** 2362 N. Fremont, 831/372-5059,

where pets are allowed, or the **Econo Lodge,** 2042 Fremont St., 831/372-5851, with its pool and spa, free continental breakfast, and some rooms with kitchenettes. Both are basic but pleasant, comfortable enough for anyone sticking to the family budget, with better deals in the off-season.

Other motels with lower-priced rooms include the pleasant **El Adobe Inn,** 936 Munras Ave., 831/372-5409, website: www.El-Adobe-Inn.com, where amenities include in-room coffeemakers and refrigerators. Another possibility is the **Motel 6,** 2124 N. Fremont, 831/646-8585, which is clean, has a pool, and isn't far from the downtown action—reachable on any eastbound bus (take number 1). It's popular, so make reservations six months or more in advance or stop by at 11 A.M. or so to check for cancellations. There's another Motel 6 in the same price range (a bit less expensive) just outside Monterey proper, at 100 Reservation Rd. in Marina, 831/384-1000. For reservations at any Motel 6, call 800/466-8356 or try website: www.motel6.com.

Quite nice, quite reasonably priced, and surprisingly homey are the locally owned Comfort Inns on Munras Avenue. **Comfort Inn-Carmel Hill,** 1252 Munras Ave., 831/372-2908, features 30 cheery rooms with the usual amenities and electronic door locks. Adjacent is the **Comfort Inn-Munras,** 1262 Munras, 831/372-8088. Both are close enough—but not too close—to local attractions, especially if you're looking forward to some vigorous walking. The best thing about the location, which is quite close to Highway 1 and the Del Monte Shopping Center, is its walkability. Directly across the way, flanking Munras all the way back downtown to its junction with Abrego, is long, narrow **Dan Dahvee Park,** with its pleasant trees, flowers, birds—and walking paths.

Other motels with at least some lower-priced rooms include the 15-room **El Dorado Inn,** 900 Munras Ave., 831/373-2921, and the very nice **Best Western Park Crest Motel,** 1100 Munras, 831/372-4576 or 800/528-1234, where rooms include in-room coffeemakers and refrigerators, and extras include TVs with free HBO, a pool, a hot tub, and free continental breakfast. There are also a number of good motels off Fremont.

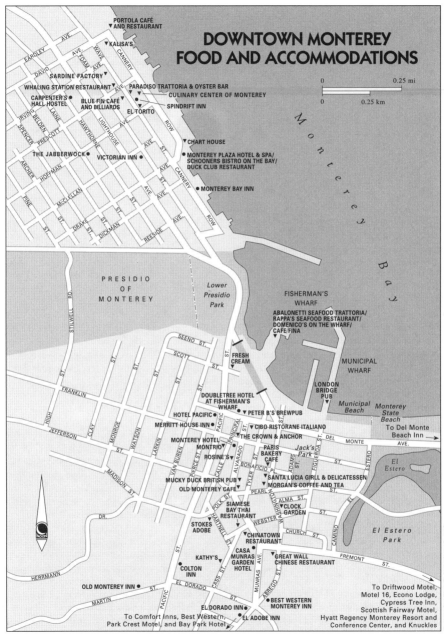

DOWNTOWN MONTEREY FOOD AND ACCOMMODATIONS

PORTOLA CAFÉ
AND RESTAURANT

KALISA'S

SARDINE FACTORY

WHALING STATION RESTAURANT
CARPENTER'S
HALL HOSTEL
BLUE FIN CAFÉ
AND BILLIARDS
EL TORITO

PARADISO TRATTORIA & OYSTER BAR
CULINARY CENTER OF MONTEREY
SPINDRIFT INN

THE JABBERWOCK
VICTORIAN INN

CHART HOUSE

MONTEREY PLAZA HOTEL & SPA/
SCHOONERS BISTRO ON THE BAY/
DUCK CLUB RESTAURANT

MONTEREY BAY INN

Monterey Bay

PRESIDIO
OF
MONTEREY

Lower
Presidio
Park

FISHERMAN'S
WHARF

ABALONETTI SEAFOOD TRATTORIA/
RAPPA'S SEAFOOD RESTAURANT/
DOMENICO'S ON THE WHARF/
CAFE FINA

FRESH
CREAM

MUNICIPAL
WHARF

LONDON
BRIDGE
PUB

Municipal
Beach

Monterey
State
Beach

To Del Monte
Beach Inn

DOUBLETREE HOTEL
AT FISHERMAN'S
WHARF

HOTEL PACIFIC
MERRITT HOUSE INN

PETER B'S BREWPUB

CIBO RISTORANE ITALIANO
THE CROWN & ANCHOR

MONTEREY HOTEL
MONTRIO
ROSINE'S

PARIS
BAKERY
CAFE

Jack's
Park

MUCKY DUCK BRITISH PUB
OLD MONTEREY CAFE

SANTA LUCIA GIRLL & DELICATESSEN
MORGAN'S COFFEE AND TEA

SIAMESE
BAY THAI
RESTAURANT

CLOCK
GARDEN

STOKES
ADOBE

CHINATOWN
RESTAURANT

El Estero
Park

KATHY'S
COLTON
INN

CASA
MUNRAS
GARDEN
HOTEL

GREAT WALL
CHINESE RESTAURANT

OLD MONTEREY INN

EL DORADO INN

BEST WESTERN
MONTEREY INN

To Comfort Inns, Best Western,
Park Crest Motel, and Bay Park Hotel

EL ADOBE INN

To Driftwood Motel,
Motel 16, Econo Lodge,
Cypress Tree Inn,
Scottish Fairway Motel,
Hyatt Regency Monterey Resort and
Conference Center, and Knuckles

El
Estero

0   0.25 mi
0   0.25 km

MONTEREY

© AVALON TRAVEL PUBLISHING, INC.

MOON

$100–150

Most of the area's less expensive motels, including those listed above, also offer pricier rooms. Centrally located, near Highway 1 and within easy reach of all area towns, is the **Bay Park Hotel**, 1425 Munras Ave., 831/649-1020 or 800/338-3564, website: www.bayparkhotel.com, featuring in-room coffeemakers, refrigerators, and hair dryers, plus on-site extras including a restaurant, pool, and hot tub. The nonsmoking **Best Western Monterey Inn**, 825 Abrego, 831/373-5345 or toll-free 877/373-5345, website: www.montereyinnca.com, is quite pleasant, with 80 spacious rooms—some with fireplaces, all with in-room coffeemakers and refrigerators. The motel also has a heated pool and hot tub. Best bets on Fremont include the **Scottish Fairway Motel**, 2075 Fremont St., 831/373-5551 or 800/373-5571, website: www.scottishfairway.com, where kitchens and kitchenettes are available.

$150–250

With a delightful Old World ambience, right downtown, the refurbished and fashionable **Monterey Hotel**, 406 Alvarado St., 831/375-3184 or 800/727-0960 (reservations), website: www.montereyhotel.com, comfortably combines the best features of a hotel with a bed-and-breakfast feel. This graceful 1904 Victorian is classic yet contemporary. The large breakfast room downstairs is reserved for complimentary breakfast (you can watch morning news programs on the TV). Just outside the cozy lobby is a wonderful small garden where wine and cheese are served every afternoon from 5 to 7:30 P.M., and cookies and milk are served 8 to 11 P.M. Rooms feature custom-made armoires (with TV sets), telephones, private baths with tub showers, antiques, queen-sized beds, and tasteful yet subtle decorating touches, all individualized. Only two rooms, smaller than standard, feature double beds. One suite (Room 217) features two separate entrances, a featherbed in the bedroom, a sofa bed in the sitting area, and an interior garden plot between. The street-facing suites feature fabulous fan-shaped windows, fireplaces, wet bars, refrigerators, Jacuzzi-style tubs, and queen-sized beds with down comforters. Back-landing suites include many of the same amenities, plus special touches like marble countertops and antique sinks. Every floor features an outdoor landing and deck area, and the third-floor interior landing boasts an intimate atrium parlor lit by a skylight. The only inconvenience is a lack of on-site parking, but an inexpensive city lot (rarely full) is nearby.

Offering good value in comfortable accommodations on acres of lovely landscape is the **Casa Munras Garden Hotel**, 700 Munras, 831/375-2411 or toll-free 800/222-2446 in California, 800/222-2558 nationwide, website: www.casamunras-hotel.com, conveniently located close to historic downtown. A restaurant is on-site.

Another good deal, right downtown, is the attractive and accommodating **Colton Inn,** 707 Pacific, 831/649-6500 or 800/848-7007, website: www.coltoninn.com, where extras include a sauna and sundeck. The comfortable **Doubletree Hotel at Fisherman's Wharf,** 2 Portola Plaza (adjacent to the Convention Center downtown at Pacific and Del Monte), 831/649-4511 or 800/222-8733 (reservations), website: www.doubletreemonterey.com, boasts a full-service fitness center and 370 rooms—all stylishly redecorated by fall 2002—and is convenient to just about everything.

$250 and up

For definite bayside luxury, head for the 290-room, Craftsman-style **Monterey Plaza Hotel & Spa**, 400 Cannery Row, 831/646-1700 or 800/368-2468, website: www.woodsidehotels.com. The Monterey Plaza's fine accommodations include Italian Empire and 18th-century Chinese furnishings, every convenience (even a complete fitness center with six Nautilus stations), and exceptional food service, including the Duck Club, one of the area's finer restaurants. The 15 Grand Suites feature grand pianos. Great on-site restaurants, rental bikes, and kayaks are available. Recently, the Monterey Plaza added a $6 million, 10,000-square-foot, Euro-style rooftop full-service spa and three spa-level suites. Coming soon to the neighborhood is a new IMAX theater.

Also deluxe and downtown is the contemporary, faux-adobe-style **Hotel Pacific,** 300 Pacific, 831/373-5700 or 800/554-5542, website: www.innsofmonterey.com. All rooms are suites and feature hardwood floors, separate sitting areas, balconies or decks, fireplaces, wet bars, honor bars, in-room coffeemakers, irons, ironing boards, two TVs, two phones, and terrycloth bathrobes. The tiled bathrooms have a separate shower and tub. Some rooms have a view. Continental breakfast, afternoon tea, and free underground parking are also available.

Surprisingly appealing is the **Spindrift Inn,** a onetime bordello at 652 Cannery Row (at Hawthorne), 831/646-8900 or 800/841-1879, website: www.innsofmonterey.com. Rooms feature hardwood floors, wood-burning fireplaces, TVs with VCRs, second telephones in the tiled bathrooms, marble tubs, featherbeds (many canopied) and goose-down comforters, all-cotton linens, and terry bathrobes. In the morning, continental breakfast and the newspaper of your choice is delivered to your room. With a rooftop garden and sky-high atrium, the Spindrift also offers a luxurious lobby with Oriental rugs and antiques.

The huge (575-room) **Hyatt Regency Monterey Resort and Conference Center,** 1 Old Golf Course Rd., 831/372-1234, toll-free 800/824-2196 (in California), or 800/233-1234 (central reservations), website: www.monterey hyatt.com, is definitely a resort. The spacious grounds here include an 18-hole golf course, six tennis courts (extra fee for both), two pools, whirlpools, and a fitness center—the works. The sports bar here, **Knuckles,** offers 200 satellite channels and 11 TV monitors.

Other upscale stays include the **Monterey Bay Inn,** 242 Cannery Row, 831/373-6242 or 800/424-6242, website: www.innsofmonterey .com, offering contemporary accommodations right on the bay (many view rooms with balconies). Near the Row is the 68-room **Victorian Inn,** 487 Foam St., 831/373-8000 or 800/232-4141, website: www.innsofmonterey.com, where gas fireplaces, complimentary continental breakfast, and afternoon wine and cheese are among the amenities. Concierge-level rooms include featherbeds and robes; some feature whirlpool tubs. Two family suites are available.

MONTEREY BED-AND-BREAKFASTS

Monterey's showcase country inn is the gorgeous ivy-covered 1929 English Tudor **Old Monterey Inn,** 500 Martin St., 831/375-8284 or 800/350-2344, website: www.oldmontereyinn.com, featuring 10 elegant rooms and suites, most with fireplaces. All have sitting areas, featherbeds, CD players, a Jacuzzi for two, and special touches such as skylights and stained glass. As if the inn itself isn't appealing enough, it is shaded by a specimen oak amid stunning gardens. Buckeye, the inn's rescued golden retriever, will probably greet you when you arrive. You'll also enjoy marvelous full breakfasts and a sunset wine hour. Rates are $250 and up.

The Jabberwock, 598 Laine St., 831/372-4777 or 888/428-7253, website: www.jabber wockinn.com, is a seven-room "post-Victorian" with a Victorian name and an Alice-through-the-looking-glass sensibility. Some rooms share baths. Rates include full breakfast (imaginative and good) plus cookies and milk at night. Rates are $100 to $250.

A classic in inimitable Monterey style is the historic **Merritt House Inn,** downtown at 386 Pacific St., 831/646-9686 or 800/541-5599, website: www.merritthouseinn.com. The original adobe, built in 1830, features three suites with 19th-century sensibility and modern bathrooms. Rates are $250 and up. The 22 surrounding motel-style rooms are more contemporary. Rates are $150 to $250.

At the European-style **Del Monte Beach Inn,** 1110 Del Monte Ave., 831/649-4410, most of the rooms share baths—which means this place is affordable for people who don't normally do B&Bs. Rates, including continental breakfast, are $50 to $100.

EATING IN MONTEREY

In Monterey, eating well *and* fairly inexpensively is easier than finding low-cost lodgings. Hard to beat is picnicking at the beaches or local parks. Happy hour—at the wharf, on the Row, and elsewhere—is a big deal in the area. In addition to cheap drinks, many bars serve good (free) food from 4 to 7 P.M. Due to an abundance of reasonably priced (and generous) breakfast places, an inexpensive alternative to three meals a day is skipping lunch (or packing simple picnic fare), then shopping around for early-bird dinners, a mainstay at many local restaurants. Do-it-yourselfers can pick up whatever suits their culinary fancy at the open-air **Old Monterey Marketplace Certified Farmers' Market** on Alvarado Street at Pearl, held every Tuesday 3 to 8 P.M. year-round (until 7 P.M. in winter). Great food, great fun. For more information, call 831/665-8070. On Thursday, head for the **Monterey Bay Peninsula College Certified Farmers' Market,** 831/728-5060, held 2:30 to 6 P.M. year-round at Fremont and Phisher.

No doubt helped along by the abundance of fresh regional produce, seafood, cheese and other dairy products, poultry, and meats, the Monterey Peninsula has also become a sophisticated dining destination. Some of the area's great restaurants are listed below (in various categories). But to get a true "taste" of the Monterey Peninsula, consider dining as well in nearby Pacific Grove and Carmel.

Monterey Standards

By "standard," we mean places people can happily—and affordably—frequent. The **Old Monterey Cafe,** 489 Alvarado, 831/646-1021, serves all kinds of omelettes at breakfast—try the chile verde—plus unusual choices like calamari and eggs, lingüiça and eggs, and pigs in a blanket. Just about everything is good at lunch, too, from homemade soups, hearty shrimp Louie, and the Athenian Greek salad (with feta cheese, Greek olives, shrimp, and veggies) to the three-quarter-pound burgers and steak or calamari sandwiches. Fresh-squeezed juices and espresso and cappuccino are featured beverages. Open daily for breakfast and lunch, 7 A.M. to 2:30 P.M.; breakfast served until closing.

Rosine's, nearby at 434 Alvarado, 831/375-1400, is locally loved at breakfast, lunch, and dinner. In addition to good pancakes, waffles, and other standards, at breakfast here you can get veggie Benedict (with avocado, sautéed mushrooms, and tomatoes instead of Canadian bacon). Lunch features homemade soups, salads, sandwiches, and burgers. Pasta, chicken, seafood, and steak appear on the menu at dinner, with prime rib available on Friday and Saturday nights.

Still reasonable (and delicious) is **Kathy's,** 700 Cass St., 831/647-9540. Pick any three items for a fluffy omelette. Your meal includes home fries, cheese sauce, bran muffins, and homemade strawberry jam for around $5. Sandwiches, similarly priced, are best when eaten on the patio.

For a casual lunch, dinner, or Sunday jazz brunch, the **Clock Garden,** 565 Abrego, 831/375-6100, is a popular place. Guests sit outside amid antique clocks planted in the garden, weather permitting. Closed Sunday evening.

Thai food fanatics should try **Siamese Bay Thai Restaurant,** 131 Webster St., 831/373-1550. You can make a meal of the appetizers—such things as veggie tempura with plum sauce and crushed peanuts. The **Great Wall Chinese Restaurant,** 724 Abrego St., 831/372-3637, has wonderful soups and an extensive vegetarian menu. At **Chinatown Restaurant,** close to downtown at 600 Munras St., 831/375-1111, arrive early for the $5 lunch buffet. The food goes fast.

Wonderful for lunch and takeout is the **Santa Lucia Grill & Delicatessen,** downtown at 484 Washington St., 831/333-1111, which serves memorable sandwiches—chicken pesto, chicken Malaysian—and thin-crusted brick oven pizza. Santa Lucia is also a full-service breakfast and dinner house. Or stop in at **Morgan's Coffee and Tea** next door, 498 Washington, 831/373-5601, for superb coffees as well as organic green, black, and herb teas—not to mention sweets like mixed nut cake and pear tarts. Unusual sandwiches and a great $4.95 pizza are available at lunch. Morgan's and Santa Lucia share pleasant outdoor street seating, complete with tables, chairs, and umbrellas. One block away, at 271 Bonifacio Place, is another pleasant, quite reasonable breakfast or lunch stop, **Paris Bakery Café,** 831/646-1620. The lunch menu includes sandwiches, salads, and soups, and the breads and pastries are wonderful.

© SUSAN PHILLIPS

Cannery Row

Monterey Pubs

For fans of British pubs, the real deal in Monterey is **The Crown & Anchor,** 150 W. Franklin St., 831/649-6496, dark and inviting with a brassy seagoing air. The full bar features 20 beers on tap, and the food is pretty darn good and reasonably priced—from the fish and chips or bangers and mash to spicy meatloaf, curries, cottage pie, and steak and mushroom pie. You'll also find salads and sandwiches and a special menu for the "powder monkeys" (Brit sailor slang for kids). Open for lunch and dinner daily. Also consider the **London Bridge Pub,** Municipal Wharf (north of Fisherman's Wharf), 831/655-2879, which specializes in authentic British cuisine and pours more than 60 different beers to wash it down with, and the **Mucky Duck British Pub,** 479 Alvarado, 831/655-3031, Monterey's original British pub.

With a logo depicting a one-eyed jack doing the proverbial 12-ounce curl, **Peter B's Brewpub,** 2 Portola Plaza (in the alley behind the Doubletree Hotel), 831/649-4511, offers 10 different Carmel Brewing Company microbrews on tap and good pub grub.

Eating at the Wharf

Named for tender squid breaded and then sautéed in butter, TV chef John Pisto's **Abalonetti Seafood Trattoria,** 57 Fisherman's Wharf, 831/373-1851, offers relaxed lunch and dinner—primarily seafood and standard Italian fare. The restaurant is fairly inexpensive with a nice view. Out on the end of the secondary pier at the wharf is **Rappa's Seafood Restaurant,** Fisherman's Wharf #1, 831/372-7562, an ocean-side oasis with outdoor dining, reasonable prices, good food, and good early-bird dinners.

Domenico's on the Wharf, another Pisto outpost, 50 Fisherman's Wharf #1, 831/372-3655, is famous for its Southern Italian accent. The menu features fresh seafood, homemade pasta, chicken, steak, and veal dishes and a long, very California wine list. An oyster bar is open from 10 A.M. daily.

But **Cafe Fina,** 47 Fisherman's Wharf #1, 831/372-5200 or 800/843-3462 (THE-FINA), is probably the best bet on the wharf—very Italian and very lively and lighthearted. On the menu you'll find everything from mesquite-barbecued fish and beef to smoked salmon on fettuccine with shallot cream sauce and a goat cheese and black olive ravioli. People go crazy over Cafe Fina's "pizzettes," little eight-inch pizzas popped hot out of the restaurant's wood-burning oven.

Eating on Cannery Row

If you're spending most of the day at the Monterey Aquarium, try the **Portola Café and Restaurant** there. Or head out onto the Row. Many of the places along Cannery Row offer early-bird dinners, so if price matters, go deal shopping before you get hungry.

Get your margarita fix and decent Mexican fare at **El Torito,** 600 Cannery Row, 831/373-0611. For something simple, an interesting choice for "views, brews, and cues" is the **Blue Fin Café and Billiards,** 685 Cannery Row, 831/375-7000. In addition to salads, sandwiches, and full dinners, the Blue Fin boasts a full bar emphasizing bourbons and scotches and also serves some 40 beers, including 22 ales and lagers on tap. There's plenty to do besides eat and drink, too, thanks to 18 pool tables, snooker, foosball, darts, and shuffleboard.

Naturally enough, seafood is the predominant dinner theme along the Row. The **Chart House,** 444 Cannery Row, 831/372-3362, brings its trademark casually elegant, nautical-themed decor to the Row, serving primarily seafood, steaks, and prime rib—predictably tasty. A bit inland but still looking to the sea for inspiration is TV chef John Pisto's casual **Whaling Station Restaurant,** 763 Wave, 831/373-3778, another locally popular dinner house offering everything from seafood and house-made pastas to mesquite-grilled Black Angus steaks. Open daily. Pisto's newest outpost is right on the Row: **Paradiso Trattoria & Oyster Bar,** 654 Cannery Row, 831/375-4155, open daily for lunch and dinner, serving fresh California-style Mediterranean food. You'll enjoy a full bar and an extensive Monterey County wine list.

The exceptional, semiformal **Sardine Factory,** 701 Wave St., 831/373-3775, serves California-style regional fare, from seafood and steaks to pasta and other specialties. Full bar. Open daily for dinner.

Another upscale Row restaurant going for the nautical theme is **Schooners Bistro on the Bay,** 400 Cannery Row (at the Monterey Plaza Hotel), 831/372-2628, specializing in California cuisine at lunch and dinner. If a bistro isn't chi-chi enough for you, consider the hotel's renowned but still casual **Duck Club Restaurant,** 831/646-1706, which serves outstanding bay views and superb American regional cuisine for breakfast and dinner daily.

Stylish Dining

Fresh Cream, across from Fisherman's Wharf and upstairs at 100-C Heritage Harbor, 99 Pacific St., 831/375-9798, has wonderful French country cuisine lightened by that fresh California touch. One of the Monterey Peninsula's best restaurants, it's more formal than most. Great views of Monterey Bay are served, too. Meals are expensive, but even travelers light in the pocketbook can afford dessert and coffee. Open for dinner only; menu changes daily. Call for information and reservations.

Still the contemporary dining hotspot downtown is the relaxed all-American bistro **Montrio,** 414 Calle Principal (at Franklin), 831/648-8880, *Esquire* magazine's New Restaurant of the Year in 1995. You might start with fire-roasted artichokes, terrine of eggplant, or Dungeness crab cakes, then continue with grilled gulf prawns, lamb tenderloins, or Black Angus New York steak. Vegetarians can dig into the oven-roasted portobello mushroom over polenta and veggie ragout. At last report, Monday was still cioppino night. You'll also enjoy marvelous sandwiches at lunch, exquisite desserts, a full bar, and a great wine list. Open Monday through Saturday for lunch, daily for dinner.

Equally stylish is the historic 1833 **Stokes Adobe,** 500 Hartnell St. (at Madison), 831/373-1110, its exteriors—including the gardens—preserving that Monterey Colonial style, its interiors beautifully recast with terra-cotta floors, plank ceilings, and a light, airy ambience. But the food is the thing. On the menu here is rustic, refined, and reasonably affordable California-style Mediterranean fare, from savory soups, salads, and tapas to seafood, chicken, lamb, and beef. Small plates might feature choices such as house-made mozzarella and ciabatta bread served with herbed olive oil and oven-roasted spinach gratin with mussels and herbed breadcrumbs. Large plates might include pasta tubes with house-made fennel sausage, manila clams, and spinach aioli; seared hanger steak with spinach cheese tart; or perhaps grilled lavender pork chops with leek-lemon bread pudding. Full bar, good wines. Open for lunch Monday through Saturday; dinner daily.

Other Mediterranean possibilities include **Cibo Ristorante Italiano,** 301 Alvarado, 831/649-8151, serving rustic but stylish Sicilian fare—plenty of pastas and pizzas, house specialties, and house-made desserts.

Serving up stylish "American country" fare, **Tarpy's Roadhouse,** inside the historic stone Ryan Ranch homestead three miles off Highway 1 on Highway 68 (at Canyon del Rey), 831/647-1444, is not to be confused with some cheap-eats-and-beer joint. The culinary challenge here is reinterpreting American classics—and that's no inexpensive task. Dinner includes such things as Indiana duck, Dijon-crusted lamb loin, baby back ribs, and grilled vegetables with succotash. Great desserts; salads and sandwiches at lunch; full bar. Open for lunch and dinner daily; brunch on Sunday.

For other high-style dining in Monterey, consider some of the choices on Cannery Row and at Fisherman's Wharf, listed above.

EVENTFUL MONTEREY

Visitors have a whale of a time at January's free **Whalefest** weekend, held at Fisherman's Wharf. Come in February for **A Day of Romance in Old Monterey**—"living history" storytelling, with 19th-century Monterey characters holding forth from the Cooper-Molera and Diaz Adobes, Larkin House, and Sherman Quarters. In late February come for the **Steinbeck Cannery Row Birthday Celebration** and **Mardi Gras on Cannery Row.** In early March, **Dixieland Monterey** brings three days of Dixie and swing to various venues around town. Later in March, come for the **Taste of Old Monterey** food and entertainment fest and the **Sea Otter Classic,** one of the world's best cycling parties. Mid-April, show up for the **Monterey Wine Festival,** when more than 200 California wineries strut their stuff. Traditionally, though, April is adobe month in Monterey, with the popular **Adobe Tour** through public and private historic buildings toward the end of the month. Monterey's **Historic Garden Tours,** beginning at the Cooper-Molera Adobe

and including the Stevenson and (usually) Larkin Houses, continue into September. Come in May for the **Marina International Festival of the Winds,** which includes the annual **Tour de Ford Ord** bike ride and the free Memorial Day weekend **Red, White & a Little Blues** music festival, staged at Custom House Plaza and along Alvarado Street in Monterey. In late May, the **Great Monterey Squid Festival** is a chic culinary indulgence for those with calamari cravings, plus arts, crafts, and entertainment.

June brings the acclaimed **Monterey Bay Blues Festival.** The **Fourth of July** celebration here is fun, with fireworks off the Coast Guard Pier, music in historic Colton Hall, and living history in Old Monterey. Come mid-month for the **Old Monterey Sidewalk Art Festival.** There's almost always something going on at nearby Laguna Seca, too, including July's **Honda International Superbike Classic.** In August, the **Monterey County Fair** comes to the fairgrounds, bringing amusement rides, livestock shows, and young faces sticky with cotton-candy residue. Also come in August for the annual **Winemaker's Celebration** and the **Downtown Celebration Sidewalk Sale.**

In early September, race car fans zoom into town for the three-day **Monterey Sports Car Championships** at Laguna Seca. Come mid-September, it's time for the city's most famous event of all: the **Monterey Jazz Festival,** the oldest continuous jazz fest in the nation. Not as daring as others, it nonetheless hosts legendary greats and up-and-coming talent. This is the biggest party of the year here, so get tickets and reserve rooms well in advance (four to six months). Birders, come in October for the annual **Monterey Bay Bird Festival** in nearby Elkhorn Slough. Other October possibilities include the annual **Old Monterey Seafood & Music Festival** and the **California Constitution Day** reenactment of California's 1849 constitutional convention. In mid-November comes the **Robert Louis Stevenson Un-Birthday Party** at the Stevenson House, as well as the **Great Wine Escape Weekend,** when area wineries all hold open houses, and the **Cannery Row Christmas Tree Lighting.** The **Christmas in the Adobes** yuletide tour in mid-December is another big event, with luminaria-lit tours of 15 adobes, each dressed up in period holiday decorations. Festivities are accompanied by music and carolers. Also come in December for the annual **Cowboy Poetry & Music Festival.** Celebrate New Year's Eve through the arts at **First Night Monterey.**

SHOPPING MONTEREY

Cannery Row is the obvious starting point for most visiting shoppers. Wander the Row's shops on the way to and from the Monterey Bay Aquarium. Intriguing possibilities include the Monterey satellite of the **National Steinbeck Center Museum Store** at 700 Cannery Row, just off Steinbeck Square, 831/373-3566, where you'll find most of the writer's works. The **Monterey Soap & Candle Works,** 685 Cannery Row Ste. 109, 831/644-9425, offers natural, handmade coconut, glycerin, and specialty soaps as well as beeswax candles. Don't overlook the gift and book shop at the nonprofit **Monterey Bay Aquarium,** 886 Cannery Row, 831/648-4800, which offers good books and a wonderful selection of educational and "eco" items. Proceeds support the aquarium and its educational and research mission.

Shopping is good in adjacent Pacific Grove, too—starting right next to Cannery Row at the **American Tin Cannery Premium Outlet** mall, 125 Ocean Ave., 831/372-1442, whose shops include Carole Little, Carter's Children's Wear, Nine West, and Woolrich. **The First Noel,** 562 Lighthouse Ave., 831/648-1250, specializes in all things Christmas, with other holidays thrown in for good measure.

The Monterey area boasts its fair share of antique and "heritage" shops. But consider actively supporting the preservation of local history. A few shops within downtown's Monterey State Historic Park actually operate out of park buildings—to help generate funds for historic preservation, garden development, and other improvements. Worth a look along Monterey's Path of History is the **Cooper Shop** in the Cooper-Molera Adobe at Polk and Munras Sts., 831/649-7111, operated by the nonprofit Old Monterey Preservation Society, which offers quality 1800s-vintage reproductions, from toys

to furniture. The **Boston Store** or Casa del Oro at the corner of Scott and Olivier, 831/649-3364, is run by the nonprofit Historic Garden League and offers antiques, collectibles, and reproductions. The garden league also operates the **Picket Fence,** an upscale garden shop.

There are many great shops downtown, and just wandering around is an enjoyable way to find them. **Avalon Beads** at 490 Alvarado St., 831/643-1847, features beads from around the globe as well as imported jewelry. The unique **California Views Historical Photo Collection,** 469 Pacific St., 831/373-3811, offers more than 80,000 historical photographs of California and Monterey. For "a superb collection of gourmet cheeses, fine wines, and gifts," the place is **Monterey Bay Vintage,** 481 Tyler St., 831/375-5087.

A first stop for books and magazines is **Bay Books,** 316 Alvarado St., 831/375-1855, with a nice selection of Steinbeck and titles of local or regional emphasis. Used-book aficionados will have a field day at places such as **Book End,** 245 Pearl St., 831/373-4046; **The Book Haven,** 559 Tyler St., 831/333-0383; and the Craftsman-style **Old Monterey Book Company,** 136 Bonifacio Place, 831/372-3111. **Carpe Diem Fine Books** at 502 Pierce St., 831/643-2754, specializes in rare and out-of-print books and is open only by appointment.

In addition to gathering up fresh produce and bakery items, head for downtown's Tuesday **Old Monterey Market Place** on Alvarado Street and Bonifacio Place (4 to 7 or 8 P.M.) for quality crafts.

For more shopping ideas and other visitor information, contact the **Monterey County Convention & Visitors Bureau,** 831/649-1770 (recorded) or toll-free 888/221-1010, website: www.montereyinfo.org, and the **Old Monterey Business Association,** 321 Alvarado St. Ste. G, 831/655-8070, website: www.oldmonterey.org.

MONTEREY INFORMATION

The **Monterey Visitor Center,** 401 Camino El Estero, is staffed by the Monterey County Convention & Visitors Bureau and offers reams of flyers on just about everything in and around the region. It's open April through October, Monday through Saturday 9 A.M. to 6 P.M., Sunday 9 A.M. to 5 P.M.; November through March, Monday through Saturday 9 A.M. to 5 P.M., Sunday 10 A.M. to 4 P.M. The Visitor & Convention Bureau also cosponsors the new **Maritime Museum Visitor Center** at 5 Custom House Plaza (near Fisherman's Wharf), open daily 10 A.M. to 5 P.M. For additional area information, including a current *Monterey County Travel & Meeting Planner,* contact **Monterey County Convention & Visitors Bureau,** P.O. Box 1770, Monterey, CA 93942-1770, 831/649-1770 or 888/221-1010, website: www.montereyinfo.org. For answers to specific questions, driving directions, and hotel reservations assistance, call the MCCVB Call Center at toll-free 877/666-8373 or inquire via email to info@mccvb.org. Another resource is the **Monterey Peninsula Chamber of Commerce,** 380 Alvarado St., Monterey, CA 93940, 831/648-5360, website: www.mpcc.com.

The *Monterey County Herald* is the mainline community news source. For an alternative view of things, pick up the free *Coast Weekly,* 831/394-5656, website: www.coastweekly.com, also offering entertainment and events information. Other free local publications detail dinner specials and current activities and entertainment.

MONTEREY TRANSPORTATION

Hitching into, out of, and around the Monterey Peninsula is difficult. Even getting around by car is a problem; finding streets is confusing due to missing signs, complex traffic signals, and one-way routes. Local traffic jams can be horrendous; save yourself some headaches and avail yourself of local public transportation. Drivers, park at the 12-hour meters near Fisherman's Wharf—the cheapest lots are downtown—and walk or take the bus. For more specific parking advice, pick up the free *Smart Parking in Monterey: How to Find Affordable Legal Public Parking* brochure at area visitors centers.

Bicycling

Bicycling is another way to go. The local roads are narrow and bike paths are few, but you can get just about everywhere by bike if you're care-

ful. Rent bikes at **Bay Bikes,** 640 Wave St. (on Cannery Row), 831/646-9090, where you can opt for mountain bikes, touring bikes, or four-wheel covered surreys known as pedalinas. Other bike rental firms include **Monterey Moped Adventures,** 1250 Del Monte Ave., 831/373-2696, and **Adventures by the Sea,** 299 Cannery Row, 831/372-1807, website: www.adventuresbythesea.com. For more about both, which also offer information on scheduled rides with the local **Velo Club Monterey,** see Outdoor Monterey, above.

Shuttles and Buses

Once parked, from Memorial Day through Labor Day you can ride Monterey's **WAVE**—Waterfront Area Visitor Express—a free shuttle bus system connecting the Tin Cannery shopping center (at the edge of Pacific Grove), the Monterey Bay Aquarium, Cannery Row, Fisherman's Wharf, and the town's historic downtown adobes with the downtown conference center, nearby motels and hotels, parking garages, and the Del Monte Shopping Center. WAVE's Monterey-Salinas transit buses are identified by a wave logo. Buses run north every 10 to 12 minutes and south every 30 minutes from 9 A.M. to 7:30 P.M. See a Monterey-Salinas Transit guide—or MST's website—for a route map.

To get around on public buses otherwise, contact **Monterey-Salinas Transit,** 1 Ryan Ranch Rd., 831/899-2555 or 831/424-7695 (from Salinas), website: www.mst.org. "The Bus" serves the entire area, including Pacific Grove, Carmel, and Carmel Valley, from Watsonville south to Salinas. Local buses can get you just about anywhere, but some run sporadically. Pick up the free Rider's Guide schedule at the downtown **Transit Plaza** (where most buses stop and where Alvarado, Polk, Munras, Pearl, and Tyler Streets converge) or at motels, the chamber of commerce, and the library. The standard single-trip fare (one zone) is $1.75; exact change required; free transfers. Some longer routes traverse multiple zones and cost more. Seniors, the disabled, and children can ride for $.85 with the transit system's courtesy card. Children under age 5 ride free. A regular adult day pass costs $3.50, and a super day pass (valid on all routes and all zones) is $7; seniors and students pay half price. From late May through mid-October, bus 22 runs south to famous Nepenthe in Big Sur (two buses per day in each direction; $3.50 one way).

Greyhound is at 1042 Del Monte Ave., 831/373-4735 or 800/231-2222 (system-wide information and reservations), website: www.greyhound.com, open daily 8 A.M. to 10 P.M.

Trains

Amtrak's Coast Starlight runs from Los Angeles to Seattle with central coast stops in Oxnard, Santa Barbara, San Luis Obispo, Salinas, and Oakland. If you'll be heading to the San Francisco Bay Area from the Monterey Peninsula, keep in mind that Amtrak also connects in San Jose with the San Francisco-San Jose **Caltrain**, 650/817-1717 or 800/660-4287 (in the service area), website: www.caltrain.com. For help in figuring out the way to San Jose—and how to get around the entire Bay Area by rapid transit—see www.transitinfo.org.

Monterey-Salinas Transit buses can get you to and from the **Amtrak** station in Salinas, 11 Station Place. Contact 831/422-7458 (depot), 800/872-7245, or website: www.amtrak.com for reservations and schedule information, including information on Amtrak's Thruway bus connections from Monterey and vicinity, a service included in some fares.

Airplanes

Not far from Santa Cruz, the **San Jose International Airport**, 408/501-7600, website: www.sjc.org, is the closest major airport served by commuter and major airlines. To get to Monterey from the airports in San Jose or San Francisco—or vice versa—you can take **Monterey-Salinas Airbus**, based at Marina Municipal Airport, 791 Neeson Rd., Marina, 831/883-2871. The buses shuttle back and forth up to 10 times daily.

You can fly directly into the Monterey Peninsula area. The **Monterey Peninsula Airport**, 200 Fred Kane Dr. #200, 831/648-7000, website: www.montereyairport.com, offers direct and connecting

flights from all domestic and foreign locales—primarily connecting flights, because this is a fairly small airport. **United Airlines/United Express,** 800/241-6522; **American/American Eagle Airlines,** 800/433-7300; and **America West Airlines/America West Express,** 800/235-9292, are all allied with major domestic and/or international carriers. You can fly directly into Monterey from San Francisco, Los Angeles, or Phoenix.

The newest peninsula airport is the **Marina Municipal Airport,** north of Monterey proper on Neeson Road in Marina, 831/582-0102, website: www.airnav.com/airport/OAR. Another possibility is the **Salinas Municipal Airport,** 831/758-7214, website: www.salinasairport.com, a mecca for private pilots and charters, helicopter tours, and flight training companies.

Other Transportation and Tours

An unusual thrill: cruising town in a facsimile Model A or Phaeton from **Rent-A-Roadster,** 229 Cannery Row, 831/647-1929, website: www.rent-a-roadster.com. The basic rate is about $30–35 an hour, but you can arrange half-day and full-day tours, too—and head south to Big Sur and San Simeon in style.

Ag Venture Tours, P.O. Box 2634, Monterey, CA 93942, 831/643-9463, website: www.whps.com/agtours, specializes in winery tours in the Salinas Valley, Carmel Valley, and Santa Cruz Mountains. A typical daylong tour includes tasting at three different wineries, a vineyard walk, and a picnic lunch.

Otter-Mobile Tours & Charters, based just south of town in Carmel, 831/649-4523 or 877/829-2224, website: www.otter-mobile.com, offers van tours of local sights ("Peninsula Highlights") as well as trips to Point Lobos, Big Sur, San Simeon and Hearst Castle, and wineries in the Salinas Valley. The company designs personalized tours around specific interests, from nature hikes to hunting down Steinbeck's haunts.

Almost a local institution, and particularly popular as an adjunct to corporate meetings and conventions, is **California Heritage Guides,** 535 Polk St., 831/373-6454, which organizes large group tours, teas, and shopping expeditions.

Pacific Grove:
Butterfly City

Pacific Grove began in 1875 as a prim, proper tent city founded by Methodists who, Robert Louis Stevenson observed, "come to enjoy a life of teetotalism, religion, and flirtation." No boozing, waltzing, zither playing, or reading Sunday newspapers was allowed. Dedicated inebriate John Steinbeck lived here for many years, in the next century, but had to leave town to get drunk. Pacific Grove was the last dry town in California: Alcohol has been legal here only since 1969. The first Chautauqua in the western states was held here—bringing "moral attractions" to heathen Californians—and the hall where the summer meeting tents were stored still stands at 16th and Central Avenues.

Nicknamed Butterfly City U.S.A. in honor of migrating monarchs (a big fine and/or six months in jail is the penalty for "molesting" one), Pacific Grove sparkles with Victorians and modest seacoast cottages, community pride, a rocky shoreline with wonderful tidepools, and an absolutely non-commercial Butterfly Parade in October. Also here is Asilomar, a well-known state-owned conference center with its own beautiful beach.

Pacific Grove is well served by Monterey-Salinas Transit buses (see Monterey Transportation). For events, accommodations, restaurants, and other current information, stop by the **Pacific Grove Chamber of Commerce** at Forest and Central, P.O. Box 167, Pacific Grove, CA 93950, 831/373-3304 or 800/656-6650, website: www.pacific-grove.org. Another interesting web portal is www.93950.com. The **Pacific Grove Public Library,** 550 Central (at Fountain), 831/648-3160, is open Monday through Thursday 10 A.M. to 8 P.M., Friday and Saturday 10 A.M. to 5 P.M.

MELISSA SHEROWSKI

Pescadero Point, along the 17-Mile Drive

Seeing and Doing Pacific Grove

From Pacific Grove, embark on the too-famous 17-Mile Drive in adjacent Pebble Beach. But better (and free), tour the surf-pounded peninsula as a populist. The city of Pacific Grove is one of few in California owning its own beaches and shores, all dedicated to public use. Less crowded and hoity-toity than 17-Mile Drive, just as spectacular, and absolutely free, is a walk, bike ride, or drive along Ocean View Boulevard. Or take the Monterey Peninsula Recreation Trail as far as you want; this path for walkers, joggers, bicyclists, skaters, and baby-stroller-pushers runs all the way from Marina to Pebble Beach. It's paved in places (right through downtown Monterey, for example), dirt in others. Or cycle from here to Carmel on the Del Monte Forest ridge via Highway 68 (the Holman Highway) for a spectacular view of the bay, surrounding mountains, and 17-Mile coastline to the south.

The "Three-Mile Drive"—or Walk

Along the Ocean View route are Berwick Park, Lovers Point, and Perkins Park; altogether, Pacific Grove boasts 13 community parks. These areas (and points in between) offer spectacular sunsets, crashing surf, craggy shorelines, swimming, sunbathing, and picnicking, plus whale-watching in season, sea otters, sea lions, seals, shorebirds, and autumn flurries of monarch butterflies. Stanford University's **Hopkins Marine Station** on Point Cabrillo (China Point) is also along the way, the crystal offshore waters and abundant marinelife attracting scientists and students from around the world. This is the first marine laboratory on the Pacific coast. (An aside for Steinbeck fans: This was the location of Chin Kee's Squid Yard in *Sweet Thursday*.) As for **Lovers Point**, the granite headland near Ocean View Boulevard and 17th Street, there is considerable disagreement over whether Pacific Grove could have been *sexual* in Methodist days, when it was named. The popular local opinion, still, is that the name was originally Lovers of Jesus Point. But conscientious researchers have established that the reference is to romance—and was, at least as far back as 1890. (For help in divining

An artist finds inspiration in Pacific Grove.

© ROBERT HOLMES/CalTour

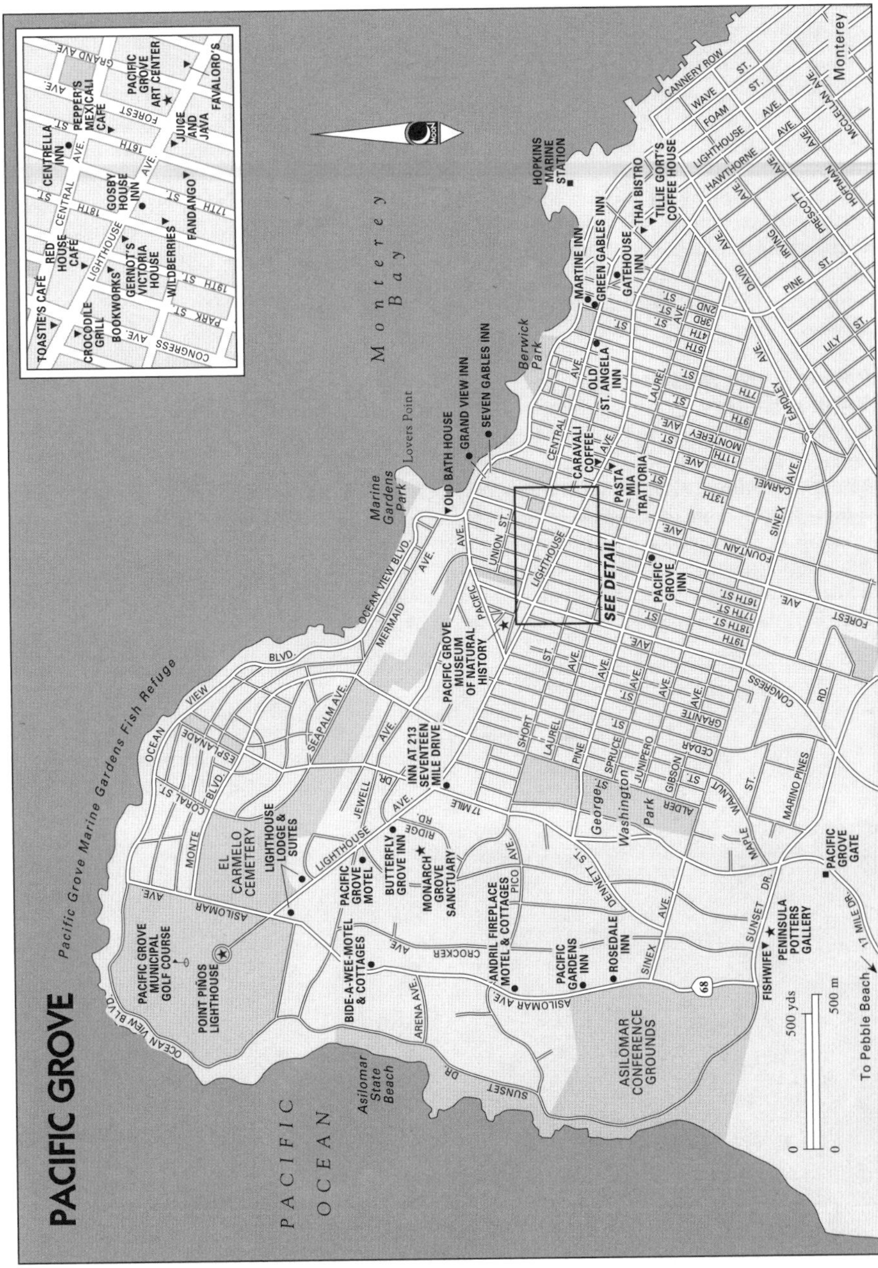

PACIFIC GROVE

Pacific Grove Marine Gardens Fish Refuge

Monterey Bay

PACIFIC OCEAN

Asilomar State Beach

DETAIL MAP:

TOASTIE'S CAFE
RED HOUSE CAFE
CROCODILE GRILL
BOOKWORKS
GERNOT'S VICTORIA HOUSE
WILDBERRIES
FANDANGO
CENTRELLA INN
GOSBY HOUSE INN
PEPPER'S MEXICALI CAFE
PACIFIC GROVE ART CENTER
JUICE AND JAVA
FAVALORO'S

GRAND AVE.
FOREST AVE.
CENTRAL AVE.
LIGHTHOUSE AVE.
18TH ST.
17TH ST.
16TH ST.
PARK ST.
CONGRESS AVE.

Lovers Point
Marine Gardens Park
Berwick Park

HOPKINS MARINE STATION
MARTINE INN
GREEN GABLES INN
THAI BISTRO
TILLIE GORT'S COFFEE HOUSE
GATEHOUSE INN
OLD ST. ANGELA INN
CARAVALI COFFEE
PASTA MIA TRATTORIA
PACIFIC GROVE INN
OLD BATH HOUSE
GRAND VIEW INN
SEVEN GABLES INN

SEE DETAIL

PACIFIC GROVE MUSEUM OF NATURAL HISTORY

INN AT 213 SEVENTEEN MILE DRIVE
LIGHTHOUSE LODGE & SUITES
EL CARMELO CEMETERY
PACIFIC GROVE MUNICIPAL GOLF COURSE
POINT PINOS LIGHTHOUSE
BIDE-A-WEE MOTEL & COTTAGES
PACIFIC GROVE MOTEL
BUTTERFLY GROVE INN
MONARCH GROVE SANCTUARY
ANDRIL FIREPLACE MOTEL & COTTAGES
PACIFIC GARDENS INN
ROSEDALE INN
FISHWIFE
PENINSULA POTTERS GALLERY
PACIFIC GROVE GATE

ASILOMAR CONFERENCE GROUNDS

To Pebble Beach
To 17 Mile Dr.

0   500 yds
0   500 m

68

PACIFIC GROVE

© AVALON TRAVEL PUBLISHING, INC.

other arcane area details, pick up a copy of *Monterey County Place Names: A Geographical Dictionary* by Donald Thomas Clark and its companion *Santa Cruz County Place Names.*) Trysting place or no, Lovers Point is not a safe place to be during heavy weather; entirely too many people have been swept away to their deaths. Picnic at **Perkins Point** instead, or wade or swim there (safe beach). **Marine Gardens Park,** an aquatic park stretching along Ocean View, with wonderful tidepools, is a good spot for watching sea otters frolic in the seaweed just offshore.

Pacific Grove Museum of Natural History

Pacific Grove's Museum of Natural History at Forest and Central showcases *local* wonders of nature, including sea otters, seabirds (a huge collection with more than 400 specimens), rare insects, and native plants. A fine array of Native American artifacts is on rotating display. Particularly impressive is the relief map of Monterey Bay, though youngsters will probably vote

for *Sandy,* the gray whale sculpture right out front. Besides the facsimile butterfly tree, the blazing feathery dried seaweed exhibit is a must-see. Many traveling exhibits visit this museum throughout the year, and the annual **Wildflower Show** on the third weekend in April is excellent. For information, contact the museum at 165 Forest Ave., Pacific Grove, CA 93950, 831/648-5716, website: www.pgmuseum.org. Open Tuesday through Sunday 10 A.M. to 5 P.M. Admission is free (donations greatly appreciated).

Point Piños Lighthouse

Built of local granite and rebuilt in 1906, this is the oldest operating lighthouse on the Pacific coast. The beacon here and the mournful foghorn have been warning seagoing vessels away from the point since the 1850s. The original French Fresnel lenses and prisms are still in use, though the lighthouse is now powered by electricity and a 1,000-watt lamp instead of whale oil. The lighthouse and the **U.S. Coast Guard Museum** inside are free and open Thursday through Sunday 1 to 4 P.M. **Doc's Great Tidepool,** yet another Steinbeck-era footnote, is near the foot of the lighthouse.

Across from the lighthouse parking lot is fascinating **El Carmelo Cemetery,** a de facto nature preserve for deer and birds. (For more birdwatching, amble down to freshwater **Crespi Pond** near the golf course at Ocean View and Asilomar Boulevards.) The Point Piños Lighthouse is two blocks north of Lighthouse Avenue on Asilomar Boulevard. For information about the lighthouse and Coast Guard Museum, call 831/648-5716, ext. 13.

Asilomar

The Young Women's Christian Association's national board of directors coined this Spanish-sounding non-word from the Greek *asilo* ("refuge") and the Spanish *mar* ("sea") when they established this facility as a YWCA retreat in 1913. **Asilomar State Beach** has tidepools and wonderful white-sand beaches, shifting sand dunes, wind-sculpted forests, spectacular sunsets, and sea otters and gray whales offshore. In-

Point Piños Lighthouse

FINDING PACIFIC GROVE

One day—I shall never forget it—I had taken a trail that was new to me. After a while the woods began to open, the sea to sound nearer hand. I came upon a road, and, to my surprise, a stile. A step or two further, and, without leaving the woods, I found myself among trim houses. I walked through street after street, parallel and at right angles, paved with sward and dotted with trees, but still undeniable streets, and each with its named posted at the corner, as in a real town. Facing down the main thoroughfare—"Central Avenue," as it was ticketed—I saw an open-air temple, with benches and sounding board, as though for an orchestra. The houses were all tightly shuttered; there was no smoke, no sound but of the waves, no moving thing. I have never been in any place that seemed so dream-like. Pompeii is all in a bustle with visitors, and its antiquity and strangeness deceive the imagination; but this town had plainly not been built above a year or two, and perhaps had been deserted overnight. Indeed, it was not so much like a deserted town as like a scene upon the stage by daylight and with no one on the boards. The barking of a dog led me at last to the only house still occupied, where a Scotch pastor and his wife pass the winter alone in this empty theater. The place was the "Pacific Camp Grounds, the Christian Seaside Resort." Thither, in the warm season, crowds come to enjoy a life of teetotalism, religion, and flirtation, which I am willing to think blameless and agreeable. The neighborhood at least is well-selected. The Pacific booms in front. Westward is Point Piños, with the lighthouse in a wilderness of sand, where you will find the light-keeper playing the piano, making models and bows and arrows, studying dawn and sunrise in amateur oil paintings, and with a dozen other elegant pursuits and interests to surprise his brave, old-country rivals. To the east, and still nearer, you will come upon a space of open down, a hamlet, a haven among rocks, a world of surge and screaming seagulls.

Excerpted from Robert Louis Stevenson's
"The Old Pacific Capital," Fraser's Magazine, 1880

land, many of Asilomar's original buildings (designed by architect Julia Morgan, best known for Hearst's San Simeon estate) are now historical landmarks.

Primarily a conference center with meeting rooms and accommodations for groups, Asilomar is now a nonprofit unit of the California state park system; subject to room availability, the general public can also stay here. Guest or not, anyone can fly kites or build sandcastles at the beach, stop to appreciate the forest of Monterey pine and cypress, and watch for deer, raccoons, gray ground squirrels, hawks, and owls. For information, contact: Asilomar Conference Center, 800 Asilomar Blvd., P.O. Box 537, Pacific Grove, CA 93950, 831/372-8016 or 831/642-4242 (reservations for leisure travelers), website: www.asilomarcenter.com. You can book online. To stay here, make reservations up to 90 days in advance, or call (not more than a week in advance) to inquire about cancellations. Rates are $100–150—full country-style breakfast included. Children ages 3–12 can stay (in the same room with an adult) for $5 more.

The 17-Mile Drive

The best place to start off on the famed 17-Mile Drive (technically in Pebble Beach) is in Pacific Grove (or, alternatively, the Carmel Hill gate off Highway 1). Not even 17 miles long anymore, since it no longer loops up to the old Del Monte Hotel, the drive still skirts plenty of ritzy digs in the 5,300-acre, privately owned Del Monte Forest in the four-gated "town" of Pebble Beach. Note the Byzantine castle of the banking/railroading Crocker family. Believe it or not, the estate's private beach is heated with underground pipes.

From **Shepherd's Knoll,** there's a great panoramic view of both Monterey Bay and the

Santa Cruz Mountains. **Huckleberry Hill** does have huckleberries, but botanically more fascinating is the unusual coexistence of Monterey pines, Bishop pines, and Gowen and Monterey cypress. **Spanish Bay,** a nice place to picnic, is named for Portolá's confused land expedition from Baja in 1769; Portolá was looking for Monterey Bay, but he didn't find it until his second trip. **Point Joe** is a treacherous, turbulent convergence of conflicting ocean currents, wet and wild even on calm days. ("Joe" has been commonly mistaken by mariners as the entrance to Monterey Bay, so countless ships have gone down on these rocks.) Both **Seal Rock** and **Bird Rock** are aptly named. **Fanshell Beach** is a secluded spot good for picnics and fishing, but swimming is dangerous.

Most famous of all is the landmark **Lone Cypress**—the official (trademarked) emblem of the Monterey Peninsula—at the route's midpoint. No longer lonely, this craggy old-timer is visited by millions each year; it's now "posed" with supporting guy wires, fed and watered in summer, and recovering well from a recent termite attack. At **Pescadero Point,** note the cypress bleached ashen and ghostlike by sun, salt spray, and wind.

PACIFIC GROVE

MELISSA SHEROWSKI

Lone Cypress at Pescadero Point

From Pacific Grove (or from other entrances), it won't cost you a cent to travel the 17-Mile Drive by bike—the only way to go if you can handle some steep grades. (On weekends, cyclists must enter the drive at the Pacific Grove Gate). By car, the drive costs $7.75, which is refundable if you spend at least $25 on food or greens fees at The Lodge at Pebble Beach. A map is available at any entrance. The drive is open for touring from sunrise to 30 minutes before sunset year-round. For more information, call Pebble Beach Resort at 831/649-8500 or 800/654-9300 or see website: www.pebble beach.com.

Pebble Beach

Very private Pebble Beach has seven world-class golf courses made famous by Bing Crosby's namesake tournament. The Crosby, now called the **AT&T Pebble Beach National Pro Am Golf Tournament,** is held each year in late January or early February. For golfing information or reservations, contact 800/654-9300 or website: www.pebblebeach.com. Only guests at the ultra-upscale resort accommodations can reserve more than 24 hours in advance. And some guests book their stays one to two years in advance. Other facilities are open to the public, including jogging paths and beautiful horse trails. Just about everything else—country clubs, yacht clubs, tennis courts, swimming pools—is private (and well guarded), though the public is welcome for a price. If you're here in August, join in the **Scottish Highland Games** or see how the rich get around at the **Concours d'Élégance** classic car fest at The Lodge.

More to See and Do

Pacific Grove boasts more than 75 local art galleries, enough to keep anyone busy. The **Peninsula Potters Gallery,** 2078 Sunset Dr., 831/372-8867, is the place to appreciate the potter's art; open Monday through Saturday 10 A.M. to 4 P.M. Also worth stopping for is the **Pacific Grove Art Center,** 568 Lighthouse, 831/375-2208.

There are hometown-style events year-round. The renowned Pacific Grove **Wildflower Show** is in mid-April, with more than 600 native species

MONARCH BUTTERFLIES AND BUTTERFLY TREES

Pacific Grove is the best known of the 20 or so places where monarch butterflies winter. Once partial to Monterey pine or cypress trees for perching, monarchs these days prefer eucalyptus introduced from Australia. Adults arrive in late October and early November, their distinctive orange-and-black Halloweenish wings sometimes tattered and torn after migrating thousands of miles. But they still have that urge to merge, first alighting on low shrubs, then meeting at certain local trees to socialize and sun themselves during the temperate Monterey Peninsula winter before heading north to Canada to mate in the spring and then die. Their offspring metamorphose into adult butterflies the following summer or fall and—mysteriously—make their way back to the California coast without ever having been here. Milkweed eaters, the monarchs somehow figured out this diet made them toxic to bug-loving birds, who subsequently learned to leave them alone.

Even when massed in hundreds, the butterflies may be hard to spot: with wings folded, their undersides provide neutral camouflage. But if fog-damp, monarchs will spread their wings to dry in the sun and "flash"—a priceless sight for any nature mystic.

Pacific Grove loves its monarch buterflies.

(150 outdoors) in bloom at the Pacific Grove Museum of Natural History. In March or April, the **Good Old Days** celebration brings a parade, Victorian home tours, and arts and crafts galore. In late July, come for the annual **Feast of Lanterns,** a traditional boat parade and fireworks ceremony that started when Chinese fishermen lived at China Point (their village was torched in 1906).

Pacific Grove's biggest party comes in October with **Welcome Back Monarch Day.** This native, naturalistic, and noncommercial community bash heralds the return of the migrating monarchs and includes the **Butterfly Parade,** carnival, and bazaar, all to benefit the PTA. Not coincidentally, from October to February the most popular destination in town is the **Monarch Grove Sanctuary** on Ridge Road (just off Lighthouse), where docent-led tours are offered daily; for reservations, call 831/375-0982 or toll-free 888/746-6627. Otherwise, come in October for the **Pacific Grove Victorian Home Tour** or in November for the **State Championship High School Marching Band Festival.** In December, check out **Christmas at the Inns,** when several local B&Bs, decorated for the holidays, hold an open house and serve refreshments.

PACIFIC GROVE

Staying in Pacific Grove

HOTELS AND MOTELS

To maintain its "hometown America" aura, Pacific Grove has limited its motel development. The local chamber of commerce provides accommodations listings. Bed-and-breakfast inns are popular in Pacific Grove—see separate listings, below—and these comfortable, often luxurious home lodgings compare in price to much less pleasant alternatives elsewhere on the peninsula.

$50–100

Especially if the monarchs are in town, consider a stay at the **Butterfly Grove Inn,** 1073 Lighthouse Ave., 831/373-4921 or 800/337-9244, website: www.butterflygroveinn.com. Butterflies are partial to some of the trees here. The inn is quiet, with a pool, a spa, some kitchens, and fireplaces. Choose rooms in a comfy old house or motel units. Closest to the beach are the 1930s-style cottages at **Bide-a-Wee-Motel & Cottages,** near Asilomar at 221 Asilomar Blvd., 831/372-2330. Some of the cottages have kitchenettes. Also comfortable is woodsy **Andril Fireplace Motel & Cottages,** 569 Asilomar Blvd., 831/375-0994, website: www.andrilcottages.com (the cottages have the fireplaces).

Always a best bet for a quiet stay is the well-located **Pacific Grove Motel** near Asilomar, close to the ocean and just west of 17 Mile Drive at Lighthouse Avenue and Grove Acre, 831/372-3218 or 800/858-8997. In addition to clean rooms with refrigerators, phones, and color TVs (some also have attractive patios), amenities include a heated pool, hot tub, barbecue area, and playground. Very low weekday rates in winter; two-night minimum stay on weekends.

$100–150

The state-owned **Asilomar Conference Center,** 800 Asilomar Ave. in Pacific Grove, 831/372-8016 or 831/642-4242 (reservations for leisure travelers), fax 831/372-7227, website: www.asilomarcenter.com, enjoys an incredible 60-acre setting on the Pacific Ocean, complete with swimming pool, volleyball nets, horseshoe pits, and miles of beaches to stroll. When it's not completely booked with businesspeople, conferences, and other groups, it can be a reasonably priced choice for leisure travelers. Adding to the earthy appeal: architect Julia Morgan designed many of the resort's pine lodges. Cheapest are the older, rustic cottages. Some units have kitchens and fireplaces. Call ahead for reservations, up to 90 days in advance, or hope for last-minute cancellations. Rates are $100–150, full country breakfast included. Children ages 3–12 stay (in same room with adult) for $5 more.

Near Asilomar is the **Pacific Gardens Inn,** 701 Asilomar Blvd., 831/646-9414 or toll-free 800/262-1566 in California, website: www.pacificgardensinn.com, where the contemporary rooms feature wood-burning fireplaces, refrigerators, TVs, and phones—even popcorn poppers and coffeemakers. Suites feature full kitchens and living rooms. Complimentary continental breakfast and evening wine and cheese are offered. Very nice. Right across from Asilomar is the all-suites **Rosedale Inn,** 775 Asilomar Blvd., 831/655-1000 or 800/822-5606, website: www.rosedaleinn.com, where all rooms have a ceiling fan, fireplace, large Jacuzzi, wet bar, refrigerator, microwave oven, in-room coffeemaker, remote-control color TV and VCR, even a hair dryer. Some suites have two or three TVs and/or a private patio.

$150 and up

The **Lighthouse Lodge and Suites,** 1150 and 1259 Lighthouse Ave., 831/655-2111 or 800/858-1249, website: www.lhls.com, are two different properties close to one another. The 31 Cape Cod–style suites feature abundant amenities—king beds, large Jacuzzi tubs, plush robes, mini-kitchens with stocked honor bars—and are the most expensive. The 64 lodge rooms feature basic motel-style comforts and are family friendly, with extras including breakfast and a complimentary poolside barbecue in the afternoon (weather permitting). Lower rates in the off-season; two-night minimum on summer weekends.

Three super-swank choices in adjacent Pebble Beach are definitely beyond the reach of most people's pocketbooks. At the **Inn at Spanish Bay,** 2700 17 Mile Dr. (at the Scottish Links Golf Course), 831/647-7500, rooms are definitely deluxe, with gas-burning fireplaces, patios, and balconies with views. Amenities include beach access, a pool, saunas, whirlpools, a health club, tennis courts, and a putting green. Also an unlikely choice for most travelers is **The Lodge at Pebble Beach,** another outpost of luxury on 17 Mile Drive, 831/624-3811. (If you don't stay, peek into the *very* exclusive shops here.) A recent addition are the elegant, estate-style cottages at the 24-room **Casa Palmero,** near both The Lodge and the first fairway of the Pebble Beach Golf Links. For still more pampering, the **Spa at Pebble Beach** is a full-service spa facility. For reservations at any of these Pebble Beach Resort facilities, contact 800/654-9300 or website: www.pebblebeach.com.

BED-AND-BREAKFASTS

Victoriana is particularly popular in Pacific Grove. The most famous Victorian inn in town is the elegant **Seven Gables Inn,** 555 Ocean View Blvd., 831/372-4341, website: www.pginns.com, which offers ocean views from all 14 rooms and an abundance of European antiques and Victorian finery. Rates include fabulous full breakfast and afternoon tea. Sharing the garden and offering equally exceptional, if more relaxed, Victorian style is the sibling **Grand View Inn** next door, 557 Ocean View Blvd., 831/372-4341. The view from all 11 rooms, with their antique furnishings and luxurious marble bathrooms, is indeed grand. Full breakfast, afternoon tea. Rates at both are $150 and up.

Another Pacific Grove grande dame is the pretty-in-pink, 23-room **Martine Inn,** 255 Ocean View Blvd., 831/373-3388 or 800/852-5588, website: www.martineinn.com, a study in Victorian refinement and propriety masquerading, on the outside, as a Mediterranean villa. Full breakfast here is served with fine china, crystal, silver, and old lace. Also enjoy wine and hors d'oeuvres in the evening, a whirlpool, spa, game room, library, and a baby grand piano in the library. Rates are $150 and up.

The lovely **Green Gables Inn,** 104 Fifth St., 831/375-2095 or 800/722-1774, website: www.foursisters.com, is a romantic gabled Queen Anne. The seaside "summer house" offers marvelous views, five rooms upstairs, a suite downstairs, and five rooms in the carriage house. Of these, seven feature private bathrooms. Rates include continental breakfast. The Green Gables, a Four Sisters Inn, was named the number one bed-and-breakfast inn in North America in 1997, according to the Official Hotel Guide's survey of travel agents. Rates are $150 and up.

The **Gosby House Inn,** 643 Lighthouse Ave., 831/375-1287 or 800/527-8828, website: www.foursisters.com, is another of the Four Sisters—this one a charming (and huge) Queen Anne serving up fine antiques, a restful garden, homemade food, and fresh flowers. All 22 rooms boast great bayside views, and most feature private bathrooms. Some have fireplaces, Jacuzzi tubs, and TVs. Rates are $100 and up.

PACIFIC GROVE

Pacific Grove Inn

The 1889 **Centrella Inn,** 612 Central Ave., 831/372-3372 or 800/233-3372, website: www .centrellainn.com, a national historic landmark, offers 20 rooms plus a Jacuzzi-equipped garden suite and five cottages with wood-burning fireplaces and wet bars. The cottage-style gardens are quite appealing, especially in summer. Rates include complimentary morning newspaper, full buffet breakfast, and a social hour in the afternoon (wine and hors d'oeuvres). Rates are $100 to $250.

The **Gatehouse Inn,** 225 Central Ave., 831/649-8436 or 800/753-1881, offers nine rooms in an 1884 Victorian that's strolling distance from the Monterey Bay Aquarium. Rates include full gourmet breakfast and afternoon wine and hors d'oeuvres. The property's comely sister inn is the Cape Cod–style **Old St. Angela Inn,** 321 Central Ave., 831/372-3246 or 800/748-6306, a converted 1910 country cottage featuring eight guest rooms decorated with antiques, quilts, and other homey touches. Amenities include a garden hot tub, solarium, living room with fireplace, complimentary breakfast,

and afternoon wine or tea and hors d'oeuvres. For a virtual preview, visit www.sueandle winns.com. Rates at both are $100 to $250.

The historic three-story (no elevator) **Pacific Grove Inn** is at 581 Pine (at Forest), 831/375-2825. Some rooms and suites in this 1904 Queen Anne have ocean views, most have fireplaces, and all have private baths and modern amenities like color TVs, radios, and telephones. Breakfast buffet every morning. Rates are $150 to $250.

Not every choice in Pacific Grove is Victorian. Perfect for aquatic sports fans—the proprietors can paddle you out to the best sea kayaking—is the **Inn at 213 Seventeen Mile Drive,** 981 Lighthouse Ave. (at 17 Mile Dr.), 831/642-9514 or 800/526-5666, website: www.innat213-17miledr .com. Guest rooms in this restored 1928 Craftsman home and affiliated cottages, all named for seabirds, feature king or queen beds and essentials like down comforters, TVs, and phones. All rooms have private baths. Generous buffet at breakfast; hors d'oeuvres and wine in the evening. Rates are $100 to $250.

Eating in Pacific Grove

Breakfast and More

Great for imaginative and very fresh fare at breakfast, lunch, and dinner is the **Red House Café,** a cozy cottage-style restaurant, tea salon, and tea shop at 662 Lighthouse Ave., 831/643-1060. You can get marvelous crêpes for breakfast or lunch, as well as good waffles and homemade soups, at **Toastie's Cafe,** 702 Lighthouse Ave., 831/373-7543, open daily 7 A.M. to 2 P.M. Or try the vegetarian dishes and cheesecake at **Tillie Gort's Coffee House** and art gallery at 111 Central, 831/373-0335.

For lattes, cappuccinos, espressos or just a good cuppa joe, head to **Caravali Coffee,** 510 Lighthouse Ave., 831/655-5633; **Juice and Java,** 599 Lighthouse Ave., 831/373-8652; or the dual-purpose **Bookworks,** 667 Lighthouse Ave., 831/372-2242, where you can sample the wares in the bookstore as well as the coffeehouse. Great for vegetarian fare as well as a wild cup or two is

the college hangout-style **Wildberries,** 212 17th St., 831/644-9836.

Lunch and Dinner

Thai Bistro, 159 Central Ave., 831/372-8700, is the place to go for outstanding Thai food. Those with a fireproof palate will love the restaurant's spicy dishes, and vegetarians will appreciate the large number of meatless entrées. Open for lunch and dinner daily. (There's another Thai Bistro in Carmel Valley at 55 W. Carmel Valley Rd., 831/659-5900.)

The **Crocodile Grill,** 701 Lighthouse Ave. (at Congress), 831/655-3311, offers eclectic and exotic decor along with fresh California-style Caribbean and Central-South American cuisine. Seafood is the specialty here—such as red snapper Mardi Gras—and for dessert, don't miss the house-made Key lime cheesecake with mango syrup. Beer and wine are served. Open for dinner nightly except Tuesday.

Popular with locals (and a favorite of the late, great Ansel Adams) is **Pablo's,** 1184 Forest Ave., 831/646-8888, featuring *real* Mexican food, including *mariscos.* Open 11 A.M. to 9 P.M. Locals say the homemade *chiles rellenos* at immensely popular **Peppers MexiCali Cafe,** 170 Forest Ave., 831/373-6892, are the best on the peninsula, but you won't go wrong with the tamales, seafood tacos, or spicy prawns. Beer and wine are served. Closed Tuesday, but otherwise open weekdays and Saturday for lunch, nightly for dinner. Also popular for seafood is the relaxed and family-friendly **Fishwife** in the Beachcomber Inn, 1996½ Sunset Dr., 831/375-7107, where such things as Boston clam chowder and grilled Cajun snapper fill out the menu. Beer and wine served. Open for lunch and dinner every day but Tuesday; brunch on Sunday.

Allegro Gourmet Pizzeria, 1184 Forest (near Prescott), 831/373-5656, offers innovative pizzas and exceptional calzones—people come from far and wide for the latter—but you can also enjoy pasta and risotto dishes, Italian-style sandwiches, and salads.

Favaloro's, 542 Lighthouse (at Fountain), 831/373-8523, is popular for traditional Italian, served in a bright location at street level in the Holman's Building. Try the gourmet specialty pizzas or the house-made pastas. Open for lunch Tuesday through Saturday and for dinner Tuesday through Sunday. Friendly **Pasta**

Mia Trattoria, 481 Lighthouse Ave. (near 13th), 831/375-7709, open nightly for dinner, serves exceptionally creative and good house-made pastas. Beer and wine served.

For boisterous Basque food, try **Fandango,** in the stone house at 223 17th St. off Lighthouse Ave., 831/372-3456. The restaurant serves up wonderful Mediterranean country fare—from mesquite-grilled seafood, steak, and rack of lamb to tapas, pastas, and paella—in several separate dining rooms warmed by fireplaces. Try the chocolate nougatine pie or *vacherin* for dessert. Sunday brunch here is superb. Formal dress prevails at dinner in the smaller dining rooms, but everything is casual in the Terrace Room. Open for lunch and dinner daily and for brunch on Sunday. Lunch is fairly inexpensive; dinners a bit pricier.

Upscale in more traditional continental style is gracious **Gernot's Victoria House,** at home in the 1892 Victorian Hart Mansion, 649 Lighthouse Ave., 831/646-1477, where fine Austrian and European fare stars. Beer and wine served. Open Tuesday through Sunday after 5:30 P.M. (reservations advised). Still one of the best restaurants on the entire Monterey Peninsula, some say, is the **Old Bath House** at Lovers Point, 620 Ocean View, 831/375-5195. It's elegant, expensive, and quite romantic, featuring lively Northern Italian and French fare, exceptional desserts, and appetizing views. Full bar, extensive wine list. Open nightly for dinner.

PACIFIC GROVE

Carmel: Cypress and Society

Vizcaíno named the river here after Palestine's Mount Carmel, probably with the encouragement of several Carmelite friars accompanying his expedition. The name Carmel-by-the-Sea distinguishes this postcard-pretty, almost too-cute coastal village of 5,000 souls from affluent Carmel Valley 10 miles inland and Carmel Highlands just south of Point Lobos on the way to Big Sur. Everything about all the Carmels, though, says one thing quite loudly: money. Despite its bohemian beginnings, these days Carmel crankily guards its quaintness while cranking up the commercialism. (Shopping is the town's major draw.) Still free at last report are the beautiful city beaches and visits to the elegant old Carmel Mission. Almost free: tours of

Robinson Jeffers's **Tor House** and fabulous **Point Lobos** just south of town.

Carmel hasn't always been so crowded or so crotchety. Open-minded artists, poets, writers, and other oddballs were the community's original movers and shakers—most of them shaken up and out of San Francisco after the 1906 earthquake. Upton Sinclair, Sinclair Lewis, Robinson Jeffers, and Jack London were some of the literary lights who once twinkled in this town. Master photographers Ansel Adams and Edward Weston were more recent residents. But, as often happens in California,

Carmel-by-the-Sea

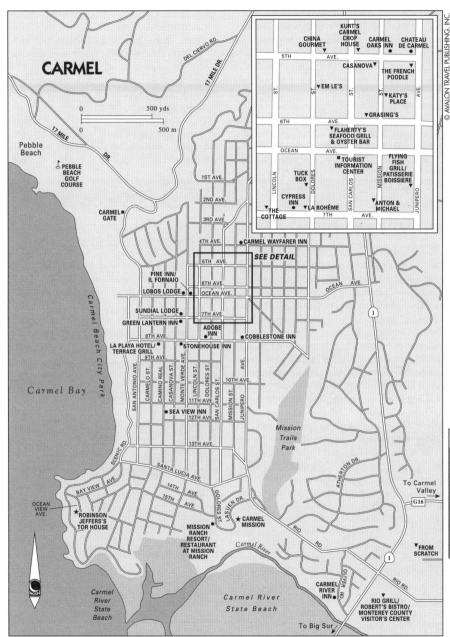

© AVALON TRAVEL PUBLISHING, INC.

CARMEL

Pebble Beach

17 MILE DR.

DEL CIERVO RD.

0   500 yds
0   500 m

17 MILE DR.

PEBBLE BEACH GOLF COURSE

CARMEL GATE

1ST AVE.

2ND AVE.

3RD AVE.

4TH AVE.

CARMEL WAYFARER INN

5TH AVE.

SEE DETAIL

PINE INN/ IL FORNAIO

LOBOS LODGE

6TH AVE.

OCEAN AVE.

OCEAN AVE.

SUNDIAL LODGE

GREEN LANTERN INN

7TH AVE.

ADOBE INN

COBBLESTONE INN

8TH AVE.

LA PLAYA HOTEL/ TERRACE GRILL

STONEHOUSE INN

9TH AVE.

SAN ANTONIO AVE.

CARMELO ST.

CAMINO REAL

CASANOVA ST.

MONTE VERDE AVE.

LINCOLN ST.

DOLORES ST.

SAN CARLOS ST.

MISSION ST.

JUNIPERO

10TH AVE.

11TH AVE.

SEA VIEW INN

12TH AVE.

Carmel Bay

Carmel Beach City Park

SCENIC RD.

13TH AVE.

Mission Trails Park

SANTA LUCIA AVE.

BAY VIEW AVE.

14TH AVE.

15TH AVE.

DOLORES ST.

LASUEN DR.

OCEAN VIEW AVE.

ROBINSON JEFFERS'S TOR HOUSE

MISSION RANCH RESORT/ RESTAURANT AT MISSION RANCH

CARMEL MISSION

Carmel River

RIO RD.

ATHERTON DR.

OCEAN AVE.

1

To Carmel Valley

G16

FROM SCRATCH

Carmel River State Beach

Carmel River State Beach

CARMEL RIVER INN

OLIVIER RD.

RIO RD.

1

RIO GRILL/ ROBERT'S BISTRO/ MONTEREY COUNTY VISITOR'S CENTER

To Big Sur

MOON

N

CARMEL

Detail inset:

CHINA GOURMET

KURT'S CARMEL CHOP HOUSE

CARMEL OAKS INN

CHATEAU DE CARMEL

5TH AVE.

CASANOVA

THE FRENCH POODLE

EM LE'S

KATY'S PLACE

GRASING'S

6TH AVE.

FLAHERTY'S SEAFOOD GRILL & OYSTER BAR

OCEAN AVE.

TOURIST INFORMATION CENTER

FLYING FISH GRILL/ PATISSERIE BOISSIERE

TUCK BOX

CYPRESS INN

LA BOHÊME

ANTON & MICHAEL

THE COTTAGE

7TH AVE.

LINCOLN

DOLORES

SAN CARLOS

MISSION

JUNIPERO

ST.

ST.

ST.

ST.

AVE.

land values shot up and the original bohemians were priced right out of the neighborhood.

Carmel-by-the-Sea is facing trying times. Sinclair Lewis predicted the future in 1933 when he said to Carmelites: "For God's sake, don't let the Babbits run the town. You've got every other city in the country beat." Growth—how much and what kind—has always been the issue here. Tourists who come here to stroll and shop (locals sometimes refer to them as "the T-shirt and ice cream people") are both loved and hated.

In summer and on most warm-weather weekends, traffic on Highway 1 is backed up for a mile or more in either direction by the Carmel "crunch." Sane people take the bus, ride bikes, or walk. The overly quaint community is so congested that parking is usually nonexistent. (Even if you do find a parking spot in downtown Carmel, you won't get to dawdle; parking is limited to one hour, and you'll risk a steep fine if you're late getting back.) Other scarce items in Carmel: streetlights, traffic signals, street signs, sidewalks, house numbers, mailboxes, neon signs, and jukeboxes.

Seeing and Doing Carmel

OUT AND ABOUT

To get oriented, take a walk. Carmel has a few tiny parks hidden here and there, including one especially for walkers—**Mission Trails Park,** featuring about five miles of trails winding through redwoods, willows, and wildflowers (in season). Finding it is challenging since Carmel doesn't believe in signs. To do the walk the easy way, start at the park's cleverly concealed Flanders Drive entrance off Hatton Road (appreciate the **Lester Rowntree Memorial Arboretum** just inside) before strolling downhill to the Rio Road trailhead near the mission. Then visit the mission or head downtown. Carmel's shops and galleries alone are an easy daylong distraction for true shoppers, but local architecture is also intriguing. The area between Fifth and Eighth Streets and Junipero and the city beach is packed with seacoast cottages, Carmel gingerbread "dollhouses," and adobe-and-post homes typical of the area.

Carmel Walks, 831/642-2700, website: www.carmelwalks.com, offers a great two-hour guided walk, with highlights including the town's original fairytale cottages, architecture by Bernard Maybeck and Charles S. Greene, onetime homes of bohemians, the local doings of photographers Edward Weston and Ansel Adams, and oddities such as a house made entirely of doors and the one built from pieces of old ships. The tour also visits Doris Day's pet-friendly hotel, includes tales of locally famous dogs, and notes local restaurants where dogs are permitted to dine with the family out on the patio. At last report, walks—$20 per person—were offered Tuesday through Friday at 10 A.M. and Saturday at 10 A.M. and 2 P.M. Reservations required.

CARMEL BEACHES

The downtown crescent of **Carmel Beach City Park** is beautiful—steeply sloping, blinding-white

COURTESY MONTEREY COUNTY CONVENTION & VISITORS BUREAU/© RANDY WILDER

Visitors and locals enjoy the sandy shore and dramatic coastline at Carmel Beach.

CARMEL

sands and aquamarine waters—but too cold and dangerous for swimming. It's also a tourist zoo in summer. (A winter sunset stroll is wonderful, though.) A better alternative is to take Scenic Road (or Carmelo Street) south from Santa Lucia off Rio Road to **Carmel River State Beach,** 831/649-2836, fringed with eucalyptus and cypress and often uncrowded (but dangerous in high surf). This is where locals go to get away. The nearby marsh is a bird sanctuary providing habitat for hawks, kingfishers, cormorants, herons, pelicans, sandpipers, snowy egrets, and sometimes flocks of migrating ducks and geese. Beyond (and almost a secret) is **Middle Beach,** a curving sandy crescent on the south side of the Carmel River and just north of **Monastery Beach** at San Jose Creek. Middle is accessible year-round by taking Ribera Road from Highway 1; in summer or fall you can also get there by walking across the dry riverbed and following the trail. Safety note: Middle Beach is hazardous for swimming and sometimes even for walking, due to freak 10-foot waves. Monastery Beach is popular for scuba diving, but its surf conditions are equally treacherous.

© ROBERT HOLMES/CALTOUR

Carmel Mission

CARMEL MISSION

The Carmel Mission, properly called Mission Basilica San Carlos Borromeo del Rio Carmelo, is wonderful and well worth a visit. California's second mission, it was originally established at the Monterey Presidio in 1770, then moved here the following year. It is the one-time headquarters and favorite foreign home of Father Junípero Serra, whose remains are buried at the foot of the altar in the sanctuary. The mission's magnificent vine-draped cathedral is the first thing to catch the eye. The romantic Baroque stone church, one of the state's most graceful buildings, complete with a four-bell Moorish tower, arched roof, and star-shaped central window, was completed in 1797.

Most of the buildings here are reconstructions, however, since the Carmel Mission fell to ruins in the 1800s. But these "new" old buildings, painstakingly rebuilt and restored in the 1930s under the direction of Sir Harry Downie, fail to suggest the size and complexity of the original

bustling mission complex: an odd-shaped quadrangle with a central fountain, gardens, kitchen, carpenter and blacksmith shops, soldiers' housing, and priests' quarters. The native peoples attached to the mission—a labor force of 4,000 Christian converts—lived separately in a nearby village. More than 3,000 "mission Indians" are buried in the silent, simple cemetery. Most graves in these gardens are unmarked, but some are decorated with abalone shells. The gardens themselves, started by Downie, are fabulous, with old-fashioned plant varieties, from bougainvillea to bird of paradise, fuchsias, and "tower of jewels."

The Carmel Mission has three museums. The "book museum" holds California's first unofficial library—the 600 volumes Padre Serra brought to California in 1769. The silver altar furnishings are also originals, as are the ornate vestments, Spanish and native artifacts, and other mission memorabilia. Serra's simple priest's cell is a lesson by contrast in modern materialism.

CARMEL

ROBINSON JEFFERS MEETS UNA

If William Hamilton Jeffers [his father] was the archetypal wise old man in Robinson's life, then Una Call Kuster was, in Jungian terms, his anima ideal. Robinson met Una the first year he attended USC [the University of Southern California], in 1906. They were in Advanced German together, reading *Faust*. Una was strikingly beautiful and very intelligent. She was also three years older than Robinson and married. Nevertheless, a friendship developed that was nurtured by a mutual love for literature and ideas. She gave him Arthur Symons' *Wordsworth and Shelley* to read, and the two spent many hours discussing this and other essays, books, and poems.

When Jeffers left USC for the University of Zurich, he sent her an occasional note. When he returned to begin medical studies, the friendship resumed and deepened.

At this time in her life, Una was struggling to define her own identity. Several years before, at eighteen, she had left Mason, Michigan, in order to enter the University of California at Berkeley. She met a young attorney there, Edward ("Teddie") Kuster, whom she promptly married. When they moved to the Los Angeles area, she lived the life of a successful lawyer's wife—with golf at the San Gabriel Country Club, social events, even road races in big, expensive cars taking up most of her time. But something was missing. . . .

Inevitably, her marriage fell apart. Her husband, trying to explain to an interested public what had happened, blamed the breakdown on Una's unconventional ideas. As he says in an interview that appeared in the February 28, 1913, edition of the *Los Angeles Times,* "my wife seemed

The mission is just a few blocks west of Highway 1 at 3080 Rio Rd., 831/624-3600 (gift shop) or 831/624-1271 (rectory), and is open for self-guided tours Mon.–Sat. 9:30 A.M. to 4:30 P.M., Sunday 10:30 A.M. to 4:15 P.M. Admission is free, but donations are appreciated.

ROBINSON JEFFERS'S TOR HOUSE

A medieval-looking granite retreat on a rocky knoll above Carmel Bay, Tor House was built by family-man poet Robinson Jeffers, who hauled the huge stones up from the beach below with horse teams. The manual labor, he said, cleared his mind, and "my fingers had the art to make stone love stone." California's dark prince of poetry, Jeffers was generally aloof from the peninsula's other "seacoast bohemians." On the day he died here, January 20, 1962, it snowed—a rare event along any stretch of California's coast.

You can only begin to appreciate Tor House from the outside (it's just a short walk up from Carmel River Beach, on Ocean View Avenue between Scenic Road and Stewart Way). Jeffers built the three-story Hawk Tower, complete

with secret passageway, for his wife, Una. The mellow redwood paneling, warm oriental rugs, and lovely gardens here soften the impact of the home's bleak tawny exterior—the overall effect

poet Robinson Jeffers

CALIFORNIA DEPARTMENT OF PARKS AND RECREATION

CARMEL

to find no solace in the ordinary affairs of life; she was without social ambition, and social functions seemed a bore to her. Her accomplishments are many, and she sought constantly for a wider scope for her intelligence. She turned to philosophy and the school of modern decadents, and she talked of things beyond the ken of those of us who dwelt upon the lower levels."

Though Teddie could not understand his wife, he knew there was someone who could—a "vile poetaster" named Robinson Jeffers.

From the first time they met, Robinson had listened to Una and shared her enthusiasms. His own extensive background in languages, philosophy, religion, and literature made him a perfect conversation partner. Moreover, he was a handsome man, rugged, poetic, melancholy, and intense.

And Una listened to Robinson. She was perhaps the only person he had ever known who could understand and appreciate the complex thoughts he brooded on. Moreover, she was unconventional and passionate. While the fashionable women wore their hair in high pompadours topped by large hats, Una often wore hers in a braid that fell loose down her back.

In time, their casual friendship grew more rich. "Without the wish of either of us," says Una, "our life was one of those fatal attractions that happen unplanned and undesired."

Excerpted with permission from the literary biography Robinson Jeffers: Poet of California *by James Karman (Ashland, OR: Story Line Press, 1995)*

---

somehow symbolizing Jeffers's hearth-centered life far removed from the world's insanity. Almost whimsical is the collection of 100-plus unicorns the poet gathered. Now a national historic landmark, Tor House is still a family-owned retreat, so don't go snooping around. Small-group guided tours are offered Friday and Saturday, advance reservations required. Adults pay $7, full-time college students $4, high school students $2. No children under 12 allowed. For

more information and reservations contact Tor House, 26304 Ocean View Ave., P.O. Box 1887, Carmel, CA 93921, 831/624-1813, website: www.torhouse.org. Make reservations by phone or via the website.

The Tor House Foundation also offers a full schedule of events, from its annual poetry prize and sunset garden parties to the Robinson Jeffers Seminars, Jeffers Country Bus Tour (of Big Sur), and Jeffers Poetry Walk.

Staying in Carmel

AREA CAMPING (UNDER $50)

Mary Austin's observation that "beauty is cheap here" may apply to the views, but little else in the greater Carmel area—with the exception of camping.

Carmel by the River RV Park, 27680 Schulte Rd. (off Carmel Valley Rd.), 831/624-9329, is well away from it all. Some 35 attractively landscaped sites sit right on the Carmel River, with full hookups, cable TV, a Laundromat, a rec room, and other amenities. Nearby **Saddle Mountain Recreation Park,** also at the

end of Schulte Rd., 831/624-1617, offers both tent and RV sites (reservations accepted for weekends only), restrooms, showers, picnic tables, a swimming pool, a playground, and other recreational possibilities—including nearby hiking trails. Another possibility is **Veterans Memorial Park** (see Monterey Camping and Area Hostels, above).

In the primitive-and-distant category, you can camp southeast of Carmel Valley at the U.S. Forest Service **White Oaks Campground,** which has seven sites, or **China Camp,** with six sites; both are first-come, first-camped and best suited for wilderness trekkers. Farther on you'll find **Tassajara Zen Mountain Center,** offering camping (and other accommodations) in summer by advance reservation—call 415/865-1899 after April 1, or try www.sfzc.com. The nearby Forest Service **Arroyo Seco Campground** has 46 sites. Camping is also plentiful to the south in Big Sur (see below). The Forest Service sites require purchase of a daily (or annual) Adventure Pass, available at Forest Service ranger stations and many sporting goods stores and other vendors. For more information on local Forest Service campgrounds, contact the Monterey District of Los Padres National Forest at 831/385-5434, website: www.r5.fs.fed.us/lospadres.

HOTELS AND INNS

$100–150

Wonderful is the only word for the historic **Pine Inn,** downtown on Ocean between Monte Verde and Lincoln, 831/624-3851 or 800/228-3851, website: www.pine-inn.com. This small hotel offers comfortable "Carmel Victorian" accommodations and fine dining at the on-site **Il Fornaio** restaurant and bakery; there's even a gazebo with a rollback roof for eating alfresco, fog permitting. Even if you don't stay, sit on the terrace, act affluent, and sip Ramos fizzes.

The **Carmel River Inn,** 26600 Oliver Rd. (south of town on Hwy. 1 at the Carmel River Bridge), P.O. Box 221609, Carmel, CA 93922, 831/624-1575 or 800/882-8142, website: www.carmelriverinn.com, is a pleasant 10-acre riverside spread with a heated pool, 24 cozy, family-friendly cottages and duplexes (some with wood-burning fireplaces and kitchens), and 19 motel rooms. Two-night minimum stay on weekends. Pets welcome for a $25-per-pet fee.

Other above-average Carmel accommodations—and there are plenty to choose from—include the **Carmel Oaks Inn,** Fifth and Mission, 831/624-5547 or 800/266-5547, attractive and convenient and a bargain by local standards, and the **Lobos Lodge,** Monte Verde and Ocean, 831/624-3874, fax 831/624-0135.

$150–250

The **Sundial Lodge,** Monte Verde and Seventh, 831/624-8578, website: www.sundiallodge.com, is a cross between a small hotel and a bed-and-breakfast. Each of the 19 antique-furnished rooms has a private bath, TV, and telephone. Other amenities include lovely English gardens and a courtyard, continental breakfast, and afternoon tea.

The **Adobe Inn,** downtown at Dolores and Eighth, 831/624-3933 or 800/388-3933, website: www.adobeinn.com, features just about every motel comfort. Rooms include gas fireplaces, wet bars and refrigerators, patios or decks, color TVs, and phones; some have ocean views. Other amenities include a sauna and heated pool. Another option is the recently upgraded, 19-room Victorian-style **Chateau de Carmel** at Fifth and Junipero, 831/624-1900 or 800/325-8515, website: www.chateaudecarmel.com.

The landmark 1929 **Cypress Inn,** downtown at Lincoln and Seventh, 831/624-3871 or 800/443-7443, website: www.cypress-inn.com, is a charming, gracious, and intimate place—another small hotel with a bed-and-breakfast sensibility, recently updated. Pets are allowed—invited, actually—since actress-owner Doris Day is an animal-rights activist. Dog beds provided. And when hotel staff place a mint on your pillow at turn-down, they'll also leave a treat for your dog or cat. How's *that* for service? Continental breakfast included.

Très Carmel, and a historic treasure, is the Mediterranean-style 1904 **La Playa Hotel,** Camino Real and Eighth, 831/624-6476 or 800/582-8900, website: www.laplayahotel.com, where lush gardens surround guest rooms and cottages on the terraced hillside. Recently remodeled, rooms at La Playa feature evocative Spanish-style furnishings. The five cottages ($250 and up) feature fireplaces, ocean-view decks, and separate living areas. Especially enjoyable when the gardens are in their glory is the on-site **Terrace Grill.**

Mission Ranch Resort

Long the traditional place to stay, just outside town, is the Mission Ranch, 26270 Dolores (at

15th), 831/624-6436 or 800/538-8221. A quiet, small ranch now owned by Clint Eastwood, Mission Ranch overlooks the Carmel River and features views of the Carmel River wetlands and Point Lobos. And the mission *is* nearby. With Eastwood ownership, the Victorian farmhouse and its outbuildings have had an expensive makeover and together now resemble a Western village. The 31 guest rooms are decorated here and there with props from Eastwood movies. Lodgings are available in the main house, the Hayloft, the Bunkhouse (which has its own living room and kitchen), and the Barn. The newer Meadow View Rooms feature, well, meadow views. Rates are $100 to $250. Another attraction is the casual on-site **Restaurant at Mission Ranch,** 831/625-9040, which serves make-my-day American fare complete with checkered tablecloths and a wood-burning stove that starred in *The Unforgiven.*

Bed-and-Breakfasts

Local inns offer an almost overwhelming amount of choice. (But keep in mind, what with the B&B craze, that "inn" in Carmel may be a revamped motel.) Local bed-and-breakfast inns are comparable in price to most Carmel area motels, and they're usually much homier.

A Carmel classic is the ivy-draped **Stonehouse Inn,** Eighth and Monte Verde, 831/624-4569 or toll-free 877/748-6618, website: www.carmelstonehouse.com, constructed by local Indians. All six rooms here are named after local luminaries, mostly writers, and all but two share bathrooms. Rates include full breakfast, wine and sherry, and hors d'oeuvres. Rates are $100 to $250. The **Cobblestone Inn,** on Junipero near Eighth, 831/625-5222 or 800/833-8836, website: www.foursisters.com, is a traditional Carmel home now transformed into a Four Sisters inn— complete with a cobblestone courtyard, gas fireplaces in the guest rooms, and English country-house antiques. Rates include a full breakfast buffet, complimentary tea, and hors d'oeuvres. Rates are $150 to $250.

The **Green Lantern Inn,** Eighth and Casanova, 831/624-4392 or toll-free 888/414-4392, website: www.greenlanterninn.com, offers 18

rustic multiunit cottages, some with lofts, others with fireplaces or sunset-viewing porches, not far from town and beaches. A generous continental breakfast with fresh-squeezed juices is served in the morning, wine and cheese in the afternoon. Rates are $100 to $250. The Victorian **Sea View Inn,** on Camino Real between 11th and 12th, 831/624-8778, website: www.seaviewinncarmel.com, is three blocks from the beach and offers eight rooms, six with private baths, and antique-filled decor. Rates include continental breakfast as well as afternoon tea and cookies or sherry. Rates are $100 to $250.

The pleasant **Carmel Wayfarer Inn,** Fourth Ave. at Mission St., 831/624-2711 or 800/533-2711, is now a bed-and-breakfast. Some rooms feature ocean views and kitchens, and most have gas fireplaces. Rates include breakfast and are $100 to $250.

STAYING IN CARMEL HIGHLANDS

The swank and well-known 1916 **Highlands Inn,** along Highway 1 four miles south of Carmel, 831/620-1234 or 800/233-1234 (Hyatt central reservations), website: www.hyatt.com, is indeed beautiful, though many people would have to forfeit their rent or house payment to stay long. That may not be a problem much longer, though, since the Highlands Inn is now beginning to sell off its luxurious rooms and suites as timeshares—a reality not too popular with long-time guests. Quite luxurious, with some of the world's most spectacular views, some suites feature wood-burning fireplaces, double spa baths, fully equipped kitchens, and all the comforts. Rates are $250 and up. Even those of more plebeian means can enjoy a stroll through the Grand Lodge to appreciate the oak woodwork, twin yellow granite fireplaces, gorgeous earth-toned carpet, leather sofas and chairs, and granite tables. Or stay for a meal—the exceptional **Pacific's Edge** features stunning sunset views and was a top 10 winner in *Wine Spectator* magazine's 1998 Reader's Choice Awards. Open for lunch, dinner, and Sunday brunch. The more casual **California Market** is open daily 7 A.M. to 10 P.M.

The nearby **Tickle Pink Inn,** just south of

Carmel Valley

the Highlands Inn at 155 Highlands Dr., 831/624-1244 or 800/635-4774, website: www.ticklepink.com, offers equally spectacular views and 35 inviting rooms and suites, an ocean-view hot tub, continental breakfast, and wine and cheese at sunset. Two-night minimum stay on weekends. Rates are $250 and up.

STAYING IN CARMEL VALLEY

Robles del Rio Lodge, 200 Punta Del Monte, 831/659-3705 or 800/883-0843, website: www.roblesdelriolodge.com, perches atop a hill overlooking Carmel Valley and is reached via winding back roads—a bit hard to find the first time. Scheduled to reopen in 2003 following an extensive remodeling, Robles del Rio is destined to become a 59-room "luxury boutique spa"—no longer the deluxe yet rustic down-home 1920s wonder it once was. Affiliated with the lodge is the excellent **The Ridge** restaurant, 831/659-0170. Call for current details and rates.

A popular local tradition is the historic **Los Laureles Country Inn,** 313 W. Carmel Valley Rd., 831/659-2233, website: www.loslaureles.com, once part of the Boronda Spanish land grant and later a Del Monte ranch. Rooms here used to be horse stables for Muriel Vanderbilt's

well-bred thoroughbreds. The inn has an excellent restaurant (American regional), pool, and conference facilities. Golf packages are available. Rates are $100 to $250.

A great choice, too, is the **Carmel Valley Lodge** on Carmel Valley Rd. at Ford, 831/659-2261 or 800/641-4646 (reservations only), website: www.valleylodge.com. After all, who can resist "Come listen to your beard grow" as an advertising slogan? The lodge features rooms fronting the lovely gardens plus one- and two-bedroom cottages with fireplaces and kitchens. Other amenities include a pool, sauna, hot tub, and fitness center. Dog friendly. Rates are $150 to $250. Two-bedroom, two-bath cottages are $250 and up.

If you must see how the other 1 percent lives, head for the five-star **Quail Lodge Resort & Golf Club** at the Carmel Valley Golf and Country Club, 8205 Valley Greens Dr., 831/624-2888, website: www.peninsula.com, now part of the Peninsula Group of international hotels. The lodge features elegant contemporary rooms and suites, some with fireplaces, plus access to private tennis and golf facilities and fine dining at **The Covey** restaurant. Rates are $250 and up.

Pricey, too, in the same vein is Wyndham Hotels's **Carmel Valley Ranch Resort,** 1 Old Ranch Rd. (off Robinson Canyon Rd.), 831/625-9500, website: www.wyndham.com, a gated resort with 100 suites, all individually decorated, with wood-burning fireplaces and private decks. Some suites feature a private outdoor hot tub. Recreation facilities include a private golf course, 12 tennis courts, pools, saunas, and whirlpools. Rates are $250 and up.

Luxurious but still something of a new concept in Carmel Valley accommodations is the **Bernardus Lodge,** 831/659-3247 or toll-free 888/648-9463, website: www.bernardus.com, a luxury resort affiliated with the Bernardus Winery and open since August 1999. Crafted from limestone, logs, ceramic tiles, and rich interior woods, the nine village-style buildings feature 57 suites for "discriminating travelers" and offer endless luxury amenities, including a different wine-and-cheese tasting every night at turn-down, a

full-service spa, and special educational forums on gardening, the culinary arts, and viticulture. On-site ballroom and restaurants. Outdoor recreation options include tennis and bocce ball, croquet, swimming, hiking and horseback riding on adjacent mountain trails, and golfing at neighboring resorts. Rates are $250 and up.

Otherwise, for a super-luxury stay—and to avoid the country clubs and other "too new" places—the choice is the 330-acre **Stonepine Estate Resort,** 150 E. Carmel Valley Rd., 831/659-2245, website: www.stonepinecalifornia.com, once the Crocker family's summer home. A Carmel version of a French chateau, Stonepine features luxury suites in the manor house, Chateau Noel, and others in Briar Rose Cottage, the Gate House, and—for horse lovers—the Paddock House. Rates are $250 and up.

Eating in Carmel

GREAT AT BREAKFAST AND LUNCH

For a perfect omelette with home fries and homemade valley pork sausage, try **The Cottage,** on Lincoln between Ocean and Seventh, 831/625-6260. Another good choice for breakfast is **Katy's Place,** on the west side of Mission between Fifth and Sixth, 831/624-0199, another quaint cottage, this one boasting the largest breakfast and lunch menu on the West Coast. Great eggs Benedict—10 different varieties to choose from! Open daily. Also cozy and crowded is **Em Le's,** Dolores and Fifth, 831/625-6780. Try the buttermilk waffles, available for lunch or dinner. The **Tuck Box** tearoom, on Dolores near Seventh, 831/624-6365, inspires you to stop just to take a photograph. It was once famous for its pecan pie, shepherd's pie, and Welsh rarebit, as well as great cheap breakfasts. New owners have changed the menu—and prices.

MORE GOOD FOOD, AT LUNCH AND DINNER

The **Rio Grill,** 101 Crossroads Blvd. (Hwy. 1 at Rio Rd.), 831/625-5436, is a long-running

favorite for innovative southwestern-style American fare. Everything is fresh and/or made from scratch, and many entrées are served straight from the oak wood smoker. Try the ice-cream sandwich. Open for lunch and dinner daily, great Sunday brunch. Interesting, too, is the inexpensive **From Scratch** restaurant at The Barnyard Shopping Center, 831/625-2448, a casual and eclectic place—with local art on the walls—serving up an abundant, ambitious, and very "local" breakfast menu, from fresh-squeezed orange and grapefruit juice to smoothies and pancakes and huevos rancheros. Look for soups, salads, pastas, and sandwiches at lunch and such things as seafood pasta with shrimp, crab, and scallops or pork chops glazed in honey-mustard sauce at dinner. Open for breakfast and lunch daily, for dinner Tuesday through Saturday, and for brunch on Sunday.

Friendly, quite reasonable **Café Rustica,** in the village of Carmel Valley, 10 Delfino Place, 831/659-4444, is brought to you by the same people who launched the Taste Café & Bistro in Pacific Grove. The fare here covers vast continental territory, so at lunch you can enjoy an egg salad sandwich on a baguette, a small pizza, or

CARMEL

a grilled vegetable salad with creamy balsamic vinaigrette. Try the Pasta Rustica at dinner.

The dinner specialty at the **Flying Fish Grill** at the Carmel Plaza shopping center, on Mission between Ocean and Seventh, 831/625-1962, is Pacific Rim seafood—from yin-yang salmon to peppered ahi tuna served with angel hair pasta. Beer and wine only. Another possibility for seafood is **Flaherty's Seafood Grill & Oyster Bar,** on Sixth between Dolores and San Carlos, 831/625-1500 (grill) or 831/624-0311 (oyster bar), an excellent two-in-one enterprise—one of Northern California's best—that offers just-off-the-boat–fresh catches of the day, great chowders, and cioppino.

Fine for takeout pastries and desserts or a light French-country lunch is **Patisserie Boissiere,** on Mission between Ocean and Seventh, 831/624-5008. **China Gourmet,** on Fifth between San Carlos and Dolores, 831/624-3941, specializes in Mandarin and Szechuan cuisine (takeout available).

FINE DINING

All the Carmels are crowded with "cuisine," some possibilities mentioned previously. Ask around if you're looking for the latest special dining experience. Some of that cuisine is pretty relaxed. Immensely popular **Grasing's** at the corner of Sixth and Mission, 831/624-6562, for example, serves "coastal cuisine." At lunch this translates into sandwiches such as grilled eggplant with roasted peppers, onions, and mushrooms, as well as a Bistro Burger with apple-wood smoked bacon, avocado, and cheddar cheese. At dinner, fish is the big deal. Dig into bronzed salmon with portabella mushrooms, roasted garlic, and Yukon golds, or try the petite filet mignon with shallot marmalade, baby carrots, asparagus, and potato cakes. Vegetarians won't starve, with choices such as lasagna with artichokes, tomatoes, spinach, Asiago cheese, and lemon vinaigrette. Somewhat less "fishy" is upbeat **Kurt's Carmel Chop House,** Fifth and San Carlos, 831/625-1199, a true steak house featuring the Chop House Caesar salad and corn-fed meat. Every entrée is served with potatoes and veggies.

Among other local stars is **Robert's Bistro,**

an outpost of French-country atmosphere in the Crossroads Shopping Center, 217 Crossroads Blvd., 831/624-9626, brought to you by the chef behind Monterey's Fresh Cream. The stylish bistro fare includes sautéed red snapper, roast duckling with sweet wild cherry sauce, and cassoulet à la Robert. Open for lunch on weekdays, dinner daily. **The French Poodle,** Junipero and Fifth, 831/624-8643, gets rave reviews for its light, award-winning French cuisine. The wine list is extensive.

Casanova, Fifth and Mission, 831/625-0501, serves both country-style French and Italian cuisine in a landmark Mediterranean-style house (complete with heated garden seating for you temperature-sensitive romantics). House-made pastas here are exceptional, as are the desserts. Impressive wine list. Open daily for breakfast, lunch, and dinner. Sophisticated yet simple is excellent **La Bohême,** Dolores and Seventh, 831/624-7500, a tiny, family-style place with French cuisine and European peasant fare for dinner. No reservations; call for the day's menu or pick up the monthly calendar when you get to town. Open daily for dinner. Beer and wine are available. Elegant **Anton & Michel,** in the Court of the Fountains on Mission between Ocean and Seventh, 831/624-2406, isn't really that expensive considering the setting and good continental fare.

Even if you can't afford to stay there, you can probably afford to eat at the Highlands Inn, on Highway 1 south of Carmel. The inn's **California Market** restaurant, 831/622-5450, serves California regional dishes with fresh local ingredients. You'll enjoy ocean-view and deck dining, plus fabulous scenery. Open for breakfast, lunch, and dinner daily. In the considerably pricier category at the Highlands is the elegant and renowned **Pacific's Edge** restaurant, 831/622-5445, open for lunch, dinner, and Sunday brunch.

More marvelous hotel dining is offered at California-French **Marinus** at Bernardus Lodge, 415 Carmel Valley Rd., 831/658-3400 or toll-free 888/648-9463, a recipient of *Wine Spectator's* Excellence Award, and at **Covey** at Quail Lodge Resort, 8205 Valley Greens Dr., 831/620-8860.

Entertaining, Eventful Carmel

ENTERTAINING CARMEL

Sunsets from the beach or from craggy Point Lobos are entertainment enough. But the **Sierra Club** folks above the shoe store, on Ocean near Dolores, 831/624-8032, provide helpful information on hikes, sights, and occasional bike rides. Open Monday through Saturday 12:30 to 4:30 P.M.

For live drama, the outdoor **Forest Theater,** Santa Rita and Mountain View, 831/626-1681, hosts light drama and musicals, Shakespeare, and concerts. (There's also an *indoor* **Forest Theater,** 831/624-1531.) The **Pacific Repertory Theatre Company** presents a variety of live stage productions at the Golden Bough Theatre, on Monte Verde between Eighth and Ninth; for information, call 831/622-0100 (Tuesday through Saturday noon to 4 P.M.).

Carmel proper has laws prohibiting live music and leg-shaking inside the city limits. **Mission Ranch,** in the county 11 blocks out of town at 26270 Dolores, 831/625-9040, has a piano bar. Otherwise, you'll have to head into rowdy Monterey for dancing and prancing. But you can always go bar-hopping locally.

EVENTFUL CARMEL

Come on New Year's Day for the annual **Rio Grill Resolution Run** and in February for the annual **Masters of Food & Wine.** Come in May for the **Jeffers Tor House Garden Party,** the annual fundraiser, and June for the Carmel Valley **California Cowboy Show.** June also kicks off the theater season in Carmel. Right around the first of the month (or slightly before), the Pacific Repertory Theatre troupe opens its performance season, part of which is devoted to the **Carmel Shakespeare Festival,** with plays presented from August into October. Plays are presented at the

Golden Bough Playhouse and other venues. The entire season runs through mid-October. For information, call 831/622-0100. The **Films in the Forest** theater series also gets underway in June at the outdoor Forest Theatre; call 831/626-1681 for information.

Johann Sebastian Bach never knew a place like Carmel, but his spirit lives here nonetheless. From mid-July to early August, Carmel sponsors its traditionally understated **Bach Festival,** honoring J. S. and other composers of his era, with daily concerts, recitals, and lectures at the mission and elsewhere, sometimes including the Hotel Del Monte at the Naval Postgraduate School in Monterey. If you're going, get your tickets *early.* For information, contact 831/624-2046 or website: www.bachfestival.org. Closer to performance dates, stop by the festival office at the Sunset Cultural Center, San Carlos at Ninth, to check on ticket availability.

At Carmel Beach, usually on a Sunday in late September or early October, the **Great Sandcastle Building Contest** gets underway. Events include Novice and Advanced Sandbox. (Get the date from the Monterey Chamber of Commerce, as Carmel locals generally "don't know," just to keep the tourists away.) Also in October, the **Tor House Festival,** the annual **Carmel Performing Arts Festival,** and the annual **Taste of Carmel** event, in recent years held at the Bernardus Lodge. In December, the **Music for Christmas** series at the Carmel Mission is quite nice. And special events take place from early in the month right up through Christmas Eve during the **Carmel Lights Up the Season** festival. For more information on special events, contact the Monterey County Visitors Center or Carmel Valley Chamber of Commerce (see Carmel Information and Transportation below for contact information).

Shopping Carmel

For something different to tote home as a souvenir, **It's Cactus** on Mission between Ocean & Seventh, 831/626-4213, offers colorful indigenous folk art from Guatemala, Indonesia, and other places around the globe. For candles, candlesticks, and oil lamps, try **Wicks & Wax** in the Doud Arcade, Ocean at San Carlos, 831/624-6044. For fine soaps, other bath products, and home scents, head for the **Rainbow Scent Company,** on Lincoln between Ocean and Seventh, 831/624-6506. **Nature's Bounty** on Lincoln between Ocean and Seventh, 831/626-0920, is a gem and mineral "gallery" featuring jewelry, sculptures, and more.

You'll find plenty of antique shops in and around Carmel. For old toys and memorable memorabilia try **Life In The Past Lane,** 24855 Outlook Court, 831/625-2121. **Sabine Adamson Antiques & Interiors,** on Dolores between Fifth and Sixth, 831/626-7464, specializes in fine European antiques and accessories. **Conway of Asia,** Seventh and Dolores, 831/624-3643, offers antiques and oriental rugs from Myanmar (Burma), India, Tibet, and Thailand. **Vermillion** in the Crossroads Shopping Center (Rio Road and Highway 1), 831/620-1502, emphasizes museum-quality Japanese items, both antique and contemporary.

For all its antique finery, Carmel has even more art galleries—dozens of them. A great place to start is the **Carmel Art Association Gallery** on Dolores between Fifth and Sixth, 831/624-6176, founded here in 1927. The art association features more than 120 local artists and regularly presents an impressive selection of their painting, sculpture, and graphic arts. The **Weston Gallery, Inc.,** on Sixth between Dolores and Lincoln, 831/624-4453, offers 19th- and 20th-century photographs by namesake local photographers Edward Weston and Brett Weston as well as Ansel Adams, Michael Kenna, Jeffrey Becom, and Jerry Uelsmann.

The **Chapman Gallery and Frame Shop,** on Seventh between San Carlos and Mission, 831/626-1766, showcases regional California artists. Wonderful for local art is the **Lyonshead Art Gallery,** 12 Del Fino Place in Carmel Valley, 831/659-4192, and **Savage Stephens Contemporary Fine Art** at Su Vecino, Dolores between Fifth and Sixth, 831/626-0800. The bronze and stone sculptures by Sharon Spencer are standouts. The impressive **Highlands Sculpture Gallery,** on Dolores between Fifth and Sixth, 831/624-0535, is Carmel's oldest contemporary art gallery.

Carmel's also no slouch when it comes to personal fashion, most of it on the pricey side. Definitely upscale is **Girl Boy Girl** at the Court of the Fountains, Mission and Seventh, 831/626-3368, featuring contemporary fashions from more than 50 designers. Worth exploring at Carmel Plaza, Ocean and Mission, are classic **Ann Taylor,** 831/626-9565, and trendier **Chico's,** 831/622-9618. Always fun for something more exotic is **Exotica** at the Crossroads Shopping Center, 831/622-0757, where you'll find handpainted and batiked natural fiber fashions along with Laurel Burch, other interesting jewelry, and folk art.

Carmel being a pet-pampering town, Fido generally fares well. The place to shop for canine and feline fashion, for example, is **Fideaux,** Ocean and Monte Verde, 831/626-7777. Buy gently used clothing, jewelry, art, books, collectibles, and antiques at the **SPCA Benefit Shop** (Society for the Prevention of Cruelty to Animals), Su Vecino Court between Fifth and Sixth, 831/624-4211 or 831/373-2631 ext. 224, to help less fortunate creatures.

For current shopping information and more suggestions, contact the **Carmel Business Association** Visitor & Information Center on San Carlos between Fifth and Sixth, 831/624-2522 or toll-free 800/550-4333, website: www.carmel california.org.

Carmel Information and Transportation

The *Carmel Pine Cone* newspaper covers local events and politics. The **Carmel Business Association** is upstairs in the Eastwood Building on San Carlos between Fifth and Sixth, P.O. Box 4444, Carmel, CA 93921, 831/624-2522 or 800/550-4333, website: www.carmelcalifornia.org. Its annual *Guide to Carmel* includes information on just about everything—from shopping hot spots to accommodations and eateries. The **Tourist Information Center** at Ocean and Mission, 831/624-1711, is quite helpful and provides assistance with lodging reservations. The **Carmel Valley Chamber of Commerce** is in the Oak Building at 71 W. Carmel Valley Rd., P.O. Box 288, Carmel Valley, CA 93924, 831/659-4000, website: www.carmelvalleychamber.com. For county-wide information, contact the **Monterey County Visitors Center,** 137 Crossroads Blvd. (in the Crossroads Shopping Center, off Hwy. 1 and Rio Rd.), Carmel, CA 93923, 831/626-1424 or toll-free 888/221-1010, website: www.montereyinfo.org. The center is open daily 10 A.M. to 6 P.M. in summer; Monday through Saturday 10 A.M. to 5 P.M. and Sunday 11 A.M. to 4 P.M. the rest of the year.

To get to Carmel from Monterey without car or bike, take Monterey-Salinas Transit bus 52 (24 hours), 831/899-2555.

Point Lobos

One of the crown jewels of California's state parks, Point Lobos State Reserve is a 1,250-acre coastal wonderland about four miles south of Carmel. Pack a picnic; this is the best the Monterey area has to offer. The relentless surf and wild winds have pounded these reddish shores for millennia, sculpting six miles of shallow aquamarine coves, wonderful tidepools, aptly named Bird Island, and jutting points: Granite, Coal, Chute, China, Cannery, Pinnacle, Pelican, and Lobos itself. From here, look to the sea, as Santa Cruz poet William Everson has, "standing in cypress and surrounded by cypress, watching through its witchery as the surf explodes in unbelievable beauty on the granite below." Local lore has it that Point Lobos inspired Robert Louis Stevenson's Spyglass Hill in *Treasure Island.* The muse for Robinson Jeffers's somber "Tamar" definitely lived (and lives) here.

SEEING AND DOING POINT LOBOS

From the dramatic headlands, watch for whales in winter. Many other marine mammals are year-round residents. Brown pelicans and cormorants preen themselves on offshore rocks. Here, the sea otters aren't shy: They boldly crack open abalone and dine in front of visitors. (The entire central coast area, from San Francisco south to beyond Big Sur, is protected as part of the **Monterey Bay National Marine Sanctuary.** And by order of former President Bill Clinton, the state's entire coastline is now protected as the California Coastal National Monument.) If you're heading south into Big Sur country, watch offshore otter antics—best with binoculars—from highway turnouts. Harbor seals hide in the coves. The languorous, loudly barking sea lions gave rise to the original Spanish name Punta de los Lobos Marinos ("Point of the Sea Wolves"). Follow the crisscrossing reserve trails for a morning walk through groves of bonsai Monterey cypress and pine, accented by colorful seasonal wildflowers (300 species, best in April). Watch for poison oak, which thrives here, too. Whalers Cove near the picnic and parking area was once a granite quarry, then a whaler's cove—the cabin and cast-iron rendering pot are still there—and an abalone cannery. It's something of a miracle that the Point Lobos headland exists almost unscarred, as cattle grazed here for decades. Fortunately for us all, turn-of-the-20th-century subdivision plans for Point Lobos were scuttled.

dramatically beautiful Point Lobos

CALIFORNIA DEPARTMENT OF PARKS AND RECREATION

CARMEL

Head for Whalers Cove to bone up on local history. **Whalers Cabin Museum,** "the shack" overlooking Whalers Cove, built by Chinese fishermen, tells the story of Point Lobos and vicinity. The adjacent **Whaling Station Museum,** once a garage, features displays about shore whaling along California's central coast—everything from harpoons and whale-oil barrels to historic Monterey Peninsula whaling photos. Guided hikes are also offered at Point Lobos; see the monthly schedule posted at the park's entrance. Curious students of history and natural history can also get an impressive area introduction via the park's website, below.

Safety First

Point Lobos is considered one of the state's "underwater parks," in recognition of its aquatic beauty. Scuba and free diving are popular but allowed by permit only; call 831/624-8413 for reservations or see the website. Diver safety is a major concern of park staff. Get permits and current information about what to expect down below before easing into the water. People aren't kidding when they mention "treacherous cliff and surf conditions" here, so think first before scrambling off in search of bigger and better tidepools. Particularly dangerous even in serene surf is the Monastery Beach area, near San Jose Creek just beyond the reserve's northern border; there's a steep offshore drop-off into submarine Carmel Canyon and unstable sand underfoot. Children should be carefully supervised, and even experienced divers and swimmers might think twice before going into the water.

Practical Point Lobos

Point Lobos is beautiful—and popular. It can be crowded in summer and sometimes on spring and fall weekends. Since only 450 people are allowed into the park at one time, plan your trip accordingly and come early in the day (or wait in long lines along Highway 1—not fun). Open for day use only (sunrise till sunset in summer; until 5 P.M. in winter); $3 per car, but free for walk-ins and bike-ins. Trail brochures are $1. Bikes must stay on pavement in the park—no trail riding.

You can also get to Point Lobos on Monterey-Salinas Transit's bus 22 (to Big Sur). From Carmel, it's a fairly easy bike ride. The weather can be cold, damp, and windy even in summer, so bring a sweater or jacket in addition to good walking shoes (and, if you have them, binocu-

lars). The park's informative brochure is printed in five languages. Guided tours are offered daily. To better appreciate local flora and the 200-plus species of birds spotted at Point Lobos, pick up the plant and bird lists at the ranger station. In May, the Department of Fish and Game's **Marine Resources and Marine Pollution Studies Laboratory** at Granite Canyon sponsors an open house. For more information, contact Point Lobos State Reserve, Rt. 1, Box 62, Carmel, CA 93923, 831/624-4909, http://pt-lobos.parks.state.ca.us.

Near Carmel

CARMEL VALLEY

The sunny (and warmer) sprawling "village" of Carmel Valley stretches some 14 miles inland via Carmel Valley Road, a well-designed but hellacious highway, at least between Carmel and these affluent suburbs and golf and tennis farms (including John Gardiner's Tennis Ranch). Locals curse tourists and others who drive the speed limit.

The village area has definite diversion value for the wealthy and the wannabes—note the shopping centers—but the valley has always been the one Carmel's just plain folks were most likely to inhabit. In 1939 Rosie's Cracker Barrel on Equiline Road became the valley's general store and soon the unofficial community center. Though Rosie's was always the place to pick up picnic supplies and whatnot, there was also a bar out back where locals held forth—definitely not a tourist joint. Rosie's is closed now; plans to reopen it as a museum are in the works. Still, some notable before-the-wealthy Carmel Valley traditions remain—like wide-open spaces. Outdoorsy types will appreciate **Garland Ranch Regional Park,** north of town at 700 W. Carmel Valley Rd., 831/659-4488. The park offers hiking trails on 4,500 hilly acres; you'll get an astounding view from the top of Snively's Ridge.

For more information about Carmel Valley and vicinity, contact the **Carmel Valley Chamber of Commerce,** 91 W. Carmel Valley Rd., 831/659-4000, website: www.carmelvalley chamber.com.

Carmel Valley and Peninsula Wineries

Not surprising in such a moderate Mediterranean climate, vineyards do well here. So do wineries and wines, recognized as eight distinct appellations. To keep up with them all, pick up the free *Monterey Wine Country* brochure and map at area visitor centers or contact the **Monterey County Vintners & Growers Association,** P.O. Box 1793, Monterey, CA 93942-1793, 831/375-9400, website: www.montereywines.org. Wine-related events well worth showing up for include the **Annual Winemakers' Celebration** in August and the **Great Wine Escape Weekend** in November. If you're short on touring time this trip, many Monterey County wines are available for tasting at **A Taste of Monterey,** 700 Cannery Row in Monterey, 831/646-5446, website: www.taste monterey.com, open daily 11 A.M. to 6 P.M.

The very small **Chateau Julien Winery,** 8940 Carmel Valley Rd., 831/624-2600, website: www.chateaujulien.com, is housed in a French-style chateau and is open daily for tasting, for tours by reservation. The winery's chardonnay and merlot have both been honored as the best in the United States at the American Wine Championships in New York. Southwest of Carmel

Valley and bordering Los Padres National Forest is the remote spring-fed "boutique" **Heller Estate/Durney Vineyards,** originally owned by the late William Durney and his wife, screenwriter Dorothy Kingsley, and still noted for its award-winning organic wines. The winery is not open to the public, but the organic wines are available for tasting in Carmel Valley Village at 69 W. Carmel Valley Rd., 831/659-6220 or 800/625-8466, website: www.durneywines.com or website: www.hellerestate.com, and are also widely available in Carmel, Monterey, and vicinity.

Bernardus Winery, 5 W. Carmel Valley Rd., 831/659-1900 or 800/223-2533, website: www.bernardus.com, has a tasting room open 11 A.M. to 5 P.M. daily. Also look around for other premium, small-production wineries, such as **Joullian Vineyards Ltd.,** with cabernet sauvignon, sauvignon blanc, merlot, zinfandel, and chardonnay. Joullian's new tasting room in Carmel Valley at 2 Village Dr., Ste. A, 831/659-8100, website: www.joullian.com, is open for tasting and sales Monday through Friday 11 A.M. to 3 P.M., excluding holidays. The winery is occasionally open for special Saturday open house events; for details call toll-free 877/659-2800.

Between Greenfield and Soledad along the inland Highway 101 corridor are a handful of good wineries. The 1978 private reserve cabernet sauvignon of **Jekel Vineyards,** 40155 Walnut Ave. in Greenfield, 831/674-5522 or 800/625-2610, website: www.usawines.com/jekel, washed out Lafite-Rothschild and other international competitors in France in 1982. Tastings daily 10 A.M. to 5 P.M., tours by appointment. **Hahn Estates/Smith & Hook Winery,** 37700 Foothill Blvd. in Soledad, 831/678-2132, website: www.hahnestates.com, is known for its cabernet sauvignon—also for the amazing view across the Salinas Valley to the Gabilan Mountains. Open daily 11 A.M. to 4 P.M.; tours by appointment. Also in the area: **Chalone Vineyard** on Stonewall Canyon Rd. (Hwy. 146), 831/678-1717, website: www.chalonewinegroup.com, the county's oldest vineyard and winery, known for its estate-bottled varietals; and noted **Paraiso Springs Vineyard,** 38060 Paraiso Springs Rd., 831/678-0300, website:www.usawines.com/paraiso, open for tasting Monday through Friday noon to 4 P.M., Saturday and Sunday 11 A.M. to 5 P.M. (tours by appointment).

Farther north is small Salinas-area **Cloninger Cellars,** 1645 River Rd., 831/675-9463, website: www.usawines.com/cloninger, which offers chardonnay, pinot noir, and cabernet sauvignon in its tasting room. Open for tasting Monday through Thursday 11 A.M. to 4 P.M., Friday through Sunday 11 A.M. to 5 P.M. Not open to the public (no tasting room) but well worth visiting during special events is **Morgan Winery** in Salinas at 590 Brunken Ave., 831/751-7777, website: www.morganwinery.com, which has garnered a glut of gold medals and other recognition for its chardonnays. Winners here, too, are the cabernet, pinot noir, and sauvignon blanc.

True wine fanatics must make one more stop—at America's most award-winning vineyard, **Ventana Vineyards,** 2999 Monterey-Salinas Hwy. (near the Monterey Airport just outside Monterey on Hwy. 68), 831/372-7415, website: www.ventanawines.com. Open daily 11 A.M. to 5 P.M., until 6 P.M. in summer.

JAMESBURG EARTH STATION

The 10-story, 34-ton AT&T Jamesburg Earth Station is a popular stop for space technology fans. The impressive parabolic COMSAT dish antenna here transmits information to and from an orbiting communications satellite more than 22,000 miles away. The visitor program includes a movie, lecture, and chance to peek into the control room. Call 831/659-6100 to arrange a tour. To get here, head southeast into the hills on Carmel Valley Road (20 miles east of Highway 1), which becomes Tularcitos Road. About 10 miles from Carmel Valley Village, turn right on Cachagua Road and hold onto your hat (and/or head) for the next five miles.

After (or instead of) the Jamesburg tour, continue on Tularcitos until it joins Arroyo Seco Road, then jog southwest toward the backside of Big Sur and the Arroyo Seco River canyon. There you can enjoy camping, picnicking, and hiking. Backpackers can head west on a long but rewarding trek to remote, undeveloped **Sykes Hot Springs,** near Horse Bridge Camp.

TASSAJARA ZEN MOUNTAIN CENTER

Not far beyond the COMSAT station is one-time Tassajara Hot Springs, a respected old resort established in 1869. (The Tassajara Road turnoff is off Cachagua Road near the southward intersection with Tularcitos.) According to Native American legend, these curative springs first flowed from the eyes of a young chief seeking help for his dying sister. Offering himself as a sacrifice to the sun, he turned to stone, and his tears became the hot springs.

Now the monastic Tassajara Zen Mountain Center, affiliated with the **San Francisco Zen Center,** Tassajara is the first Soto Zen monastery outside of Asia, open to the general public from May 1 until early September. Most people come here for the hot springs (bathing suits required), but fabulous wilderness access and marvelous vegetarian meals are also available. A wide variety of accommodations—most fairly simple and in the $100 to $150 price category—are available. Dorm accommodations are $50 to $100. A stay here includes three vegetarian meals per day and use of all facilities. You can even camp here. Advance reservations are a must. With confirmed reservations, the center will send a map and directions. Also here: serene surroundings, a swimming pool, and picnicking. Feel free to join in the monastery's prayers and meditations.

For current details, try the Zen Center's website, website: www.sfzc.com. For reservations, after April 1 call 415/865-1899. For information and help in planning your stay, especially if you haven't visited Tassajara before, first call 415/865-1895. For a printed brochure, write to **Tassajara Mailing List, San Francisco Zen Center, 300 Page St., San Francisco, CA 94102.** There is no phone at Tassajara—and no cell phones, radios, tape players, TVs, or cars allowed.

MIRA OBSERVATORY

If for some reason you decide to drive the last six miles of unpaved Tassajara Road, this is where you'll end up. Not officially open to the public, the MIRA Observatory, built by the Monterey Institute for Research in Astronomy (MIRA), is a barrel-shaped, roll-top professional observatory 12 miles inland from Big Sur. MIRA's earth-tone, two-story corrugated Oliver Observing Station—named after a retired Hewlett-Packard vice president who kicked in some cash, some advanced electronics, and a 36-inch telescope—includes office and living space. It has earned design awards from the American Institute of Architects. For information, contact: MIRA, 200 Eighth St., Marina, CA 93933, 831/883-1000, ext. 58, website: www.mira.org.

Big Sur: The Big South

The poet Robinson Jeffers described this redwood and rock coast as "that jagged country which nothing but a falling meteor will ever plow." It's only fitting, then, that this area was called Jeffers Country long before it became known as Big Sur. Sienna-colored sandstone and granite, surly waves, and the sundown sea come together in a never-ending dance of creation and destruction. Writer Henry Miller said Big Sur was "the face of the earth as the creator intended it to look," a point hard to argue. But Big Sur as a specific *place* is difficult to locate. It's not only a town, a valley, and a river, but the entire coastline from just south of Carmel Highlands to some-

where north of San Simeon (some suggest the southern limit is the Monterey County line) is considered Big Sur country.

Once "in" Big Sur, wherever that might be, visitors notice some genuine oddities—odd at least by California standards. Until recently, most people here didn't have much money and didn't seem to care. (This situation is changing as the truly wealthy move in.) They built simple or unusual dwellings—redwood cabins, glass tepees, geodesic domes, even round redwood houses with the look of wine barrels ready to roll into the sea—both to fit the limited space available and to express that elusive Big Sur sense of *style*.

Bixby Creek Bridge

Because the terrain itself is so tormented and twisted, broadcast signals rarely arrive in Big Sur. In the days before satellite dishes, there was virtually no TV; electricity and telephones with dial service have been available in Big Sur only since the 1950s, and some people along the south coast and in more remote areas still have neither.

Social life in Big Sur consists of bowling at the naval station, attending a poetry reading or the annual Big Sur Potluck Revue at the Grange Hall in the valley, driving into "town" (Monterey) for a few movie cassettes, or—for a really wild night—drinks on the deck at sunset and dancing cheek to cheek at Nepenthe. Big Sur is a very *different* California, where even the chamber of commerce urges visitors "to slow down, meditate," and "catch up with your soul."

It's almost impossible to catch up with your soul, however, when traffic is bumper-to-bumper. Appreciating Big Sur while driving or, only for the brave, bicycling in a mile-long coastline convoy is akin to honeymooning in Hades—a universal impulse but entirely the wrong ambience. As it snakes through Big Sur, California's Coast Highway (Highway 1), the state's first scenic highway and one of the world's most spectacular roadways, slips around the prominent ribs of the Santa Lucia Mountains, slides into dark wooded

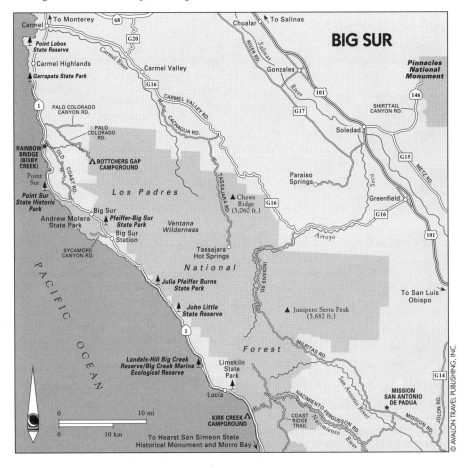

canyons, and soars across graceful bridges spanning the void. Though its existence means that a trip into Monterey no longer takes an entire day, people here nonetheless resent the highway that brings the flamed out and frantic.

To show some respect, come to Big Sur during the week, in balmy April or early May, when wildflowers burst forth, or in late September or October to avoid the thick summer fog. Though winter is generally rainy, weeks of sparkling warm weather aren't uncommon. In April, Big Sur hosts the annual **Big Sur International Marathon,** with 1,600 or more runners hugging the highway curves from the village to Carmel.

THE BIG SUR STORY

The earliest Big Sur inhabitants, the Esselen people, once occupied a 25-mile-long and 10-mile-wide stretch of coast from Point Sur to

© KIM WEIR

"That same prehistoric look. The look of always," Henry Miller said of Big Sur. "Nature smiling at herself in the mirror of eternity."

near Lucia in the south. A small group of Ohlone, the Sargenta-Ruc, lived from south of the Palo Colorado Canyon to the Big Sur River's mouth. Though most of the area's Salinan peoples lived inland in the Salinas Valley near what is now Fort Hunter-Liggett, villages were also scattered along the Big Sur coast south of Lucia. Little is known about area natives, since mission-forced intertribal marriages and introduced diseases soon obliterated them. It is known, though, that the number of Esselens in Big Sur was estimated between 900 and 1,300 after the Spanish arrived in 1770 and that the Esselen people lived in the Big Sur valley at least 3,000 years ago.

The Esselen people were long gone by the time the first area settlers arrived. Grizzly bears were the greatest 18th-century threat to settlement, since the terrain discouraged any type of travel and the usual wildlife predation that came with it. The name Big Sur ("Big South" in Spanish, a reference point from the Monterey perspective) comes from Rio Grande del Sur, or the Big Sur River, which flows to the sea at Point Sur. The river itself was the focal point of the 1834 Mexican land grant and the Cooper family's Rancho El Sur until 1965.

In the early 1900s came the highway, a hazardous 15-year construction project between Big Sur proper and San Simeon. Hardworking Chinese laborers were recruited for the job along with less willing workers from the state's prisons. The highway was completed in 1937, though many lives and much equipment were lost to the sea. Maintaining this remote ribbon of highway and its 29 bridges is still a treacherous year-round task. Following the wild winter storms of 1982–83, for example, 42 landslides blocked the highway; the "big one" near Julia Pfeiffer Burns State Park took 19 bulldozers and more than a year to clear.

Big Sur's Semi-Civil Wars and Big Surbanization

Today only 1,300 people live in Big Sur country—just 300 more than in the early 1900s. Yet "Big Surbanization" is underway. Land not included in Los Padres National Forest and the Ventana Wilderness is largely privately owned.

Plans for more hotels, restaurants, and civilized comforts for frazzled travelers continue to come up, and the eternal, wild peace Robinson Jeffers predicted would reign here forever has at last been touched by ripples of civilization. Nobody wants the character of Big Sur to change, but people can't agree on how best to save it.

As elsewhere in California, some Big Sur landowners believe that private property rights are sacrosanct, beyond the regulation of God or the government. Others argue that state and local land-use controls are adequate. Still others contend that federal intervention is necessary, possibly granting the region scenic area or national park status—an idea fought sawtooth and nail by most residents. The reason Big Sur is still ruggedly beautiful, they say, is because local people have kept it that way. A favorite response to the suggestion of more government involvement: "Don't Yosemite-cate Big Sur." In March 1986, both of California's senators proposed that the U.S. Forest Service take primary responsibility for safeguarding Big

Sur's scenic beauty—with no new logging, mining claims, or grazing privileges allowed. The final plan, which limits but doesn't eliminate new development, seems to please almost everyone—except when new controversies arise.

Some proposed changes create no controversy, such as the late 2000 acquisition by Los Padres National Forest of 784 acres along San Carpoforo Creek and the 2001 purchase of the 1,226-acre Bixby Ocean Ranch by the Trust for Public Land for eventual inclusion in the national forest. The Bixby Ranch, once owned by the late Allen Funt, host of TV's *Candid Camera,* was prime Big Sur property otherwise slated for development. Other proposals, though, raise quite a ruckus, such as the Hearst Corporation's 1998 plan to build a luxury golf result just south of Big Sur near San Simeon and the famed Hearst Castle. Negotiations to sell development rights for the corporation's 83,000-acre Piedra Blanca Ranch, or White Rock Ranch, which surrounds Hearst's castle, were continuing, at last report.

Seeing and Doing Big Sur

SEEING BIG SUR

Garrapata State Park

Garrapata State Park stretches north along the coast for more than four miles from Soberanes Point, where the Santa Lucia Mountains first dive into the sea. Southward, the at-first unimpressive **Point Sur** and its lighthouse beacon stand out beyond 2,879-acre Garrapata State Park and beach, the latter named after the noble wood tick and featuring a crescent of creek-veined white sand, granite arches, caves and grottos, and sea otters. Ticks or no ticks, the unofficial nude beach here is one of the best in Northern California. Winter whale-watching is usually good from high ground. On weekends in January, ranger-led whale-watch programs are held at Granite Canyon. Or, if it's not foggy, take the two-mile loop trail from the turnout for the view.

For more information about the park, call 831/624-4909, or call the **Big Sur Station** joint

State Parks/U.S. Forest Service office at 831/667-2315.

South of Garrapata and inland is private **Palo Colorado Canyon,** reached via the road of the same name. Dark and secluded even in summer, the canyon is often cut off from the rest of the world when winter storms stomp through. The name itself is Spanish for "tall redwood." About eight miles in at the end of the road is isolated **Bottchers Gap Campground,** complete with restrooms, picnic tables, and multiple trailheads into the Ventana Wilderness. A few miles farther south on the highway is the famous **Rainbow Bridge** (now called Bixby Creek Bridge), 260 feet high and 700 feet long, the highest single-arch bridge in the world when constructed in 1932 and still the most photographed of all Big Sur bridges.

Point Sur State Historic Park

Up atop Point Sur stands the Point Sur Lightstation, an 1889 sandstone affair still standing guard at this shipwreck site once known as the Graveyard of the Pacific. In the days when the only way to get here was on horseback, 395 wooden steps led to the lighthouse, originally a giant multi-wick kerosene lantern surrounded by a Fresnel lens with a 16-panel prism. The Point Sur Lightstation is now computer-operated and features an electrical aero-beacon, radio-beacon, and fog "diaphone." This 34-acre area and its central rocky mound (good views and whale-watching) is now a state park, though the Coast Guard still maintains the lighthouse. Guided three-hour lighthouse walking tours are offered five or six times a week in summer, three times weekly in winter. Full moon tours are also offered monthly, spring through fall. Tours are $5 adults, $3 teens, $2 children. Current tour information is posted throughout Big Sur. For details, call the park at 831/625-4419 or see website: www.lighthouse-pointsur-ca.org. For information about winter whale-watching programs here and at both Garrapata and Julia Pfeiffer Burns State Parks, call 831/667-2315.

Andrew Molera State Park

Inland and up, past what remains of the pioneering Molera Ranch (part of the original Rancho El Sur), is marvelous Andrew Molera State Park, a 2,100-acre park first donated to the Nature Conservancy by Frances Molera in honor of her brother, then deeded to the state for management. There's no pavement here, just a run-down dirt parking lot and a short trail winding through sycamores, maples, and a few redwoods along the east fork of the Big Sur River to the two-mile beach and adjacent seabird sanctuary-lagoon below. (The big breakers cresting along the coast here are created by the Sur Breakers Reef.) The trail north of the river's mouth leads up a steep promontory to Garnet Beach, noted for its colorful pebbles. Except when firefighting crews are camped here and on major holiday weekends, it's usually uncrowded at Andrew Molera.

Among its other attractions, the park features a primitive yet peaceful 10-acre walk-in campground just one-quarter mile from the parking lot (three-night limit, $3 per person, dogs allowed only with a leash and proof of current rabies vac-

© CALIFORNIA DEPARTMENT OF PARKS AND RECREATION

Andrew Molera State Park

cination). Day use at Andrew Molera is $2. For more information about the park, contact: Andrew Molera State Park, 831/667-2315.

Also at the park: **Molera Horseback Tours,** P.O. Box 111, Big Sur, CA 93920, 831/625-5486 or 800/942-5486, website: www.molera horsebacktours.com, which offers regularly scheduled one- to three-hour rides along the beach and through meadows and redwood groves. Guides explain the history, flora, and fauna of the area. Private rides are also available by appointment. Rates are $25 to $35 an hour.

Pfeiffer–Big Sur State Park

Inland, on the other side of the ridge from Andrew Molera State Park, is protected, sunny Big Sur Valley, a visitor-oriented settlement adjoining the Ventana Wilderness and surrounding picnic, camping, and lodge facilities at 821-acre Pfeiffer–Big Sur State Park. Take the one-mile nature trail or meander up through the redwoods to **Pfeiffer Falls,** a verdant, fern-lined canyon at its best in spring and early summer, then to **Valley View** for a look at the precipitous Big Sur River gorge below. Redwoods, sycamores, bigleaf maples, cottonwoods, and willows hug the river, giving way to oaks, chaparral, and Santa Lucia bristlecone fir at higher elevations. There's abundant poison oak, and raccoons can be particularly pesky here, like the begging birds, so keep food out of harm's way.

To hike within the Ventana Wilderness, head south on the highway one-half mile to the U.S. Forest Service office, 831/667-2315, for a permit and current information (trails begin here). About a mile south of the entrance to Pfeiffer-Big Sur is the road to Los Padres National Forest's **Pfeiffer Beach** (take the second right-hand turnoff after the park) and its cypresses, craggy caves, and mauve and white sands streaked with black. It's heaven here on a clear, calm day, but the hissing sand stings mercilessly when the weather is up. On any day, forget the idea of an ocean swim. The water's cold, the surf capricious, and the currents tricky; even expert divers need to register with rangers before jumping in. Pfeiffer Beach is open to the public from 6 A.M. to sunset; $5 fee.

The outdoor amphitheater at Pfeiffer-Big Sur State Park (which hosts many of the park's educational summer campfires and interpretive programs) and lagoons were built by the Civilian Conservation Corps during the depression. The large developed year-round campground features more than 218 campsites with picnic tables and hot showers ($12 per night). Group campsites are $26, hike- or bike-in sites, $1. To make camping reservations—advisable in summer, when the park is particularly crowded, and on good-weather weekends—contact ReserveAmerica, 800/444-7275, website: www.reserveamerica.com. The day-use fee for short park hikes and picnicking is $3. For more information, contact Pfeiffer–Big Sur State Park, Big Sur, CA 93920, 831/667-2315.

Urban Big Sur

Nowhere in Big Sur country are visitors really diverted from the land, because there are no big-time boutiques, gaudy gift shops, or even movie theaters. But urban Big Sur starts at Big Sur Valley and stretches south past the post office and U.S. Forest Service office to the vicinity of Deetjen's Big Sur Inn. This "big city" part of Big Sur includes the area's most famous and fabulous inns and restaurants: the Ventana Inn, the Post Ranch Inn, Nepenthe, and Deetjen's. (For more on all of these, see Practical Big Sur, below). Fascinating about Nepenthe is that although cinematographer Orson Welles was persona non grata just down the coast at San Simeon (for his too-faithful portrayal of William Randolph Hearst in *Citizen Kane*), when he bought what was then the Trails Club Log Cabin in Big Sur for his wife Rita Hayworth in 1944, he was able to haunt Hearst from the north. Welles's place became Nepenthe ("surcease from sorrows" in the *Odyssey*) shortly after he sold it in 1947. More or less across the street from Nepenthe is the **Hawthorne Gallery,** 48485 Hwy. 1, 831/667-3200, website: www.hawthornegallery.com, something of a Hawthorne family enterprise also offering Albert Paley forged metal sculptures, Max DeMoss bronze castings, Jesus Bautista Moroles granite sculptures, and the landscape creations of Frederick L. Gregory, among others.

North of Deetjen's is the **Henry Miller Memorial Library,** a collection of friendly clutter about the writer and his life's work, located on the highway about one mile south of the Ventana Inn but almost hidden behind redwoods and an unassuming redwood double gate. Henry Miller lived, wrote, and painted in Big Sur from 1944 to 1962. The library is housed not in Henry Miller's former home but in that of the late Emil White. A good friend of Miller's, White said he started the library "because I missed him." Now a community cultural arts center, the library sponsors exhibits, poetry readings, concerts, and special events throughout the year. Original art and prints, posters, and postcards are available in the gallery. Miller's books, including rare editions, are also available. In summer the library is often open daily, but year-round it is typically open Wednesday through Sunday 11 A.M. to 6 P.M. and for special events. For current information, contact: Henry Miller Library, Hwy. 1, Big Sur, CA 93920, 831/667-2574, website: www.henrymiller.org.

South of Deetjen's is the noted **Coast Gallery** at Lafler Canyon (named for editor Henry Lafler, a friend of Jack London), 831/667-2301, website: www.coastgalleries.com, open daily 9 A.M. to 5 P.M. Rebuilt from redwood water tanks in 1973, the Coast Gallery offers fine local arts and crafts, from jewelry and pottery to paintings—including watercolors by Henry Miller—plus sculpture and woodcarvings.

Julia Pfeiffer Burns State Park

Partington Cove is about one mile south of Partington Ridge, the impressive northern boundary of Julia Pfeiffer Burns State Park. To get to the cove, park on the east side of the highway and head down the steep trail that starts near the fence (by the black mailbox) on the west side of the road. The branching trail leads back into the redwoods to the tiny beach at the stream's mouth, or across a wooden footbridge, through a rock tunnel hewn in the 1880s by pioneer John Partington, and on to the old dock where tan bark was once loaded onto seagoing freighters. A fine place for a smidgen of inspirational solitude.

There's a stone marker farther south at the park's official entrance, about seven miles south of Nepenthe. These spectacular 4,000 acres straddling the highway also include a large underwater park offshore. Picnic in the coast redwoods by McWay Creek (almost the southern limit of their range) or hike up into the chaparral and the Los Padres National Forest. After picnicking, take the short walk along McWay Creek (watch for poison oak), then through the tunnel under the road to **Saddle Rock** and the cliffs above **Waterfall Cove,** the only California waterfall that plunges directly into the sea. The cliffs are rugged here; it's a good place to view whales and otters. Only experienced scuba divers, by permit, are allowed to dive offshore.

The park also features limited year-round camping at walk-in environmental sites and group campgrounds. For more information about the park, including winter whale-watching programs on weekends, contact Julia Pfeiffer Burns State Park, Big Sur, CA 93920, 831/667-2315.

The still-raw, 1,400-foot-wide slash of earth just north of Julia Pfeiffer Burns State Park, which stopped traffic through Big Sur for more than a year, has earned the area's landslide-of-all-time award (so far). Heading south from the park, the highway crosses Anderson Creek and rugged Anderson Canyon, where an old collection of highway construction cabins for convicts sheltered such bohemians as Henry Miller and his friend Emil White in the 1940s. A few human residents and a new population of bald eagles now call Anderson Canyon home.

The Esalen Institute

The Esselen and Salinan peoples frequented the hot springs here, supposedly called *tok-i-tok,* "hot healing water." In 1939, Dr. H. C. Murphy (who officiated at John Steinbeck's birth in Salinas) opened Slate's Hot Springs resort on the site. The hot springs were transformed by grandson Michael Murphy into the famed Esalen Institute, where human-potential practitioners and participants including Joan Baez, Gregory Bateson, the Beatles, Jerry Brown, Carlos Castaneda, Buckminster Fuller, Aldous Huxley, Linus Pauling, B.F. Skinner, Hunter S. Thompson, and Alan Watts taught or learned in residential workshops.

Esalen is the Cadillac of New Age retreats, according to absurdist/comedian/editor Paul

Krassner. Even writer Alice Kahn who, before arriving at Esalen, considered herself the "last psycho-virgin in California" and "hard-core unevolved," eventually admitted that there was something about the Esalen Institute that defied all cynicism.

Esalen's magic doesn't necessarily come cheap. The introductory "Experiencing Esalen" weekend workshop runs $485 or so, including simple but pleasant accommodations and wonderful meals ($230 if a sleeping bag is all you'll need). Five-day workshops are substantially more—in the $750-and-up range. But Esalen tries to accommodate the less affluent with scholarships, a work-study program, senior citizen discounts, family rates, and bunk bed or sleeping bag options. You can also arrange just an overnight or weekend stay (sans enlightenment) assuming space is available.

Esalen offers more than 400 workshops each year, these "relating to our greater human capacity." Topics cover everything from the arts and creative expression to "intellectual play," from dreams to spiritual healing, from martial arts to shamanism. Equally mythic are Esalen's baths. In February 1998 a mudslide roared down the hill to demolish the previous bathhouse facilities, though an ambitious rebuilding project is now underway. The new, improved Esalen baths, scheduled to open in the summer of 2002, will include a geothermally heated swimming pool and a handicapped-accessible hot tub and massage area—at a cost of $5.3 million. In the meantime, Esalen's "temporary baths" are available—but only to Esalen guests. When the new bath house opens, Esalen will again satisfy the California Coastal Commission's public access requirement, by allowing the general public access to the hot tubs (at the fairly unappealing hours of 1–3 A.M. daily). Call for details. The massages at Esalen are world-renowned, from $50 an hour. Nudity is big at Esalen, particularly in the hot tubs, swimming pool, and massage area, though not required.

Entrance to Esalen and its facilities is strictly by reservation only. For information on workshops and lodgings and to request a copy of Esalen's current catalog, contact: Esalen Institute, Big Sur, CA 93920, 831/667-3000, website: www.esalen.org. The website's online *In the Air* magazine offers a good sense of what Esalen is all about and also includes a complete current workshop catalog (which you can download). To make workshop reservations, call 831/667-3005 or fax completed registration forms to 831/667-2724.

Nature Reserves

Just south of the Esalen Institute is the **John Little State Reserve,** 21 acres of coast open to the public for day use (frequently foggy). For information, call the state parks Monterey District office (weekdays only), 831/649-2836. About five miles south of Esalen, beyond the Dolan Creek and dramatic Big Creek bridges, is the entrance to **Landels-Hill Big Creek Reserve,** more than 4,200 acres owned by the University of California. Adjacent is the 1,200-acre **Big Creek Marine Ecological Reserve.** The two are co-managed as the Big Creek Reserve. Safe behind these rusted cast-iron gates are 11 different plant communities, at least 350 plant species, 100 varieties of birds, and 50 types of mammals. A 10-acre area is open as a public educational center; groups are welcome. Access is by permit only (in advance or sign in at the entrance), for educational field trips and research. Camping is available. For more information, write **Big Creek Reserve,** Big Sur, CA 93920, call 831/667-2543, or see website: www.redshift.com/~bigcreek.

Lucia and the New Camaldoli Hermitage

The tiny "town" of Lucia is privately owned, with a gas station and a good down-home restaurant, open from 7 A.M. until dark, when they shut off the generator. Try the homemade split pea soup. Different, too, is a stay in one of the 10 rustic coastal cabins at **Lucia Lodge.** Rates are $100 to $150. Come nightfall, kerosene lanterns provide the ambience. A simple yet spectacular spot. Call 831/667-2391 for current information (no reservations).

South of Lucia (at the white cross), the road to the left leads to the New Camaldoli Hermitage, a small Benedictine monastery at the former Lucia Ranch. The sign says that the monks "regret we cannot invite you to camp, hunt, or enjoy a walk on our property" due to their customary solitude and avoidance of "unnecessary speaking." But visitors *can* come to buy crafts and homemade fruitcake and to attend daily mass.

In addition, the hermitage is available for very serene retreats of up to two weeks, though few outsiders can stand the no-talk rules for much longer than a few days. Simple meals are included. The suggested offering is $60 per day for the retreat rooms, $70 per day for trailer hermitages. For more information, contact: New Camaldoli Hermitage, Big Sur, CA 93920, 831/667-2456, website: www.contemplation.com.

Limekiln State Park

About two miles south of Lucia is the newest Big Sur state park, open since 1995. It encompasses 716 acres in an isolated and steep coastal canyon, preserving some of the oldest, largest, and most vigorous redwoods in Monterey County. Named for the towering wood-fired kilns that smelted quarried limestone into powdered lime—essential for mixing cement—here in the late 1800s, Limekiln State Park offers a steep one-mile round-trip, creekside hike through redwoods to the four kilns, passing a waterfall (to the right at the first fork), pools, and cascades along the way. The park includes a day-use area for picnicking ($3 fee) and a very appealing 43-site family campground with minimal amenities but abundant ambience. To get there, take the signed turnoff (on the inland or landward side of the highway) just south of the Limekiln Canyon Bridge. For more information, contact Limekiln State Park, 63025 Hwy. 1, Big Sur, CA 93920, 831/667-2403. See also Public Camping in Big Sur, below.

DOING BIG SUR

The ultimate activity in Big Sur is just bumming around, scrambling down to beaches to hunt for jade, peer into tidepools, or scuba dive or surf where it's possible. Cycling, sight-seeing, and watching the sunset are other entertainments. Along the coastline proper there are few long hiking trails, since much of the terrain is treach-

erous, and most of the rest privately owned, but the Big Sur backcountry offers good hiking and backpacking.

Ventana Wilderness

Local lore has it that a natural land bridge once connected two mountain peaks at Bottchers Gap, creating a window (or *ventana* in Spanish) until the 1906 San Francisco earthquake brought it all tumbling down. The Big Sur, Little Sur, Arroyo Seco, and Carmel Rivers all cut through this 161,000-acre area, creating dramatic gorges and wildland well worth exploring. Steep, sharp-crested ridges and serrated V-shaped valleys are clothed mostly in oaks, madrones, and dense chaparral. Redwoods grow on north-facing slopes near the fog-cooled coast; pines at higher elevations. The gnarly spiral-shaped bristlecone firs found only here are in the rockiest, most remote areas, their total range only about 12 miles wide and 55 miles long.

Most of all, the Ventana Wilderness provides a great escape from the creeping coastal traffic (a free visitor permit is required to enter) and offers great backpacking and hiking when the Sierra Nevada, Klamath Mountains, and Cascades are still snowbound—though roads here are sometimes impassible during the rainy season. Hunting, fishing, and horseback riding are also permitted. Crisscrossing Ventana Wilderness are nearly 400 miles of backcountry trails and 82 vehicle-accessible campgrounds (trailside camping possible with a permit).

The wilderness trailheads are at Big Sur Station, Carmel River, China Camp, Arroyo Seco, Memorial Park, Bottchers Gap, and Cone Peak Road. The Ventana Wilderness recreation map, available for $4 from ranger district offices, shows all roads, trails, and campgrounds. Fire-hazardous areas, routinely closed to the public after July 1 (or earlier), are coded yellow on maps.

Trail and campground traffic fluctuates from year to year, so solitude seekers should ask rangers about more remote routes and destinations. Since the devastating Marble Cone fire of 1978 (and other more recent fires), much of what once was forest is now chaparral and brush. As natural succession progresses, dense undergrowth obliterates trails not already erased by erosion. Despite dedicated volunteer trail work, lack of federal trail maintenance has also taken its toll.

Backcountry travelers should also heed fire regulations. Because of the high fire danger in peak tourist season, using a camp stove or building a fire outside designated campgrounds requires a fire permit. Also, bring water—but think twice before bringing Fido, since flea-transmitted plague is a possibility. Other bothersome realities include ticks (especially in winter and early spring), rattlesnakes, poison oak, and fast-rising rivers and streams following rainstorms.

For more Ventana Wilderness information, contact the Big Sur Station office (see above) or **Los Padres National Forest** headquarters, 6755 Hollister Ave., Ste. 150, Goleta, CA 93117,805/968-6640, website: www.r5.fs.fed.us/lospadres. Additional information is available from the **Ventana Wilderness Society,** 831/455-9514, website: www.ventanaws.org, and the **Ventana Wilderness Alliance,**831/423-3191, website: www.ventanawild.org. For guided trips on horseback, contact **Ventana Wilderness Guides and Expeditions,** 38655 Tassajara Rd., Carmel Valley, CA 93924, 831/659-2153, website: www .nativeguides.com, operated by members of the Esselen tribe.

Big Sur Hikes

The grandest views of Big Sur come from the ridges just back from the coast. A great companion is *Hiking the Big Sur Country* by Jeffrey P. Schaffer (Wilderness Press). The short but steep **Valley View Trail** from Pfeiffer-Big Sur State Park is usually uncrowded, especially midweek; there are benches on top for sitting and staring off the edge of the world. Those *serious* about coastal hiking should walk all the way from Pfeiffer-Big Sur to Salmon Creek near the southern Monterey County line. The trip from Bottchers Gap to Ventana Double Cone via **Skinner Ridge Trail** is about 16 miles one way and challenging, with a variety of possible campsites, dazzling spring wildflowers, and oak and pine forests.

Otherwise, take either the nine-mile **Pine Ridge Trail** from Big Sur or the 15-mile trail from China Camp on Chews Ridge to undevel-

oped Sykes Hot Springs, just 400 yards from Sykes Camp (very popular these days). Another good, fairly short *visual* hike is the trip to nearby Mount Manuel, a nine-mile round trip. The two-mile walk to **Pfeiffer Beach** is also worth it—miles from the highway, fringed by forest, with a wading cove and meditative monolith.

Big Sur Back Roads

For an unforgettable dry-season side trip and a true joy ride, take the **Old Coast Road** from just north of the Bixby Bridge inland to the Big Sur Valley. You'll encounter barren granite, a thickly forested gorge, and good views of sea and sky before the road loops back to Highway 1 south of Point Sur near the entrance to Andrew Molera State Park. **Palo Colorado Road,** mostly unpaved and narrow, winds through a canyon of redwoods, ferns, and summer homes, up onto hot and dry Las Piedras Ridge, then down into the Little Sur watershed.

Marvelous for the sense of adventure and the views is a drive along the **Nacimiento-Fergusson Road** from the coast inland to what's left of old Jolon and the fabulous nearby mission, both included within the Fort Hunter-Liggett Military Reservation. (Taking this route is always somewhat risky, particularly on weekends, since all roads through Hunter-Liggett are closed when military exercises are underway.) Even more thrilling is driving rough-and-ready **Los Burros Road** farther south, an unmarked turnoff just south of Willow Creek and Cape San Martin that leads to the long-gone town of Manchester in the Los Burros gold mining district. An indestructible vehicle and plenty of time are required for this route, and it's often closed to traffic after winter storms.

Big Sur back roads leading to the sea are rarer and easy to miss. About one mile south of the entrance to Pfeiffer-Big Sur State Park is **Sycamore Canyon Road,** which winds its way downhill for two exciting miles before the parking lot near Pfeiffer Beach. At Willow Creek there's a road curling down from the vista point to the rocky beach below, and just south of Willow Creek a dirt road leads to Cape San Martin (good for views any day but especially fine for whale-watching).

HEARST'S CASTLE: PLEASURE HE COULD AFFORD

The **Hearst San Simeon State Historic Monument** just south of Big Sur ranks right up there with Disneyland as one of California's premier tourist attractions. Somehow that fact alone puts the place into proper perspective. Media magnate William Randolph Hearst's castle is a rich man's playground filled to overflowing with artistic diversions and other expensive toys, a monument to one man's monumental ego and equally impressive poor taste.

In real life, of course, Hearst was quite a wealthy and powerful man, the man many people still believe was the subject of the greatest American movie ever made, Orson Welles's 1941 *Citizen Kane.* (These days even Welles's biographers say the movie was about the filmmaker himself.) Yet there's something to be said for popular opinion. "Pleasure," Hearst once wrote, "is worth what you can afford to pay for it." And that attitude showed itself

Hearst Castle, San Simeon

quite early; for his 10th birthday little William asked for the Louvre as a present. One scene in the movie, in which Charles Foster Kane shouts across the cavernous living room at Xanadu to attract the attention of his bored young mistress, endlessly working jigsaw puzzles while she sits before a fireplace as big as the mouth of Jonah's whale, won't seem so surreal once you see San Simeon.

Designed by Berkeley architect Julia Morgan, the buildings themselves are odd yet handsome hallmarks of Spanish Renaissance architecture. The centerpiece La Casa Grande alone has 100 rooms (including a movie theater, a billiards room, two libraries, and 31 bathrooms) adorned with silk banners, fine Belgian and French tapestries, Norman fireplaces, European choir stalls, and ornately carved ceilings virtually stolen from continental monasteries. The furnishings and art Hearst collected from around the world complete the picture, one that includes everything but humor, grace, warmth, and understanding.

The notably self-negating nature of this rich but richly disappointed man's life is somehow fully expressed here in the country's most ostentatious and theatrical temple to obscene wealth. In contrast to Orson Welles's authentic artistic interpretation of either his own or Hearst's life, William Randolph's idea of hearth, home, and humanity was full-flown fantasy sadly separated from heart and vision.

Touring Hearst Castle

In spring when the hills are emerald green, from the faraway highway Hearst Castle appears as if by magic up on the hill. (Before the place opened for public tours in the 1950s, the closest view commoners could get was from the road, with the assistance of coin-operated telescopes.) One thing visitors *don't* see on the tour shuttle up to the enchanted hill is William Randolph Hearst's 2,000-acre zoo—"the largest private zoo since Noah," as Charles Foster Kane would put it—once the country's largest. The inmates have long since been dispersed, though survivors of Hearst's exotic elk, zebra, Barbary sheep, and Himalayan goat herds still roam the grounds.

JULIA MORGAN: LETTING THE WORK SPEAK FOR ITSELF

Julia Morgan, San Simeon's architect, supervised the execution of almost every detail of Hearst's rambling 165-room pleasure palace. This 95-pound, teetotaling, workaholic woman was UC Berkeley's first female engineering graduate, and the first woman to graduate from the école des Beaux-Arts in Paris. She was credited only after her death for her accomplishments, but if acclaim came late for Morgan, it was partly her preference. She loathed publicity, disdained the very idea of celebrity, and believed that architects should be like anonymous medieval masters and let the work speak for itself.

Morgan's work with Hearst departed dramatically from her belief that buildings should be unobtrusive, the cornerstone of her brilliant but equally unobtrusive career. "My style," she said to those who seemed bewildered by the contradiction, "is to please my client." Pleasing her client in this case was quite a task. Hearst arbitrarily and habitually changed his mind, all the while complaining about slow progress and high costs. And she certainly didn't do the job for money, though Hearst and her other clients paid her well. Morgan divided her substantial earnings among her staff, keeping only about $10,000 annually to cover office overhead and personal expenses.

The perennially private Morgan, who never allowed her name to be posted at construction sites, designed almost 800 buildings in California and the West, among them the original Asilomar in Pacific Grove; the Berkeley City Club; the Oakland YWCA; and the bell tower, library, social hall, and gym at Oakland's Mills College. She also designed and supervised the reconstruction of San Francisco's Fairmont Hotel following its devastation in the 1906 earthquake. Other Hearst commissions included the family's Wyntoon retreat near Mount Shasta as well as the *Los Angeles Herald-Examiner* building.

The four separate tours of the Hearst San Simeon State Historic Monument take approximately two hours each. Theoretically you could take all the San Simeon tours in a day, but don't try it. So much Hearst in the short span of a day could be detrimental to one's well-being. A dosage of two tours per day makes the trip here worthwhile yet not overwhelming. Visitors obsessed with seeing it all should plan a two-day stay in the area or come back again some other time. Whichever tour, or combination of tours, you select, be sure to wear comfortable walking shoes. Lots of stairs.

Tour One is a good first-time visit, taking in the castle's main floor, one guesthouse, and some of the gardens—a total of 150 steps and a half mile of walking. Included on the tour is a short showing in the theater of some of Hearst's "home movies." Particularly impressive in a gloomy Gothic way is the dining room, where silk Siennese banners hang over the lord's table. The poolroom and mammoth great hall, with Canova's *Venus,* are also unforgettable. All the tours include both the Greco-Roman Neptune Pool and statuary and the indoor Roman Pool with its mosaics of lapis lazuli and gold leaf. It's hard to imagine Churchill, cigar in mouth, cavorting here in an inner tube. Tour One also includes the National Geographic movie, *Hearst Castle—Building the Dream.*

Tour Two requires more walking, covering the mansion's upper floors, the kitchen, the libraries, and Hearst's Gothic Suite, with its frescoes and rose-tinted Venetian glass windows (he ran his 94 separate business enterprises from here). The delightfully lit Celestial Suite was the nonetheless depressing extramarital playground of Hearst and Marion Davies. **Tour Three** covers one of the guesthouses plus the "new wing," with 36 luxurious bedrooms, sitting rooms, and marble bathrooms furnished with fine art.

Gardeners will be moved to tears by **Tour Four** (offered April–Aug. only), which includes a long stroll through the San Simeon grounds but does not go inside the castle itself. Realizing that all the rich topsoil here had to be manually carried up the hill makes the array of exotic plantlife, including unusual camellias and about

6,000 rosebushes, all the more impressive—not to mention the fact that gardeners at San Simeon worked only at night because Hearst couldn't stand watching them. Also included on the fourth tour is the lower level of the elegant, 17-room Casa del Mar guesthouse (where Hearst spent much of his time), the recently redone underground Neptune Pool dressing rooms, the never-finished bowling alley, and Hearst's wine cellar. David Niven once remarked that, with Hearst as host, the wine flowed "like glue." Subsequently, Niven was the only guest allowed free access to the castle's wine cellar.

CITIZEN HEARST

The name San Simeon was originally given to three Mexican land grants—40,000 acres bought by mining scion George Hearst in 1865. George, the first millionaire Hearst, owned Nevada's Comstock Lode silver mine, Ophir silver mine, and the rich Homestake gold mine in South Dakota, and also staked-out territory in California's goldfields. George Hearst later expanded the family holdings to 250,000 acres (including 50 miles of coastline) for the family's "Camp Hill" Victorian retreat and cattle ranch. With his substantial wealth, he was even able to buy himself a U.S. Senate seat.

But young William Randolph had even more ambitious plans—personally and for the property. The only son of the senator and San Francisco schoolteacher, socialite, and philanthropist Phoebe Apperson, the high-rolling junior Hearst took a fraction of the family wealth and his daddy's failing *San Francisco Examiner* and created a successful yellow-journalism chain, eventually adding radio stations and movie production companies.

Putting his newfound power of propaganda to work in the political arena, Hearst (primarily for the headlines) goaded Congress into launching the Spanish-American War in 1898. But unlike his father, William Randolph was unable to buy much personal political power. Though he aspired to the presidency, he had to settle for two terms as a congress member from New York.

Fairly new at San Simeon are the **Hearst Castle Evening Tours,** two-hour adventures featuring the highlights of other tours—with the added benefit of allowing you to pretend to be some Hollywood celebrity, just arrived and in need of orientation. (Hearst himself handed out tour maps, since newcomers often got lost.) Guides dress in period costume and show you around. It's worth it just to see the castle in lights. At last report, evening tours were offered on Friday and Saturday nights March–May and Sept. –Dec., but call for current details. December **Christmas at the Castle** tours are particularly festive.

Practical Hearst Castle

San Simeon is open daily except Thanksgiving, Christmas, and New Year's Day, with the regular two-hour tours leaving the visitor center area on the hour from early morning until around dusk. Tour schedules change by season and day of the week. Reservations aren't required, but the chance of getting tickets on a drop-in, last-minute basis is small. For current schedule information and reservations, call ReserveAmerica toll-free at 800/444-4445 and have that credit card handy. For cancellations and refunds, in the U.S. call toll-free 800/695-2269. (To make ticket reservations from outside the U.S., call 916/414-8400 ext. 4100.) Wheelchair-access tours of San Simeon are offered on a different schedule; call 805/927-2070 for reservations and information. The toll-free TDD number is 800/274-7275.

Admission to Tour One is $14 adult, $7 youth (ages 6–17). Each of the other three San Simeon day tours is $10 adults, $5 youth. Evening tour rates are $20 adults, $10 children. A special brochure for international travelers (printed in Japanese, Korean, French, German, Hebrew, Italian, and Spanish) is available. With a little forethought—head for Cambria or the town of San Simeon—visitors can avoid eating the concession-style food here.

Adjacent to the visitor center is the Hearst Castle's giant-screened **National Geographic Theater,** tel. 805/927-6811, where at last report the larger-than-life *Hearst Castle—Building the*

the Neptune Pool at Hearst Castle

Dream and *Everest* were showing on the 70-foot by 52-foot screen. Call for current times and details (no reservations required).

For other information, contact: Hearst San Simeon State Historic Monument, 750 Hearst Castle Rd., San Simeon, CA 93452, tel. 805/927-2020 (recorded) or 805/927-2000, www.hearstcastle.org.

Practical Big Sur

STAYING IN BIG SUR
Public Camping in Big Sur
In the accommodations category, nothing but camping is truly inexpensive in Big Sur, so to travel on the cheap, make campground reservations *early* (where applicable) and stock up on groceries and sundries in Monterey up north or in San Luis Obispo to the south. All the following options are Under $50. The U.S. Forest Service **Bottchers Gap Campground** on Palo Colorado Canyon Road has primitive, walk-in tent sites (first-come, first-camped). Rough road, no drinking water. The Forest Service **Kirk Creek Campground** is far south of urban Big Sur and just north of the intersection with Nacimiento-Fergusson Road. It consists of 33 first-come, first-camped sites, picnic tables, and grills, all situated on a grassy seaside bluff. Inland,

halfway to Jolon, are two small creekside campgrounds managed by Los Padres National Forest. They are free, since there's no reliable drinking water, and are popular with deer hunters. Also run by the Forest Service and even farther south, north of Gorda, is the 43-site **Plaskett Creek Campground.**

For more information on the area's national forest campgrounds and for free visitor permits, fire permits, maps, and other information about Los Padres National Forest and the Ventana Wilderness, stop by the **Big Sur Station** State Parks/U.S. Forest Service office at Pfeiffer-Big Sur State Park, open daily 8 A.M. to 4:30 P.M., 831/667-2315, or the **Monterey Ranger District** office at 406 S. Mildred Ave. in King City, 831/385-5434.

At state park facilities, for secluded camping try **Andrew Molera State Park,** with 50 walk-in tent sites not far from the dusty parking lot, three-night maximum; or **Julia Pfeiffer Burns State Park,** almost as nice, with two separate environmental campgrounds (far from RVs). More comforts (including flush toilets and hot showers) are available at the attractive family campground at **Pfeiffer–Big Sur State Park.** It has 218 campsites, plus a regular summer schedule of educational and informational programs. There are no hookups. Another possibility, just south of Lucia, is the postcard-pretty **Limekiln State Park,** 63025 Hwy. 1, 831/667-2403, which takes up most of the steep canyon and offers some good hiking in addition to attractive tent and RV sites (no hookups, but water, hot showers, and flush toilets are available). For information about any of the area's state park campgrounds, stop by the office at Pfeiffer-Big Sur State Park or call 831/667-2315. For ReserveAmerica reservations (usually necessary May through early September and on warm-weather weekends) at Pfeiffer–Big Sur and

Limekiln, call 800/444-7275 or reserve online at website: www.reserveamerica.com.

Private Camping in Big Sur

Not far from the state campgrounds at Pfeiffer–Big Sur State Park is the private riverside **Big Sur Campground,** Hwy. 1, 831/667-2322, with tent sites and RV sites including hookups. Tent cabins and cabins are also available, as well as hot showers, laundry facilities, a store, telephone access, and a playground. Also on the Big Sur River, with similar facilities and prices, is the **Riverside Campground,** Hwy. 1, 831/667-2414, with tent or RV sites plus cabins. The private **Ventana Campgrounds,** managed by the Ventana Inn, Hwy. 1, 831/667-2712, website: www.ventanabigsur.com, has 80 very private, pretty sites in a scenic 40-acre redwood setting along Post Creek. There are some RV hookups, hot showers (three bathhouses), fireplaces, and picnic tables. Rates for all the above are Under $50.

NEPENTHE

Nepenthe, about a mile south of the Ventana Inn, was built almost exactly on the site of the cabin Orson Welles bought for Rita Hayworth. So it's not too surprising that the restaurant is almost as legendary as Big Sur itself. A striking multilevel structure complete with an arts and crafts center, the restaurant was named for an ancient drug mentioned in Homer's *The Odyssey,* taken to help people forget their grief. Naturally enough, the bar here does a brisk business.

As is traditional at Nepenthe, relax on the upper deck (the "gay pavilion," presided over by a sculpted bronze and redwood phoenix) with drink in hand to salute the sea and setting sun—surreal views. The open-beamed restaurant and its outdoor above-ocean terrace isn't nearly as rowdy as all those bohemian celebrity stories would suggest. Nonetheless, thrill-seekers insist on sitting on the top deck, though there's often more room available downstairs at the Café Kevah health food deli and deck, open March-Dec. for brunch and lunch. The fare at Nepenthe is good, but not as spectacular (on a clear day) as the views. Try the

homemade soups, the hefty chef's salad, any of the vegetarian selections, or the world-famous Ambrosia burger (an excellent cheeseburger on French roll with pickles and a salad for a hefty price) accompanied by a Basket o' Fries. Good pies and cakes for dessert.

To avoid the worst of the tourist traffic and to appreciate Nepenthe at its best, come later in September or October. And although Nepenthe is casual any time of year, it's not *that* casual. Local lore has it that John F. Kennedy was once turned away because he showed up barefoot. Nepenthe is open for lunch and dinner daily, with music and dancing around the hearth at night. For more information or reservations, call 831/667-2345. To reach Café Kevah, call 831/667-2344.

And if at the moment you can't be here in person, you can be here in spirit—much easier now that Nepenthe has an online weather camera pointing south over the back deck. To "see" what's happening along Nepenthe's coastline, try www.nepenthebigsur.com.

Affordable Big Sur Accommodations

Always a best bet for cabins and affordable for just plain folks is the charming **Ripplewood Resort,** about a mile north of Pfeiffer-Big Sur, 831/667-2242, website: www.ripplewoodresort.com. The primo units, most with fireplaces and kitchens (bring your own cookware), are down by the Big Sur River (and booked months in advance for summer). Rates are $100 to $150. Convenient on-site café, too; open for breakfast and lunch. Other options include the adobe **Glen Oaks Motel,** 831/667-2105, website: www.glenoaks bigsur.com, and the **Fernwood Resort,** 831/667-2422, both on Highway 1 and both with rates of $50 to $150. The **Big Sur River Inn,** on Highway 1 in Big Sur Valley, 831/625-5255 or 800/548-3610, is a motel-restaurant-bar popular with locals and featuring views of the river and live music most weekends. The 61-room **Big Sur Lodge** nearby, just inside the park's entrance at 47225 Hwy. 1, 831/667-3100 or 800/424-4787, website: www.bigsurlodge.com, is quiet, with a pool, sauna, restaurant, and circle of comfy cabins, each with its own porch or deck. Some rooms feature wood-burning fireplaces or fully stocked kitchens. Rates start at $50. A lodge stay includes a complimentary pass to all area state parks.

Deetjen's Big Sur Inn

Just south of the noted Nepenthe restaurant and the Henry Miller Library is the landmark Norwegian-style Deetjen's Big Sur Inn in Castro Canyon, 831/667-2377, a rambling, ever-blooming inn with redwood rooms—now listed on the National Register of Historic Places. *Very* Big Sur. The 20 eccentric, rustic rooms and cabins—one's named Chateau Fiasco, after the Bay of Pigs invasion—are chock-full of bric-a-brac and feature thin walls, front doors that don't lock, fireplaces, books, and reasonably functional plumbing. No TVs, no telephones. Forget about trendy creature comforts. People love this place—and have ever since it opened in the 1930s—because it has *soul.* Private or shared baths. Reservations advised because rooms are usually booked up many months in advance. Rooms are $100 and up. Eating at Deetjen's is as

big a treat as an overnight. Wonderfully hearty, wholesome breakfasts are served 8 to 11:30 A.M., and dinner starts at 6:15 P.M. Reservations are also taken for meals.

Ventana Inn & Spa

Perhaps tuned into the same philosophical frequency as Henry Miller—"There being nothing to improve on in the surroundings, the tendency is to set about improving oneself"—the Ventana Inn didn't provide distractions like TV or tennis courts when writer Lawrence A. Spector first built the place in 1975. Though it's still a hip, high-priced resort, and there are still no tennis courts, things have changed. Now the desperately undiverted *can* phone home, if need be, or watch in-room TV or videos. But the woodsy, world-class Ventana high up on the hill in Big Sur, 831/667-2331 or 800/628-6500, website: www.ventanainn.com, still offers luxurious and relaxed contemporary lodgings on 240 acres overlooking the sea, outdoor Japanese hot baths, and heated pools. Rates are $250 and up; reservations usually essential; two-night minimum stay on weekends. Children are discouraged at Ventana, which is not set up to entertain or otherwise look after them.

This rough-hewn and hand-built hostelry comprises 12 separate buildings with rooms featuring unfinished cedar interiors, parquet floors, and down-home luxuries like queen- or king-sized beds with hand-painted headboards, handmade quilted spreads, and lots of pillows. All rooms are reasonably large and have in-room refrigerators; most have fireplaces. Rooms and suites with both fireplaces and hot tubs are at the top of the inn's price range. The Ventana Inn also has a library, not to mention hiking trails and hammocks. Complimentary group classes—so very *California*—include Native American tai chi, Chi Gong, guided meditation, yoga, and hiking. Complimentary continental breakfast is served (delivered to your room by request), and in the afternoon from 4 to 5:30 P.M. you can enjoy the complimentary wine and cheese buffet in the main lodge.

Ranked number two of the 25 "Best Small Hotels in the World" in the 1998 *Travel &*

Leisure reader survey, the Ventana Inn became the Ventana Inn & Spa with the 1999 debut of its full-service spa. For a price, expect world-class massage, wraps, facials, scrubs, and other body therapies.

If a stay here or a self-pampering spa session seems just *too rich*, try drinks with a view or a bite of enticing California cuisine served in the inn's lovely two-tiered **Cielo** restaurant overlooking the ocean, a pleasant stroll through the woods. The Ventana Inn is located 0.8 miles south of Pfeiffer–Big Sur State Park; look for the sign on the left.

Post Ranch Inn

For good reason, new Big Sur commercial development has been rare in the 1990s. If further coastal development must come, the environ-

mentally conscious Post Ranch Inn offers the style—if not the price range—most Californians would cheer. All the upscale travel mags rave about the place, open since 1992, calling it "one of the best places to stay in the world" *(Condé Nast Traveler)* and "the most spectacular hotel on the Pacific Coast" *(Travel & Leisure)*. This place is something special. Developer Myles Williams, of New Christy Minstrels folksinging fame, and architect Mickey Muennig took the Big Sur region's rugged love of the land to heart when they built the very contemporary Post Ranch Inn. They also acknowledged the community's increasing economic stratification and took other real-world problems into account, adding 24 housing units for workers (affordable housing is now scarce in these parts) and donating land for Big Sur's first fire station.

HEADING SOUTH: CRUISING THE CENTRAL COAST

Just south of rugged Big Sur and San Simeon, and always worth a stop, is the scenic coastal town of Cambria. With its lush Monterey pines, galleries, and shops, it is considered by some the Carmel of the southern Big Sur coast.

The biggest city immediately south from San Simeon is San Luis Obispo, a convenient stop halfway between L.A. and San Francisco along Hwy. 101 and most famous for inventing both the word and the modern concept of "motel," a contraction of "motor hotel." Agriculture is big business in and around San Luis Obispo. If you can time your trip right, roll into town on a Thursday evening to enjoy the Higuera Street Farmers' Market, one of the best anywhere (cancelled only in the event of rain).

Well worth going out of your way to discover is Mission San Antonio de Padua, north of San Luis Obispo and smack-dab in the middle of Fort Hunter-Liggett (security check at the gate). Not the grandest or most spruced-up, San Antonio de Padua is perhaps the most genuinely evocative of all the California missions. Nearby Lake San Antonio is popular in winter for guided bald eagle-watching tours.

Off in the other direction, via Hwy. 58, is the Carrizo Plain Preserve, earthquake territory once

sacred to the Chumash people and refuge to some of the state's most endangered animal species. If you head east from Paso Robles toward the San Joaquin Valley via Hwy. 46, you'll come to the shrine marking (almost) the spot where actor James Dean *(Rebel Without a Cause, Giant,* and *East of Eden)* died in a car accident in 1955. Paso Robles itself and nearby Templeton anchor an increasingly popular—and increasingly impressive—wine region.

Morro Rock, California's little Gibraltar, spotted by Cabrillo in 1542, is the first thing people notice at Morro Bay on the coast west of San Luis Obispo. But the Morro Bay Chess Club maintains its giant outdoor chessboard downtown, and Morro Bay State Park, Montana de Oro State Park, and area beaches are also worth exploring. The one-time port towns and piers along San Luis Obispo Bay to the south also have their attractions.

Santa Maria just over the border in Santa Barbara County is most noted for its own unique culinary heritage—"Santa Maria Barbecue," a tradition preserved since the days of the vaqueros. Near town is the Guadalupe-Nipomo Dunes Preserve, a coastal wildlife and plant preserve also protecting the remains of Cecil B. DeMille's *The Ten Commandments* movie set, buried under the sand here once filming was finished.

Perched on a ridge overlooking the grand Pacific Ocean, the Post Ranch Inn is a carefully executed aesthetic study in nature awareness. The 30 redwood-and-glass "guest houses" are designed and built to harmonize with—almost disappear into—the hilltop landscape. The triangular "tree houses" are built on stilts, to avoid damaging the roots of the oaks with which they intertwine; the spectacular sod-roofed "ocean houses" literally blend into the ocean views; and the gracious "coast house" duplexes impersonate stand-tall coastal redwoods. Absolute privacy and understated, earth-toned luxury are the main points here. Each house includes a wood-burning fireplace, a two-person spa tub in the stunning slate bathroom, a good sound system, in-room refrigerators stocked with complimentary snacks, a private deck, a king-sized bed—and views. Extra amenities include plush robes, in-room coffeemakers and hair dryers, even walking sticks. Priced for Hollywood entertainment execs and Silicon Valley survivors, rates are $250 and up, continental breakfast included.

Guests can also enjoy the **Post Ranch Spa**—offering massage, wraps, and facials—and the exceptional California-style **Sierra Mar** restaurant, where the views are every bit as inviting as the daily changing menu. Full bar. Open for lunch and dinner.

The Post Ranch Inn is 30 miles south of Carmel on Highway 1, on the west (seaward) side of the road. As at Ventana, children are discouraged here. For more information, contact Post Ranch Inn, P.O. Box 219, Big Sur, CA

Lompoc is noted for its blooming flower fields—this is a major seed-producing area—and is home to Vandenberg Air Force Base as well as Mission La Purisima State Historic Park four miles east of town, California's only complete mission compound.

Farther south, Solvang is a Danish-style town founded in 1911 and now a well-trod tourist destination. If you've got time, worth exploring nearby are the towns of Los Olivos and Los Alamos, center of northern Santa Barbara County's impressive wine country.

Technically speaking, Point Conception just below Vandenberg marks the spot where California turns on itself—that pivotal geographical point where Northern California becomes Southern California, where rugged and rocky coastline gives way to broad white sandy beaches. The climatic and terrain changes are unmistakable by the time you arrive in Santa Barbara, a richly endowed city noted for its gracious red-tile-roofed California Spanish-style buildings and cultural attractions.

Continue south from Santa Barbara to Ventura to set off on whale-watching trips and guided boat tours of California's Channel Islands National Park, often visible from Santa Barbara and vicinity.

© ROBERT HOLMES/CalTour

Highway 1 is California's first scenic highway.

93920, 831/667-2200, website: www.postranch inn.com. For inn reservations, call 800/527-2200. For restaurant reservations, call 831/667-2800.

EATING WELL IN BIG SUR

Look for fairly inexpensive fare in and around the Big Sur Valley. Good for breakfast is the **Ripplewood Resort** just north of Pfeiffer-Big Sur near the tiny Big Sur Library, 831/667-2242, where favorites include homemade baked goods and French toast. **Deetjen's,** 831/667-2377, is special for breakfast—wholesome and hearty fare served in the open-beamed, hobbit-style dining rooms. Dinner is more formal (fireplace blazing to ward off the chill mist, classical music, and two seatings, by reservation only), with entrées including steaks, fish, California country cuisine, and vegetarian dishes. Tasty home-baked pies are an after-meal specialty at the casual and cheery **Big Sur Lodge Restaurant** at the Big Sur Lodge, 831/667-3111, overlooking the river and also known for red snapper and California-style fare. Beer and wine. Another draw is the lodge's **Espresso House,** perfect for coffee, tea, or a quick snack.

Everyone should sample the view from famed **Nepenthe,** 831/667-2345, at least once in a lifetime; just below Nepenthe is **Café Kevah,** 831/667-2344, open March through December for brunch and lunch. A culinary hot spot is the locally popular **Bonito Roadhouse** (previously the Glen Oaks Restaurant) at the Glen Oaks Motel, next door to the Ripplewood Resort, 831/667-2264. It is diverse, low-key, and likable à la Big Sur. Entrées emphasize what's local and fresh and include crêpes, good vegetarian dishes, seafood gumbo, and chicken pot pie. Open for dinner Wednesday through Monday nights. The roadhouse also serves a fine Sunday brunch, with omelettes, eggs Benedict, and cornmeal hotcakes. A quarter-mile north of Palo Colorado Rd. on Highway 1 is the **Rocky Point Restaurant,** 831/624-2933, a reasonably well-heeled

steak and seafood place overlooking the ocean. Open for lunch, dinner, and cocktails daily.

The finest of local fine dining is served at the area's luxury-hotel restaurants—at **Cielo** at the Ventana Inn & Spa and **Sierra Mar** at the Post Ranch Inn—which both serve lunch and dinner daily. For information, see listings above.

INFORMATION, SERVICES, AND TRANSPORTATION

For general information about the area, contact the **Big Sur Chamber of Commerce,** P.O. Box 87, Big Sur, CA 93920, 831/667-2100, website: www.bigsurcalifornia.org. (Send a stamped, self-addressed legal-sized envelope for a free guide to Big Sur, or download it from the website.) Combined headquarters for area state parks and the U.S. Forest Service is **Big Sur Station** on the south side of Pfeiffer-Big Sur on Hwy. 1, Big Sur, CA 93920, 831/667-2315. Open daily 8 A.M. to 4:30 P.M., this is the place to go in search of forest and wilderness maps, permits, and backcountry camping and recreation information. There's a **laundromat** at Pfeiffer-Big Sur State Park in the Big Sur Lodge complex.

Bicycling Big Sur can be marvelous, except when you're fighting RVs and weekend speedsters for road space. Forewarned, fearless cyclists should plan to ride from north to south to take advantage of the tailwind. (Driving south makes sense, too, since most vistas and turnouts are seaward.) It takes *at least* five hours by car to drive the 150 miles of Highway 1 between Monterey and San Luis Obispo.

Hitchhiking is almost as difficult as safely riding a bicycle along this stretch of road, so don't count on thumbs for transportation. More reliable is **Monterey-Salinas Transit** Bus 22, which runs to and from Big Sur daily mid-April to October, stopping at Point Lobos, Garrapata State Park, the Bixby Creek Bridge, Point Sur Lightstation, Pfeiffer-Big Sur and the River Inn, Pfeiffer Beach, the Ventana Inn, and Nepenthe; call 831/899-2555 for information.

Salinas and Vicinity

The sometimes bone-dry Salinas River starts in the mountains above San Luis Obispo and flows north through the Salinas Valley, much of the time underground, unseen. Named for the salt marshes, or *salinas,* near the river's mouth, the Salinas River is the longest underground waterway in the United States. The 100-mile-long Salinas Valley, with its fertile soil and lush lettuce fields, is sometimes referred to as the nation's Salad Bowl. To the west is the Santa Lucia Range; to the east are the Gabilan and Diablo Mountains. Cattle graze in the hills.

No longer such a small town, Salinas is the blue-collar birthplace of novelist John Steinbeck, who chronicled the lives and hard times of California's down-and-out. Some things don't change

much. More than 60 years after the 1939 publication of Steinbeck's Pulitzer Prize–winning *The Grapes of Wrath,* the United Farm Workers (UFW) are still attempting to organize the primarily Hispanic farm laborers and migrant workers here. The idea of a unionized agricultural labor force has never been popular in the United States, and certainly not with Salinas Valley growers. In 1936, during a lettuce workers' strike, Salinas was at the center of national attention. Reports to the California Highway Patrol that communists were advancing on the town—"proven" by red flags planted along the highway, some of which were sent as evidence to politicians in Sacramento—led to tear gas and tussling between officers, growers, and strikers. The state highway commission later insisted that the construction warning banners be returned to the area's roadsides.

south of Salinas

Seeing and Doing Salinas

A Salinas tradition (since 1911) is the four-day **California Rodeo,** held on the third weekend in July. It is one of the world's largest rodeos, with bronco busting and bull riding, roping and tying, barrel racing, and a big western dance on Saturday night. The rowdiness here—cowboy-style, of course—rivals Mardi Gras. For information, contact the California Rodeo, 1034 N. Main St., P.O. Box 1648, Salinas, CA 93902, 831/775-3100 (office), 831/775-3113 (event information), or 831/775-3131 (advance ticket sales), website: www.carodeo.com. There's western high art, too. See the massive triptych sculpture by Claes Oldenburg, titled *Hat in Three Stages of Landing,* on the lawn of the nearby Salinas Community Center, 940 N. Main St. The series of 3,500-pound yellow hats appear to have been tossed from the nearby rodeo grounds.

The **Boronda Adobe,** 333 Boronda Rd. (at W. Laurel), 831/757-8085, is an outstanding example of a Mexican-era Monterey Colonial adobe. Built between 1844 and 1848 by Jose Eusebio Boronda and virtually unaltered since, the tiny structure has been refurbished and now features museum displays and exhibits, including a few handsome original furnishings. Note the wood shingles, a considerable departure from traditional red-clay tiles. Open Monday through Friday 10 A.M. to 2 P.M. and Sunday 1 to 4 P.M. for tours (donation requested). Also here is the one-room 1897 **Old Lagunita School House** and a turn-of-the-20th-century home designed by architect William H. Weeks.

Toro Park, on the way to Monterey via Highway 68, is a pleasant regional park with good hiking, biking, and horseback trails. For an invigorating walk and views of both Monterey Bay and Salinas Valley, take the 2.5-mile trail to Eagle Peak. The park is open daily 8 A.M. to dusk. The day-use fee is $3 on weekdays, $5 on weekends and holidays. For information call 831/484-1108.

A satellite community southeast of Salinas, the town of **Spreckels** was developed by Claus Spreckels in the late 1890s to house employees of his sugar beet factory. This is a genuine "company town," down to the sugar beet architectural motifs in the roof gables of many historic homes. **Natividad** is a onetime stage station about seven miles north of Salinas and the site of the 1846 **Battle of Natividad,** where Californios attacked Yankee invaders herding 300 horses to Frémont's troops in Monterey.

STEINBECK'S LEGACY
Salinas Valley's Despised Star

The Grapes of Wrath didn't do much for John Steinbeck's local popularity. Started as a photojournalism project chronicling the "Okie" Dust Bowl migrations to California during the Depression, Steinbeck's *Grapes* instead became fiction. The entire book was a whirlwind, written between June and October 1938. After publication, it became a bestseller and remained one through 1940. Steinbeck was unhappy about the book's incredible commercial success; he believed there was something wrong with books that became so popular.

Vilified here as a left-winger and Salinas Valley traitor during his lifetime, Steinbeck never came back to Salinas. (The only way the town would ever take him back, he once said, was in a six-foot wooden box. And that's basically how it happened. His remains are at home at the local Garden of Memories Cemetery.) Most folks here have long ago forgiven their local literary light for his political views, so now you'll find his name and book titles at least mentioned, if not prominently displayed, all around town.

Steinbeck's Rehabilitation: The National Steinbeck Center

Some people have long been trying to make it up to Steinbeck. After all, he was the first American to win both the Pulitzer and Nobel Prizes for literature. Efforts to establish a permanent local Steinbeck center finally succeeded, and in summer 1998 the doors of the $10.3 million National Steinbeck Center opened to the public.

Billed as a "multimedia experience of literature, history, and art," the Steinbeck Center provides at least one answer to the question of how to present literary accomplishment to an increasingly nonliterary culture. And that answer is—ta da—high-tech interactivity. In addition to changing exhibits, seven themed permanent galleries—incorporating sights, sounds, and scents—introduce Steinbeck's life, work, and times, in settings ranging from Doc Rickett's lab on Cannery Row and the replica boxcar of "ice-packed" lettuce to the (climbable) red pony in the barn. Seven theaters show clips from films derived from Steinbeck's writings. But some appreciations are strictly literal, including John Steinbeck's trusty green truck and camper Rocinante (named after Don Quixote's horse), in which the writer sojourned while researching *Travels with Charley.* The **Art of Writing Room,** with literary exhibits and all kinds of technical interactivity, explores the themes of Steinbeck's art and life. The 30,000-piece **Steinbeck Archives** here, open only to researchers by appointment, was originally housed in the local John Steinbeck Library on Lincoln Avenue. The archival collection includes original letters, first editions, movie posters, and taped interviews with local people who remember Steinbeck. Some of the barbed remarks, made decades after the publication of *The Grapes of Wrath,* make it clear that local wrath runs at least as deep as the Salinas River.

Other attractions include the sunny **Steinbeck Center Café** and the **museum store,** which features a good selection of books in addition to gift items. (To visit some of the actual places Steinbeck immortalized in his fiction, be sure to pick up the 24-page *Steinbeck Country: A Guide to Exploring John Steinbeck's Monterey County.* Also see if you can find a used copy of *The John Steinbeck Map of America,* now out of print.) The center's new 6,500-square-foot wing, the **Salinas Valley Agricultural History and Education Center,** opened in 2000 and showcases the Salinas Valley's agricultural heritage.

The center is open daily 10 A.M. to 5 P.M., but is closed on Easter, Thanksgiving, Christmas, and New Year's Day. Admission is $7.95 adults, $6.95 seniors (over age 62) and students with ID, $5.95 youths (ages 13 to 17), $3.95 children (age 6 to 12), free for age 5 and under. For more information about the center and its

the National Steinbeck Center

MELISSA SHEROWSKI

SALINAS AND VICINITY

THE RED PONY

John Steinbeck's short story "The Red Pony" nestles into the Salinas region like a young boy might bury his face in the earthy, sweet smell of his pony's neck. Most memorable is the story's bittersweetness nature. "The Red Pony" is often considered a children's story because of the protagonist, the young boy Jody, who soon learns about the depths of love and loss when his beloved red pony, Gabilan, gets the strangles and dies, despite everyone's heroic efforts to save him. Yet love and loss are steps in an endless emotional dance; that theme is woven throughout the story, which also depicts the grandfather's loss of his own "story"—certainly a willing audience for his storytelling—and the similar U.S. loss of its storied western frontier. As Jody's grandfather tells it: "No place to go, Jody. Every place is taken. But that's not the worst—no, not the worst. Westering has died out of the people. Westering isn't a hunger anymore. It's all done."

To decide for yourself whether "westering" is done or not, read *The Red Pony*, available in paperback.

events and activities, contact National Steinbeck Center, 1 Main St., Salinas, CA 93901, 831/775-7240 or 831/796-3833, website: www.steinbeck.org.

Other Steinbeck Attractions

On the first weekend in August, come for the annual **Steinbeck Festival**—four days of films, lectures, tours, and social mixers. And in late February or early March, the town throws a Piscean **Steinbeck Birthday Party.** For information on either event, call 831/796-3833. The **Western Stage** performs occasional Steinbeck works, other dramatic productions, and popular concerts on the Hartnell College campus, 156 Homestead Ave. For information and reservations call 831/755-6816 or 831/375-2111.

Steinbeck described the family home—a jewel-box Victorian, located just two blocks from the National Steinbeck Center—as "an immaculate and friendly house, grand enough, but not pretentious." And so it still is, as both a dining and

historic destination. The Salinas Valley Guild serves up gourmet lunches for Steinbeck fans and literary ghosts alike, featuring Salinas Valley produce and Monterey County wines and beer, at **Steinbeck House,** the author's birthplace and "a living museum" at 132 Central St., open Monday through Saturday 11 A.M. to 2:30 P.M. The menu changes weekly, served by volunteers dressed in period Victorian costumes. Call 831/424-2735 for information and reservations (suggested but not required). The house is also open for guided tours (call for information), and there's a "Best Cellar" book and gift shop in the basement, 831/757-0508. All proceeds maintain and support the Steinbeck House and local charities.

PRACTICAL SALINAS

Staying in Salinas

Camp at the **Laguna Seca Raceway** facility near Monterey (see Monterey chapter). **Fremont Peak State Park,** on San Juan Canyon Road (southeast from San Juan Bautista), 831/623-4255, has some first-come, first-camped primitive campsites.

In the Soledad and King City areas, **Arroyo Seco** features several U.S. Forest Service campgrounds; take Arroyo Seco Road west off Highway 101, just south of Soledad, or take Carmel Valley Road south to its end and turn right. Or camp at **Los Coches Wayside Camp,** just south of Soledad, or **Paraiso Hot Springs,** nearby on Paraiso Springs Road, 831/678-2882. **San Lorenzo County Park,** on the Salinas River near King City, 831/385-5964, boasts some 200 campsites with hot showers and picnic tables; call 831/385-1484 for information and reservations. The **Monterey County Agricultural & Rural Life Museum** in San Lorenzo Park at 1160 Broadway, 831/385-8020, features Spreckels farmhouse, a barn with antique farm equipment, a cook wagon, a schoolhouse, and a historic railroad depot. Continuing south toward San Luis Obispo, both **Lake San Antonio** (north and south shore, call 831/385-8399 for information) and **Lake Nacimiento** have abundant campsites. All camping options are under $50.

For something a tad more uptown, Salinas has two **Motel 6** locations: 140 Kern, 831/753-1711, and 1257 De La Torre Blvd., 831/757-3077. Both feature the basics plus a pool and in-room color TV. Rates are under $50. For reservations at any Motel 6, contact 800/466-8356 or website: www.motel6.com. Most other motels lining Highway 101 are a bit more upscale. Rooms at the **Comfort Inn,** just off the freeway at 144 Kern St., 831/758-8850 or 800/888-3839, feature in-room coffeemakers; some have microwaves and refrigerators. Rates are $100 to $150.

For something different, head for casual **Barlocker's Rustling Oaks Ranch Bed & Breakfast,** off River Road at 25252 Limekiln Rd., 831/675-9121. There are five guest rooms. Extras include horseback trails, a swimming pool, a pool table, and a genuine country breakfast. Rates are $100 to $250.

Eating in Salinas

Get up to speed on the local politics of food production, then sample that famed Salinas Valley produce. The **Old Town Salinas Certified Farmers' Market** is held downtown along the 200 block of Main Street (near Alifal Street) every Wednesday from 3 to 7 P.M. (until 8 P.M. in summer). Call 831/758-0725 for details. If you're here on the weekend, head for the **Salinas Certified Farmers' Market** at the Northridge Mall, 796 Main St., 831/728-5060, held on Sunday from 8 A.M. to noon. Another possibility is **The Farm,** on Highway 68 just west of Salinas off the Spreckels exit, 831/455-2575—just look for the giant murals—featuring certified organic fruits and vegetables, specialty products, agricultural memorabilia, and the opportunity to get out in the fields and commune with the vegetables. Open Monday through Saturday 10 A.M. to 6 P.M. Farm tours are available by reservation.

A wonderful coffee stop just a couple blocks from the Steinbeck Center is the **Cherry Bean Gourmet,** 332 Main St., 831/424-1989. (And if you're really in a hurry—just passin' through—Salinas has an **In-N-Out Burger,** at 151 Kern Street.) For breakfast downtown, try the breakfast specialists at **First Awakenings,** 171 Main,

831/784-1125, where the pancakes are reputedly the best in the county. Open daily 7 A.M. to 2:30 P.M. Cheap and good is the locally popular **Rosita's Armory Cafe,** 231 Salinas St., 831/424-7039. Always a best bet for literary lunch, especially for Steinbeck fans, is the historic **Steinbeck House,** just two blocks from the National Steinbeck Center at 132 Center St., open Monday through Saturday 11 A.M. to 2:30 P.M., 831/424-2735 (see above for more information).

The **Salinas Valley Fish House,** 172 Main St., 831/775-0175, offers various "fresh catches" plus an oyster bar. For Italian food try **Spado's,** 66 W. Alisal, 831/424-4139, featuring fresh pastas, a daily stew, and lamb dishes. **Smalley's Roundup,** 700 W. Market, 831/758-0511, is locally famous for its oak-wood barbecue and other cowboy-style fine dining. (Reservations advised at dinner.)

the California Rodeo in Salinas

SALINAS AND VICINITY

Salinas Information and Transportation

The **Salinas Valley Chamber of Commerce,** 119 E. Alisal, P.O. Box 1170, Salinas, CA 93902, 831/424-7611, website: www.salinaschamber .com, offers information on accommodations and sights, as well as a great little brochure: ***Steinbeck Country Starts in Salinas.*** The Salinas chamber is also a county-wide visitors center, so stop here for any Monterey County information. Open 8:30 A.M. to 5 P.M. Monday through Friday, 9 A.M. to 3 P.M. on Saturday (closed Sunday). **Amtrak** is at 11 Station Place; contact 831/422-7458 or 800/872-7245, or website: www.amtrak.com for fare and schedule information. There's no train station in Monterey, but you can connect from there to Salinas via **Monterey-Salinas Transit** bus 20 or 21 (or via the Amtrak Thruway bus as part of your train fare). For more information, contact Monterey-Salinas Transit, 1 Ryan Ranch Rd., Monterey, 831/424-7695 or 831/899-2555, website: www.mst.org. **Greyhound** is at 19 W. Gabilan St., 831/424-4418 or 800/231-2222. The **Salinas Municipal Airport** is on Airport Boulevard, 831/758-7214.

Southeast from Salinas

SOLEDAD

Soledad, a sleepy town where no one hurries, is the oldest settlement in the Salinas Valley. Stop by the local bakery *(panaderia)* on Front Street for fresh Mexican pastries and hot tortillas. **Misión Nuestra Señora de La Soledad** was founded here in 1791 to minister to the Salinas Valley natives. Our Lady of Solitude Mission three miles southwest of town was quite prosperous until 1825. But this, the 13th in California's mission chain, was beset by problems ranging from raging Salinas River floods to disease epidemics before it crumbled into ruin. The chapel was reconstructed and rededicated, and another wing has since been restored. The original 1799 mission bell still hangs in the courtyard of this active parish church. Outside is a lovely garden. The mission, 831/678-2586, which also offers a museum and gift shop, is open daily 10 A.M. to 4 P.M. Just three miles south of Soledad (west at the Arroyo Seco interchange from Highway 101) is another historic survivor, the 1843 **Richardson Adobe,** at Los Coches Rancho Wayside Campground.

PARAISO HOT SPRINGS

Nestled in a grove of lovely palm trees, with a sweeping valley view, this serene, scenic 240-acre old resort a few miles southwest of Soledad has an indoor hot mineral bath (suits required), outdoor pools, picnic tables and barbecues, campgrounds, and Victorian cabins—a genuinely restful getaway and rarely crowded. There's not much to do here but loll around in the waters and soak up the sun, but visitors can use the lending library and recreation room and enjoy free coffee

MELISSA SHEROWSKI

This marker commemorates the original Misión de Nuestra Señora de la Soledad, which was destroyed by a flood.

SALINAS AND VICINITY

MELISSA SHEROWSKI

Paraiso Hot Springs

and cookies. Nothing much happens after 6 P.M. but the sunset and moonrise. Facilities include indoor and outdoor baths and pools, tent cabins, and furnished cabins. Weekly and monthly rates are available. For more information and reservations, contact Paraiso Hot Springs, Soledad, CA 93960, 831/678-2882.

PINNACLES NATIONAL MONUMENT

Exploring these barren 16,000 acres of volcanic spires and ravines is a little like rock climbing on the moon. The weird dark-red rocks are bizarrely eroded, unlike anywhere else in North America, forming gaping gorges, crumbling caverns, terrifying terraces. Rock climbers' heaven (not for beginners), this stunning old volcano offers excellent trails, too, with pebbles the size of houses to stumble over. Visitors afraid of earthquakes should know that the Pinnacles sit atop an active section of the San Andreas Fault. Spring is the best time to visit, when wildflowers brighten up the chaparral, but sunlight on the rocks creates rainbows of color year-round. Rock climbing is the major attraction, for obvious reasons.

Climbers come during the cool weather. But you can also hike, and in winter watch the raptors: golden eagles, red-shouldered hawks, kestrels, and prairie falcons.

Though it was Teddy Roosevelt who first utilized presidential decree on behalf on the Pinnacles—protecting it as a national monument in 1906—in early 2000 President Bill Clinton announced plans to expand the park by some 5,000 acres. Some of that acreage, when acquired, may encourage gentler, more family-oriented recreation.

Hiking the Pinnacles

Of Pinnacles' existing (pre-expansion) 16,000-plus acres, nearly 13,000 are protected as wilderness. Only hiking trails connect the park's east and west sides. Some trails are fairly easy, while others are rugged. Pinnacles has four self-guided nature trails; the **Geology Hike** and **Balconies Trail** are quite fascinating. The short **Moses Spring Trail** is one of the best. Longest is the trek up the **Chalone Peak Trail,** 11 miles round-trip, passing fantastic rock formations (quite a view of Salinas once you get to the top of North Chalone Peak). Less ambitious is the **Condor Gulch Trail,** an easy two-mile hike into Balconies Caves from the Chalone Creek picnic area. Various interconnecting trails encourage creativity on foot. The best caves, as well as the most fascinating rock formations and visitors center displays, are on the park's east side. The fit, fast, and willing can hike east to west and back in one (long) day. Easiest return trip is via the Old Pinnacles Trail, rather than the steep Juniper Canyon Trail. Pack plenty of water.

Practical Pinnacles

As lasting testament to the land's rugged nature, there are two districts in the Pinnacles—west and east—and it's not possible to get from one to the other by road. Within the monument, bicycles and cars may only be used on paved roads. If coming from the west, get visitor information at the **Chaparral Ranger Station,** reached via Highway 146 heading east (exit Highway 101 just south of Soledad). For most visitors, Pinnacles is most accessible from this route, but it's a narrow road, not recommended for campers and trailers. If coming from the east, stop by the **Bear Gulch Visitor Center,** reached via Highway 25, then Highway 146 heading west. From Hollister, it's about 34 miles south, then about five miles

west to the park entrance. Pinnacles is open for day use only; the vehicle entry fee is $5, the walk-in fee is $2; valid for seven days. An annual pass costs $15. Within the monument, bicycles and cars may only be used on paved roads. For additional information, contact Pinnacles National Monument, 5000 Hwy. 146, Paicines, CA 95043, 831/389-4485, website: www.nps.gov/pinn.

Good rules of thumb in the Pinnacles: Carry water at all times and watch out for poison oak, stinging nettles, and rattlesnakes. Spelunkers should bring good flashlights and helmets. Pick up guides to the area's plantlife and natural history at the visitors centers, and also topo maps. Rock climbers can thumb through old guides there for climbing routes.

No camping is offered (or allowed) within the park. The closest private camping is **Pinnacles Campground, Inc.,** near the park's entrance on the east side, 2400 Hwy. 146, 831/389-4462, website: www.pinncamp.com. The campground is quite nice, featuring flush toilets, hot showers, fire rings, picnic tables, a swimming pool, some RV hookups, and group facilities. Under $50. Basic supplies and some food are available at the campground's store.

entrance to Pinnacles National Monument

MELISSA SHEROWSKI

Northeast from Salinas

Travelers heading from Monterey north on Highway 1 will pass through the towns of Castroville, Moss Landing, and Watsonville en route to Santa Cruz. Northeast from Watsonville via Highway 152 is Gilroy, famous for its annual Gilroy Garlic Festival. Southeast of Watsonville is historic San Juan Bautista, the mission and the town.

SAN JUAN BAUTISTA AND VICINITY

The tiny town of San Juan Bautista is charming and charmed, as friendly as it is sunny. (People here say the weather in this pastoral valley is "salubrious." Take their word for it.) Named for John the Baptist, the 1797 Spanish mission of San Juan Bautista is central to this serene community at the foot of the Gabilan Mountains. But the historic plaza, still bordered by old adobes and now a state historic park, is the true center of San Juan—rallying point for two revolutions, onetime home of famed bandit Tiburcio Vasquez, and the theatrical setting for David Belasco's *Rose of the Rancho.* Movie fans may remember Jimmy Stewart and Kim Novak in the mission scenes from Alfred Hitchcock's *Vertigo,* which were filmed here.

One of the most colorful characters ever to stumble off the stage in San Juan Bautista was one-eyed stagecoach driver Charley Parkhurst, a truculent, swaggering, tobacco-chewing tough. "He," however, was a woman, born Charlotte Parkhurst in New Hampshire. (Charley voted in Santa Cruz in 1866, more than 50 years before American women won the right to vote.)

In addition to history, San Juan Bautista has galleries, antiques and craft shops, and an incredible local theater troupe. To get oriented, pick up a walking tour brochure at the **San Juan Bautista Chamber of Commerce,** 1 Polk St., P.O. Box 1037, San Juan Bautista, CA 95045, 831/623-2454, website: www.sanjuanbautista.com. In June experience mid-1800s mission days at **Early Days in San Juan Bautista,** a traditional celebration complete with horse-drawn carriages, period dress,

music, and fandango. The barroom at the Plaza Hotel is even open for card games. Also fun in June is the **Peddler's Faire and Street Rod Classic Car Show.** The **Flea Market** here in August, with more than 200 vendors, is one of the country's best. Later in the month, **San Juan Fiesta Day** is the most popular venue of the wandering **Cabrillo Music Festival.** But the event of the year is *La Virgen del Tepeyac* or *La Pastorela* (they alternate yearly), traditional Christmas musicals that attract visitors from around the world. (For details, see El Teatro Campesino, below.) Christmas chorale music is also offered at the mission.

Historic San Juan Bautista

Partly destroyed by earthquakes in 1800 and 1906 (the San Andreas Fault is just 40 feet away), **Mission San Juan Bautista** has been restored many times. The 15th and largest of the Franciscan settlements in California, the mission here is not as architecturally spectacular as others in the Catholic chain. Visitors can tour sections of the mission—which still features an active parish church—though it's not really part of the adjacent state historic park. After visiting the small museum and gardens, note the old dirt road beyond the wall of the mission cemetery. This is an unspoiled, unchanged section of the 650-mile El Camino Real, the "royal road" that once connected all the California missions. Archaeological excavations at the mission by CSU Monterey, Hartnell College, and Cabrillo College students unearthed the foundations of the mission's original quadrangle, tower, well, and convent wing (which many historians previously believed had never existed). Students also cleared the 1799 Indian Chapel of debris and restored it; inside is an ornate altar built in the 1560s and moved to the chapel for the Pope's visit in 1987. Many of the students' other discoveries are on display in the mission's museum.

San Juan Bautista's oldest building is the **Plaza Hotel** at Second and Mariposa Streets on the west side of the plaza, originally barracks built in

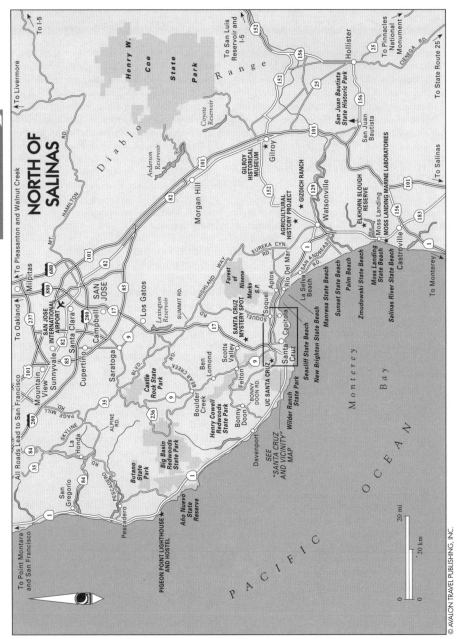

1813 for Spanish soldiers. In horse and buggy days, San Juan Bautista was a major stage stop between San Francisco and Los Angeles, and the hotel was famous statewide. (Note the two-story outhouse out back.) Also fascinating are the stable—with its herd of fine old horse-drawn vehicles and the "Instructions for Stagecoach Passengers" plaque out front—and the restored blacksmith shop. Also worth a peek: the jail, washhouse, and cabin.

Above the town of San Juan Bautista is **Pagan Hill.** Today a giant concrete cross stands where mission fathers once put up a wooden one, intended to ward off evil spirits supposedly summoned by Indian neophytes secretly practicing their traditional earth religion. The park is open daily 9:30 A.M. to 4 P.M., in summer until 5 P.M. For information, contact San Juan Bautista State Historic Park, 19 Franklin St., P.O. Box 116, San Juan Bautista, CA 95045, 831/623-4881.

El Teatro Campesino

Don't pass through San Juan Bautista without trying to attend a performance by San Juan Bautista's El Teatro Campesino. Chicano playwright Luis Valdez founded this small theater group as guerrilla theater on the United Farm Workers' picket lines more than two decades ago. But Valdez's smash hits *Zoot Suit* and *Corridos* have since brought highly acclaimed nationwide tours and the birth of other Chicano *teatros* throughout the American Southwest. El Teatro's Christmas-season *La Pastorella,* the shepherd's story that alternates with the miracle play *La Virgen del Tepeyac,* is a hilarious and deeply poetic spectacle, a musical folk pageant about shepherds trying to get past comic yet terrifying devils to reach the Christ child. Besides Spanish-language plays, concerts, and film festivals, the company also presents contemporary and traditional theater in English. El Teatro Campesino's permanent playhouse is at 705 Fourth St., 831/623-2444. For a current calendar of events, call or see the website, www.elteatrocampesino.com.

Practical San Juan Bautista

A few tent sites and 165 RV hookups are available at the private **Mission Farm Campground and RV Park,** in a walnut orchard at 400 San Juan-Hollister Rd., 831/623-4456. Under $50. Motel accommodations are available at the **San Juan Inn,** Hwy. 156 and Alameda, 831/623-4380, rates $50 to 100, and the **Posada de San Juan Hotel,** 310 Fourth St., 831/623-4030, with fireplace and whirlpool tubs in every room. Rates $100 to 150.

For farm-fresh produce, pick up a copy of the free guide to nearby family farms and ranches. (Fresh cherries are available in June; apricots in July; and apples, walnuts, and kiwis in the fall.)

The **Mission Cafe,** 300 Third St., 831/623-2635, is good for families at breakfast and lunch. Try **Felipe's,** 313 Third St., 831/623-2161, for Mexican and Salvadoran food.

La Casa Rosa, 107 Third St., 831/623-4563, is famous for its butter lettuce salads with fresh herb dressing, fresh rolls, and hearty Peruvian-style casseroles (a Californio favorite). **Doña Esther,** 25 Franklin, 831/623-2518, serves Mexican fare—and the best margaritas in town. More upscale is **Jardines de San Juan,** 115 Third St., 831/623-4466, where you can get *pollos borachos* (drunken chickens) at lunch and dinner daily. Despite the ominously accurate name, well worth a stop for continental-style lunch and dinner (and the view of the San Juan Valley) is the **Fault Line Restaurant** nearby at 11 Franklin, 831/623-2117.

Fremont Peak State Park

In March 1846, Gen. John C. Frémont and Kit Carson built a "fort" here in defiance of the Mexican government, unfurled their flags on Gabilan Peak (now Fremont Peak), and waited for the supposedly imminent attack of Californio troops. When no battle came, they broke camp and took off for Oregon. Fremont Peak State Park, a long, narrow, isolated strip in the Gabilan Mountains northeast of Salinas, has rolling hills with oaks, madrones, Coulter pines, and spring wildflowers that attract hundreds of hummingbirds. The park offers good hiking in spring and good views from the top of Fremont Peak. Another attraction at Fremont Peak is an observatory with a 30-inch Challenger reflecting telescope, open to the public at least twice monthly for free programs including lectures and observation; call 831/623-2465 for details (recorded) or see www.fpoa.net.

Camping is available in about 25 primitive campsites (some in the picnic area) and a group camp. To get to the park from Highway 156, head 11 miles south on San Juan Canyon Road (County Road G1)—paved but very steep and winding (trailers definitely not recommended). For information, contact Fremont Peak State Park, P.O. Box 1110, San Juan Bautista, CA 95045, 831/623-4255.

Hollister

If Gilroy is the garlic capital of the world, then Hollister is the earthquake capital. Because of the region's heavy faulting, some say this San Benito County town moves every day, however imperceptibly. (A small 1985 quake shook loose a 20,000-gallon oak wine cask and flooded the Almaden Winery just south of town.) Agricultural Hollister is as historic as San Juan Bautista, but the "feel" here is straight out of the Old West. Stop by the **San Benito County Historical Society Museum,** 498 Fifth St. (at West), 831/635-0335 (open Saturday and Sunday 1 to 3 P.M.; other times by appointment), then wander

through Old Town (particularly along Fifth) to appreciate Hollister's old Victorians.

Traditional cowboy events and some unique competitions are the name of the game during June's **San Benito County Rodeo,** an event dedicated to the vaquero. The **Fiesta-Rodeo** in July dates back to 1907, when it was first held to raise funds for rebuilding Mission San Juan Bautista after the big quake in 1906. Up-and-coming on the events scene here is a big motorcyclists gathering (à la Sturgis, South Dakota) on the **Fourth of July** weekend.

GILROY AND VICINITY
Gilroy and Garlic

Will Rogers supposedly described Gilroy as "the only town in America where you can marinate a steak just by hanging it out on the clothesline." But Gilroy, the "undisputed garlic capital of the world," dedicates very few acres to growing the stinking rose these days. The legendary local garlic farms have been declining due to soil disease since 1979—ironically, the first year of the now-famous and phenomenally successful Gilroy Garlic Festival. Gilroy now

Gilroy celebrates its garlic-ness.

SALINAS AND VICINITY

MELISSA SHEROWSKI

Fortino Winery vineyard

grows housing subdivisions—former *San Francisco Chronicle* columnist Herb Caen defined modern Gilroy as the place "where the carpet ends and the linoleum begins"—and the San Joaquin Valley grows most of California's garlic. Nonetheless, that unmistakable oily aroma still permeates the air in summer, since more than 90 percent of the world's garlic is processed or packaged here.

Other attractions in Gilroy include the **Indian Motorcycle** production facility (call 408/847-2221 to arrange factory tours) and Goldsmith Seeds' seasonal six-acre **Field of Dreams** experimental flower seed garden. Call 408/847-7333 for tour information. Downtown Gilroy has its historic attractions, too. The best place to start exploring is the **Gilroy Historical Museum** at Fifth and Church, 408/848-0470, open weekdays 9 A.M. to 5 P.M.

For more information about what's cookin' in and around Gilroy, contact the **Gilroy Visitor Bureau,** 7780 Monterey St., Gilroy, CA 95020, 408/842-6436, website: www.gilroyvisitor .org, and the **Gilroy Chamber of Commerce,** 7471 Monterey, 408/842-6437, website: www .gilroy.org.

The Gilroy Garlic Festival

It's chic to reek in Gilroy. On the last full weekend in July, 150,000 or more garlic lovers descend on the town for several dusty days of sampling garlic perfume, garlic chocolate, and all-you-can-eat garlic ice cream (for some reason, just a few gallons of the stuff takes care of the entire crowd). Who wouldn't pay the $10 admission for belly dancing, big bands, and the crowning of the Garlic Queen? For more information, contact the **Gilroy Garlic Festival Association,** 7473 Monterey, 408/842-1625, website: www.gilroy garlicfestival.com. If you're looking for garlic gifts and accessories at other times, Gilroy boasts a number of garlic-themed shops; get a current listing from the city's website, www.gilroy.org.

Gilroy Wineries

Besides sniffing out local Italian scallions, tour the Gilroy "wine country." Most of the area's wineries are tucked into the Santa Cruz Mountain foothills west of the city, seven of these along Highway 152's Hecker Pass. The hearty, full-flavored red wines produced here are still made by hand. **Solis Winery,** 3920 Hecker Pass Rd., 408/847-6306, offers tastings of its chardonnay and merlot Wednesday through Sunday 11 A.M. to 5 P.M. (tours by appointment). Come by **Sarah's Vineyard** Saturday noon to 4 P.M. (otherwise by appointment only), 4005 Hecker Pass Rd., 408/842-4278, to meet delightful proprietor Marilyn Otteman, who refers to her fine white wines as "ladies," or visit the nearby **Thomas Kruse Winery,** 4390 Hecker Pass Rd., 408/842-7016, with its eclectic collection of antique equipment, presided over by philosopher-winemaker Thomas Kruse. His Gilroy Red and other wines sport handwritten, offbeat labels. Open for tasting and tours most days noon to 5 P.M. The **Fortino Winery,** 4525 Hecker Pass Rd., 408/842-3305, and **Hecker Pass Winery,** 4605 Hecker Pass Rd., 408/842-8755, are both run by the Fortino family and specialize in hearty old-country red wines.

For more information about these and other regional wineries, contact the **Santa Clara Valley Wine Growers Association,** P.O. Box 1192, Morgan Hill, CA 95037, 408/778-1555 or 408/779-2145, website: www.scvwga.com.

Bonfante Gardens

The region's most amazing new visitor attraction, Gilroy's glorious, $100 million Bonfante Gardens Theme Park, reopened in May 2002 after a brief hiatus.

The appeal of 75-acre Bonfante Gardens is rooted in its inspired horticultural ambience. That's right—*horticultural.* Trees and shrubs, in particular. Some 23 years were spent planning and developing the park's unique landscape before Bonfante Gardens finally opened its gates in June 2001. Botanical oddities abound, from the five themed gardens to the 25 wonderful "circus trees" created by the late Axel Erlandson—wonders created by grafting and pleaching, feats that have never been successfully duplicated. Kids are equally impressed by the Monarch Garden's immense greenhouse with a monorail, train, and river running through it.

Though the pace here is relaxed and the thrills understated, traditional theme park attractions haven't been neglected. Bonfante Gardens includes 40 family-friendly rides and attractions, from the cheerful 1927 Illions Supreme Carousel

and the Quicksilver Express roller coaster to the very cool antique car ride. The latter allows you to "tour" either the 1920s or 1950s—dig those old gas stations—depending on where you climb on. Still, encouraging people to appreciate trees is the main point of Bonfante Gardens. All attractions are literally woven into the landscape.

The not-for-profit Bonfante Gardens closed in late September 2001—just days after the World Trade Center and Pentagon disasters—in order to "conserve capital, concentrate on future funding requirements, and complete additional attractions rather than deplete resources by keeping the park open during times of economic uncertainty," according to founder Michael Bonfante. During its first three months of operation the park attracted 28,000 visitors; hopes are high that the park will again flourish, now that it has reopened.

At last report, park admission was $29.95 adults, $26.95 seniors, and $19.95 children ages 3–12 (age 2 and under free); parking, $7 per vehicle. For current details, contact: Bonfante Gardens, 3050 Hecker Pass Hwy. (Hwy. 152 West), Gilroy, CA 95020, 408/840-7100, website: www.bonfantegardens.com.

Casa de Fruta and Coyote Reservoir

Unforgettable is one word for Casa de Fruta on Pacheco Pass Highway, 831/637-0051, website: www.casadefruta.com. The sprawl of neon-lit, truck stop–type buildings is complete with trailer park and swimming pool, motel, petting zoo, merry-go-round, and miniature train and tunnel. Stop off at the Casa de Fruta Coffee Shop (open 24 hours) and read about the Casa de Fruta Country Store, Casa de Fruta Gift Shop, Casa de Fruta Fruit Stand, Casa de Burger, Casa de Sweets Bakery and Candy Factory, Casa de Choo-Choo, and Casa de Merry-Go-Round on the "mail me" souvenir paper placemats. (To see the coffee cups "flip," ask the coffee shop staff for a show.)

Coyote Reservoir, eight miles north of Gilroy, is great for sailboarding, sailing, and fishing. Open year-round 8 A.M. to sunset for day use; 75 campsites. For information, contact **Coyote Lake Park,** 10840 Coyote Lake Rd., Gilroy, CA 95020, 408/842-7800. To get to Coyote Lake, take the Leavesley Road/Highway 152 exit east from Highway 101; after two to three miles, head north on New Avenue then east on Roop Road to Gilroy Hot Springs Road. The Coyote Reservoir Road turnoff is about a mile farther, the campground two miles more.

North to Santa Cruz

MOSS LANDING AND VICINITY

Near the mouth of Elkhorn Slough on the coast, Moss Landing is a crazy quilt of weird shops and roadside knickknack stands, watched over by both a towering steam power plant (formerly under PG&E [Pacific Gas & Electric] control and now owned and recently expanded by Duke Energy), built circa 1948, the second largest in the world, and a Kaiser firebrick-making plant. All of which makes for an odd-looking community.

First a Salinas Valley produce port, then a whaling harbor until 1930, Moss Landing is now surrounded by artichoke and broccoli fields. The busy fishing harbor and adjoining slough are home to hundreds of bird and plant species, making this an important center for marinelife studies.

These days the area is also noted for its indoor recreational opportunities, with more than two-dozen antique and junk shops along Moss Landing Road. Show up on the last Sunday in July for the annual **Antique Street Fair,** which draws more than 350 antiques dealers and at least 12,000 civilian antiquers. October brings the **Monterey Bay Bird Festival.**

For more information about the area, contact the **Moss Landing Chamber of Commerce,** P.O. Box 41, Moss Landing, CA 95039, 831/633-4501, website: www.monterey-bay.net/ml.

Moss Landing Marine Laboratories

The laboratories here, at 895 Blanco Circle, 831/755-8650, are jointly operated by nine campuses of the California State Universities and Colleges system. Students and faculty study local marinelife, birds, and tidepools, but particularly Monterey Bay's spectacular underwater submarine canyons, which start where Elkhorn Slough enters the bay at Moss Landing. Stop for a visit

Moss Landing State Beach

MELISSA SHEROWSKI

Moss Landing: marina and refinery

and quick look around, but don't disturb classes or research projects. Better yet, come in spring—usually the first Sunday after Easter—for the big open house, when you can take a complete tour; explore the "touch tank" full of starfish, sea cucumbers, sponges, snails, and anemones; and see slide shows, movies, and marinelife dioramas.

Elkhorn Slough Reserve

Most people come here to hike and bird-watch, but the fishlife in this coastal estuary, the second largest in California, is also phenomenal. No wonder the Ohlone people built villages here some 5,000 years ago. Wetlands like these, oozing with life and nourished by rich bay sediments, are among those natural environments most threatened by "progress." Thanks to the Nature Conservancy, the Elkhorn Slough (originally the mouth of the Salinas River until a 1908 diversion) is now protected as a federal and state estuarine sanctuary and recognized as a National Estuarine Research Reserve—California's first. Elkhorn Slough is managed by the California Department of Fish and Game.

These meandering channels along a seven-mile river are thick with marshy grasses and wildflowers beneath a plateau of oaks and eucalyptus.

In winter an incredible variety of shorebirds (not counting migrating waterfowl) call this area home. Endangered and threatened birds, including the brown pelican, the California clapper rail, and the California least tern, thrive here. The tule elk once hunted by the Ohlone are long gone, but harbor seals bask on the mudflats, and bobcats, gray foxes, muskrats, otters, and black-tailed deer are still here. Come in fall for the annual **Monterey Bay Bird Festival.**

Though this is a private nature sanctuary, not a park, the public can visit. Some 4.5 miles of trails pass by tidal mudflats, salt marshes, and an old abandoned dairy. The reserve and visitors center, which offers a bird-watchers map/guide to the Pajaro Valley, are open Wednesday through Sunday 9 A.M. to 5 P.M. There's a small day-use fee to use the trails. Docent-led walks are offered year-round on Saturday and Sunday at 10 A.M. and 1 P.M. On the first Saturday of the month, there's also an Early Bird Walk at 8:30 A.M. Still, there's no better way to see the slough than from the seat of a kayak. Stop by the visitors center at the entrance to arrange a guided tour or contact the **Elkhorn Slough Foundation,** 1700 Elkhorn Rd., P.O. Box 267, Moss Landing, CA 95039, 831/728-2822 or

831/728-5939, website: www.elkhornslough.org. Arrange kayak tours through **Monterey Bay Kayaks,** 693 Del Monte Ave., Monterey, 831/373-5357 or 831/633-2211, or **Kayak Connections,** 831/724-5692. For a guided tour aboard a 27-foot pontoon boat, contact **Elkhorn Slough Safari** in Moss Landing, 831/633-5555, website: www.elkhornslough.com.

Practical Moss Landing

Time-honored people's eateries abound, particularly near the harbor. Most serve chowders and seafood and/or ethnic specials. Quite good, right on the highway, is **The Whole Enchilada,** 831/633-3038, open for lunch and dinner daily and specializing in Mexican seafood entrées. (The "whole enchilada," by the way, is filet of red snapper wrapped in a corn tortilla and smothered in enchilada sauce and melted cheese.) The Enchilada's associated **Moss Landing Inn and Jazz Club,** 831/633-9990, is a bar featuring live jazz on Sunday 4:30 to 8:30 P.M. A best bet for fish is **Phil's Fresh Fish Market and Eatery** on Sandholdt Road, 831/633-2152. (To get there from Moss Landing Road, take the first and only right-hand turn and cross the one-lane bridge; it's the

wooden warehouse just past the research institute.) Stop for fresh fruit smoothies and generous deli sandwiches at the associated **Phil's Snack Shack,** 7921 Moss Landing Rd.

"En route camping" for self-contained RVs is available at **Moss Landing State Beach.**

Castroville: Artichokes and Marilyn

The heart of Castroville is Swiss-Italian, which hardly explains the artichokes all over the place. Calling itself "Artichoke Capital of the World," Castroville grows 75 percent of California's artichokes, though that delicious leathery thistle grows throughout Santa Cruz and Monterey Counties. Come for the annual **Artichoke Festival** every May; contact 831/633-6545 or website: www.artichoke-festival.org for information. It's some party, too, replete with artichokes fried, baked, mashed, boiled, and added as colorful ingredients to cookies and cakes. Nibble on french-fried artichokes with mayo dip and artichoke nut cake, sip artichoke soup, and sample steamed artichokes. Sometimes Hollywood gets in on the action: In 1947 Marilyn Monroe reigned as California's Artichoke Queen. If you miss the festival there are other artichoke options, including

MELISSA SHEROWSKI

Get your deep-fried artichokes here.

Giant Artichoke Fruits and Vegetables at 11261 Merritt St., 831/633-3501, and the **Thistle Hut,** just off Highway 1 at Cooper-Molera Road, 831/633-4888. The **Franco Restaurant,** 10639 Merritt, 831/633-2090, sponsors a Marilyn Monroe look-alike contest in June. But come by otherwise just to grab a burger—some say the best in the county—and to ogle the Marilyn memorabilia. The Italian **Ristorante La Scuola** is housed in Castroville's first schoolhouse, 10700 Merritt, 831/633-3200.

WATSONVILLE AND VICINITY

Watsonville, an agriculturally rich city of over 25,000, is the mushroom capital of the United States, though the town calls this lovely section of the Pajaro Valley the Strawberry Capital of the World and Apple City of the Ives. Farming got off to a brisk clod-busting start during the gold rush, when produce grown here was in great demand. Among the early settlers were Chinese, Germans, Yugoslavs, and immigrants from the Sandwich Islands and the Azores. None gained as much notoriety as Watsonville stage driver Charley Parkhurst, one of the roughest, toughest, most daring muleskinners in the state—a "man" later unveiled as a woman, the first to ever vote in California.

Watsonville made history still earlier. Nothing remains today to commemorate the site of the 1920s "Mother House" of California's Vallejo clan, yet the **House of Glass** once stood about 2.5 miles southeast of Watsonville near Highway 1. General Mariano Guadalupe Vallejo was one of five sons and eight daughters born to his parents there, in a house with 20-inch-thick walls and hand-hewn redwood window frames and joists. It was called the House of Glass for its completely glassed-in second story veranda. Legend has it the veranda got its unique fishbowl design when Don Ignacio Vincente Ferrer Vallejo mistakenly received a shipment of 12 dozen windows instead of one dozen. It was from the Vallejo ranch that Jose Castro, Juan Bautista Alvarado, and their rebel troops launched their 1835 attack on Monterey to create the free state of Alta California. The victorious single shot

(fired by a lawyer who consulted a book to figure out how to work the cannon) hit the governor's house, and he surrendered immediately.

Seeing and Doing Watsonville

For the local **Country Crossroads** farm trails map and other visitor information, contact the **Pajaro Valley Chamber of Commerce,** 444 Main St., P.O. Box 470, Watsonville, CA 95077, 831/724-3900, website: www.pvchamber.com. Or stop by Country Crossroads headquarters at the farm bureau office, 141 Monte Vista Ave., 831/724-1356. Get up to speed on local agricultural history at the **Agricultural History Project** at the Santa Cruz County Fairgrounds, 831/724-5898. Museum exhibits and demonstrations are open to the public on Friday and Saturday noon to 4 P.M. An almost mandatory stop, from May through January, is **Gizdich Ranch,** 55 Peckham Rd., 831/722-1056, website: www.gizdichranch.com, fabulous from late summer through fall for its fresh apples, homemade apple pies, and fresh-squeezed natural apple juices. Earlier in the season, this is a "Pik-Yor-Sef" berry farm, with raspberries, olallieberries, and strawberries (usually also available in pies, fritters, and pastries). Another best bet is **Emile Agaccio Farms,** 4 Casserly Rd., 831/728-2009, known for its you-pick raspberries and chesterberries (a blackberry variety). Also worth seeking in Watsonville are Mexican and Filipino eateries, many quite good, most inexpensive. Watsonville has its share of motels, too, in addition to camping at Pinto Lake (see below) and at the Santa Cruz KOA.

Watsonville Area Beaches

At **Manresa State Beach,** 1445 San Andreas Rd., 831/724-3750, stairways lead to the surf from the main parking lot and Sand Dollar Drive; restrooms, an outdoor shower, and walk-in tent camping are available. Rural San Andreas Road also takes you to **Sunset State Beach,** 201 Sunset Beach Rd., 831/763-7062 or 831/763-7063, four miles west of Watsonville in the Pajaro Dunes (take bus 54B from Santa Cruz). Sunset offers 3.5 miles of nice sandy beaches, plus 90 campsites (tents and RVs) and 60 picnic sites, but also way too many RVs and not much privacy. Even so, after sunset the beach is open only to campers. Day use at both is $3, camping $12. To reserve campsites at all state beaches and parks, call ReserveAmerica, 800/444-7275, or try www.reserveamerica.com.

Parking for pretty **Palm Beach** near Pajaro Dunes—a great place to find sand dollars—is near the end of Beach Street. Also here are picnic facilities, a par course, and restrooms. **Zmudowski State Beach** is near where the Pajaro River reaches the sea. You'll find good hiking and surf fishing. The beach is rarely crowded. Next, near Moss Landing, are **Salinas River State Beach** on Potrero Road, 831/384-7695, and **Jetty State Beach.**

Other Area Attractions

Just a few miles northwest of Watsonville is tiny **Pinto Lake City Park,** 451 Green Valley Rd., 831/722-8129, website: www.pintolake.com, where you can go swimming, sailing, pedalboating, sailboarding, fishing, or RV camping (28 sites with full hookups, $24; no tent camping) or enjoy a 180-acre urban nature refuge and picnic area.

The **Ellicott Slough National Wildlife Refuge,** a 180-acre ecological reserve of coastal uplands for the Santa Cruz long-toed salamander, is four miles west along San Andreas Road. To get there, turn west off Highway 1 at the Larkin Valley Road exit and continue west on San Andreas Road to the refuge, next to the Santa Cruz KOA. For information about the reserve, call 510/792-0222.

Eventful Watsonville

The area also offers unusual diversions. The biggest event here is the annual **West Coast Antique Fly-In** in May (Memorial Day weekend), when more than 50,000 people show up to appreciate hundreds of classic, antique, and home-built airplanes on the ground and in the air. Originally held over Memorial Day weekend but now usually scheduled for early August is the annual **Monterey Bay Strawberry Festival.** Come in mid-September for the **Santa Cruz County Fair.**

Santa Cruz:
Sunshine and Silicon

Still in tune with its gracefully aging Boardwalk, Santa Cruz is a middle-class tourist town enlightened and enlivened by retirees and the local University of California campus. It's possible to live here without a lot of money, though it's getting harder, with the advent of Silicon Valley commuters. Still, Santa Cruz is quite a different world from the affluent and staid Monterey Peninsula.

The Santa Cruz attitude has little to do with its name, taken from a nearby stream called Arroyo de Santa Cruz ("Holy Cross Creek") by Portolá. No, the town's relaxed good cheer must be karmic compensation for the morose mission days and the brutishness of nearby Branciforte. The Gay Nineties were happier here than anywhere else in Northern California, with trainloads of Bay Area vacationers in their finest summer whites stepping out to enjoy the Santa Cruz waterfront, the Sea Beach Hotel, and the landmark Boardwalk and amusement park. The young and young at heart headed straight for the amusement park, with its fine merry-go-round, classic wooden roller coaster, pleasure pier, natatorium (indoor pool), and dancehall casino. More decadent fun lovers visited the ships anchored offshore to gamble or engage the services of prostitutes.

Santa Cruz still welcomes millions of visitors each year, yet it somehow manages to retain its dignity—except when embroiled in hot local political debates or when inundated by college students during the annual rites of spring. A

the Santa Cruz Beach Boardwalk

GREATER SANTA CRUZ

Just east of Santa Cruz, along the south-facing coast here, are the towns of Soquel, Capitola, and Aptos—the Santa Cruz 'burbs. High-rent **Soquel,** once a booming lumber town and the place where Portolá and his men were all but stricken by their first sight of coastal redwoods, is now noted for antiques and oaks.

The wharf in **Capitola** has stood since 1857, when the area was known as Soquel Landing. The name "Camp Capitola" was an expression of Soquel locals' desire to be the state capital—the closest they ever came. The city was, however, the state's first seaside resort. Nowadays, Capitola is big on art galleries and fine craft shops—take a stroll along Capitola Avenue from the trestle to the creek—but it's still most famous for its begonias. The year's big event is the **Begonia Festival,** usually held early in September. Stop by **Antonelli Bros. Begonia Gardens,** 2545 Capitola Rd., tel. 831/475-5222, to see a 10,000-square-foot greenhouse display of begonias, best in August and September.

Aptos, on the other side of the freeway, is more or less the same community as Capitola but home to Cabrillo College and the **World's Shortest Parade,** usually held on the July 4th weekend and sponsored by the Aptos Ladies' Tuesday Evening Society.

Heading north on Hwy. 9 from Santa Cruz will take you through the Santa Cruz Mountains and the towns of Felton, Ben Lomond, and Boulder Creek before winding down the other side of the mountains into Saratoga on the flank of Silicon Valley. This route is the gateway to several beautiful redwood state parks, including Henry Cowell, Fall Creek, Big Basin, and Castle Rock.

tourist town it may be, but some of the best things to do here are free: watching the sun set from East or West Cliff Drive, beachcombing, bike riding (excellent local bike lanes), swimming, surfing, and sunbathing.

The "People's Republic of Santa Cruz"

Old-timers weren't ready for the changes in community consciousness that arrived in Santa Cruz along with the idyllic UC Santa Cruz campus in the 1960s. More outsiders came when back-to-the-landers fled San Francisco's Haight Ashbury for the hills near here, and when Silicon Valley electronics wizards started moving in. The city's boardwalk-and-beach hedonism may be legendary, but so are the Santa Cruz City Council's foreign policy decisions opposing contra aid, proclaiming the city a "free port" for Nicaragua, and calling for divestiture of South African investments. In October 2000 Santa Cruz passed its own "living wage" law, mandating a minimum pay rate of $11 per hour ($12 without benefits) for city workers and companies that contract with the city.

Though there's always some argument, the city's progressive politics are now firmly entrenched, as are other "dancing-on-the-brink" attitudes. The

"People's Republic of Santa Cruz" is also a way station for the spiritually weary, with its own unique evangelical crusade for higher consciousness. Dreams and dreamers run the show.

The Santa Cruz Story

The charming Santa Cruz blend of innocence and sleaze has roots in local history. The area's earliest residents were the Ohlone people, who avoided the sacred redwood forests and subsisted on seafood, small game, acorns, and foods gathered in woodland areas. Then came the mission and missionaries, a Spanish military garrison, and the den-of-thieves culture of Branciforte; the latter community posed an active threat to the holy fathers' attempted good works among the heathens. Misión Exaltación de la Santa Cruz declined, was abandoned, then collapsed following an earthquake in 1857.

A small trading town, borrowing the mission's name, grew up around the old mission plaza in the 1840s. The town supplied whalers with fruits and vegetables. Nearby Branciforte became a smugglers' haven, hosting bullfight festivals and illicit activities until 1867. The "education" and excitement imported by foreigners proved to be too much for the Ohlone; the only traces of their culture today are burial grounds. Branciforte disappeared, too, absorbed as a suburb when loggers and "bark strippers" (those who extracted tannin from tan oaks for processing leather) arrived to harvest the forests during the gold rush.

By the late 1800s, Santa Cruz was well established as a resort town. Logging continued, however. In the early 20th century, the local lumber industry was ready to log even majestic Big Basin. But those plans were thwarted by the active intervention of the Sempervirens Club, which successfully established California's first state park.

Seeing and Doing Santa Cruz

THE BOARDWALK

Santa Cruz Beach Boardwalk

The Boardwalk may be old, but it's certainly lively, with a million visitors per year. This is the West Coast's answer to Atlantic City. The original wood planking is now paved over with asphalt, stretching from 400 Beach Street for a half mile along one of Northern California's finest swimming beaches. A relatively recent multi-million-dollar facelift didn't diminish the Boardwalk's charms one iota. Open daily from Memorial Day to Labor Day and on weekends the rest of the year, the Boardwalk is an authentic amusement park, with 27 carnival rides, odd shops and eateries, good-time arcades, even a big-band ballroom. Ride the **Sky Glider** to get a good aerial view of the Boardwalk and beach scene.

None other than *The New York Times* has declared the 1924 **Giant Dipper** roller coaster here one of the nation's 10 best. A gleaming white wooden rocker 'n' roller, the Dipper is quite a

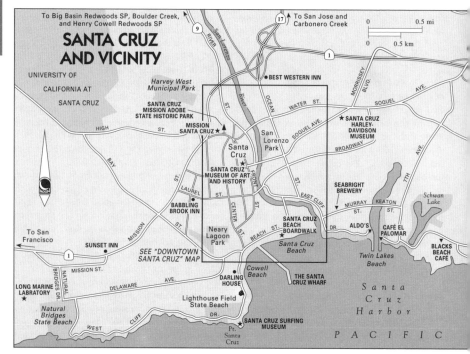

sight anytime, but it's truly impressive when lit up at night. The 1911 **Charles Looff carousel,** one of a handful of Looff creations still operating in the United States, has 70 handcrafted horses, two chariots, and a circa-1894 Ruth Band pipe organ—all now lovingly restored to their original glory. (Both the Dipper and the carousel are national historic landmarks.)

New rides feature more terror, of course. The bright lights and unusual views offered by the Italian-made **Typhoon** are just part of the joys of being suspended upside down in midair. The **Hurricane** is the Boardwalk's modern high-tech roller coaster, providing a two-minute thrill ride with a maximum gravitational force of 4.7 Gs and a banking angle of 80 degrees. There's only one other coaster of its kind in the United States. Also state of the art in adrenaline inducement at the Boardwalk is the **Wave Jammer**—not to mention **Chaos, Crazy Surf, Tsunami,** and **Whirl Wind.**

The antique devices in the penny arcades at the Boardwalk's west end cost a bit more these days, but it's worth it to Measure the Thrill of Your Kisses or Find Your Ideal Mate. Playing miniature golf at the new, two-story, $5.2 million **Neptune's Kingdom** amusement center—housed in the Boardwalk's original "plunge" building, or natatorium—is a nautical-themed adventure in special effects, with an erupting volcano, firing cannons, and talking pirates. It's the perfect diversion for the video-game generation and their awestruck parents. Though the rest of the Boardwalk's attractions are seasonal, Neptune's Kingdom and the arcade are open daily year-round. Nearby is the esteemed **Cocoanut Grove** casino and ballroom, a dignified old dancehall that still swings with nostalgic tunes from the 1930s and '40s at special shindigs. Sunday brunch in the Grove's Sun Room, with its Victorian-modern decor and galleria-style retracting glass roof, is a big event.

To fully appreciate the Boardwalk then and now, pick up the *Walking Tour of the Historical Santa Cruz Boardwalk* brochure, as well as a current attractions listing/map. Both will help you locate yourself, then and now. Annual events held at the Boardwalk include the **Clam Chowder Cook-Off and Festival** in late February; the **Central Coast Home & Garden Expo** in early April; the **Santa Cruz Band Review** in October, a fundraiser for local high school bands; and the **Santa Cruz Christmas Craft and Gift Festival** held at the Cocoanut Grove during Thanksgiving weekend. On Friday nights in summer, starting in June, come for free **Summertime, Summer Nights** concerts.

Admission to the Boardwalk is free, though enjoying its amusements is not. If you'll be staying all day, the best deal is usually the all-day ride ticket, $22.95 at last report, or Unlimited Rides Plus," $27.95, which offers unlimited rides plus two other attractions. During **1907 Nights,** on certain Monday and Tuesday evenings in summer, ride prices revert to 1907 equivalents—$.50 per ride. Season passes are available. Height, age, and chaperone requirements are enforced. For current complete information, contact the **Santa Cruz Seaside**

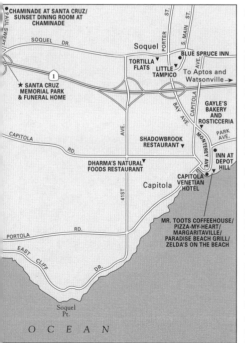

SANTA CRUZ

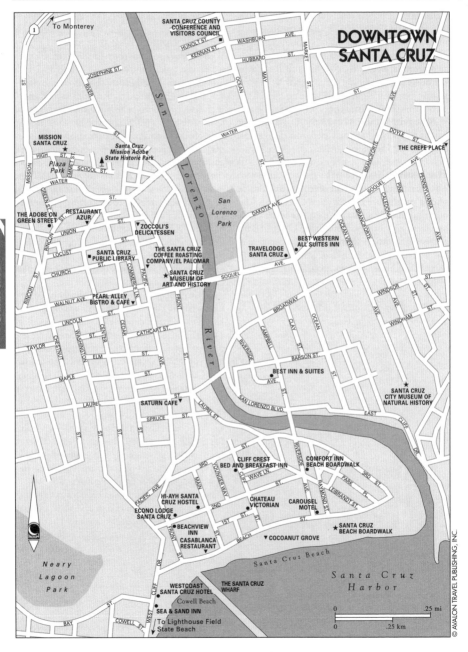

SANTA CRUZ

DOWNTOWN SANTA CRUZ

To Monterey

SANTA CRUZ COUNTY CONFERENCE AND VISITORS COUNCIL

THE CREPE PLACE

MISSION SANTA CRUZ

Santa Cruz Mission Adobe State Historic Park

Plaza Park

San Lorenzo Park

THE ADOBE ON GREEN STREET

RESTAURANT AZUR

ZOCCOLI'S DELICATESSEN

SANTA CRUZ PUBLIC LIBRARY

THE SANTA CRUZ COFFEE ROASTING COMPANY/EL PALOMAR

BEST WESTERN ALL SUITES INN

TRAVELODGE SANTA CRUZ

SANTA CRUZ MUSEUM OF ART AND HISTORY

PEARL ALLEY BISTRO & CAFÉ

BEST INN & SUITES

SANTA CRUZ CITY MUSEUM OF NATURAL HISTORY

SATURN CAFE

CLIFF CREST BED AND BREAKFAST INN

COMFORT INN BEACH BOARDWALK

HI-AYH SANTA CRUZ HOSTEL

CHATEAU VICTORIAN

CAROUSEL MOTEL

ECONO LODGE SANTA CRUZ

BEACHVIEW INN

SANTA CRUZ BEACH BOARDWALK

CASABLANCA RESTAURANT

COCOANUT GROVE

Neary Lagoon Park

Santa Cruz Beach

Santa Cruz Harbor

WESTCOAST SANTA CRUZ HOTEL

THE SANTA CRUZ WHARF

Cowell Beach

SEA & SAND INN

To Lighthouse Field State Beach

0   .25 mi

0   .25 km

© AVALON TRAVEL PUBLISHING, INC.

Company, 400 Beach St., Santa Cruz, CA 95060-5491, 831/423-5590, website: www .beachboardwalk.com. While you're at it, inquire about special vacation packages, including accommodations at the Sea & Sand Inn or the Carousel Motel.

For current Boardwalk hours, call 831/ 426-7433. For information on special Boardwalk activities, call 831/423-5590. To find out what's happening at the Cocoanut Grove, call 831/423-2053.

The Santa Cruz Wharf

The pier at the western end of Santa Cruz Beach, once a good place to buy cheap, fresh fish, did booming business during the state's steamship heyday. Today, the place is packed instead with tourists, and most fish markets, restaurants, and shops here charge a pretty penny. Still, the wharf's worth a sunset stroll. (Peer down into the fenced-off "holes" to watch the sea lions.) A few commercial fishing boats still haul their catches of salmon and cod ashore in summer, doubling as whale-watching tour boats in winter. Worth a look, too, are the kiosk displays on wharf and fishing history.

OTHER SANTA CRUZ SIGHTS

Historic Homes Walking Tour

If you're over- or underwhelmed by the Boardwalk, take the Santa Cruz walking tour. This expedition is a lot quicker than it used to be— since many of the city's unusual Victorians— with frilly wedding-cake furbelows and "witch's hat" towers on the Queen Annes—departed to that great Historical Register in the Sky during the 1989 earthquake. But some grande dames remain. To find them, stop by the visitors center and pick up the *Historic Santa Cruz Walking Tours and Museum Guide* brochure. Most houses are private homes or businesses, so don't trespass.

To find out more about area history, stop by the Santa Cruz Museum of Art and History. In particular, the museum staff can fill you in on regional historical sites under their care, including the Davenport Jail (1917), up the coast in Davenport, though no longer open to the public, and the Evergreen Cemetery (established 1850) at Evergreen and Coral Streets, one of the oldest Protestant cemeteries in California. Next door to the museum is the visitors center.

SANTA CRUZ

MELISSA SHEROWSKI

a view of the Santa Cruz wharf and nearby boardwalk

CIRCLE OF ENCHANTMENT

Tour the eclectic scenery of Santa Cruz greenbelt areas on the area's Circle of Enchantment Trail, also known as the Circle Trail. The 23-mile trail is actually two separate loops; each segment can be hiked in a half day.

Begin either loop in downtown Santa Cruz at the San Lorenzo River pedestrian bridge, just off Front Street.

The circle's western loop, about a 12-mile hike, follows the river down to the Boardwalk. It then climbs to the bayside recreation trail along W. Cliff Drive and continues on to Natural Bridges State Park and the Long Marine Lab be-

fore angling inland. The route then follows Delaware Avenue into wooded Arroyo Seco Canyon, then up the hill to the UC Santa Cruz campus—redwoods and fabulous views—and the Pogonip grasslands before circling back to the river levee.

The eastern loop is more urban, yet it eventually leads to the "Top of the World" lookout, Arana City Park, Santa Cruz Yacht Harbor, and along E. Cliff Drive and the Pleasure Point area before returning to Lorenzo Park downtown.

A general route map and detailed directions are available at www.ecotopia.org.

Santa Cruz Museum of Art and History

A sure sign that downtown Santa Cruz is almost done digging out from the rubble of the devastating 1989 earthquake is the Museum of Art and History at the McPherson Center, 705 Front

St. (Front and Cooper), 831/429-1964, website: www.santacruzmah.org. Traveling exhibits and local artists get prominent play. Recent shows include 2001's *Art Undercover: Tom Killion, Gay Schy, Peter and Donna Thomas,* an examination of "small press art," and *The Home Front: Santa Cruz County's War Front During World War II.* The museum is open Tuesday through Sunday 11 A.M. to 5 P.M. (until 7 P.M. on Friday); a small admission fee is charged. Adjacent to the museum is The Octagon, an eight-sided 1882 brick building relocated here, now the museum store. Inside is an intriguing collection of gift and art items, including—at least sometimes—the marvelously whimsical work (including greeting cards) of Santa Cruz artist James Carl Aschbacher.

Santa Cruz Museum of Art and History

Santa Cruz Mission Adobe State Historic Park

Restored and open to the public is the Santa Cruz Mission Adobe, a state historical park just off Mission Plaza at 144 School St., 831/425-5849. This is one of the county's last remaining original adobes, built by and for Native Americans "employed" at Mission Santa Cruz. It was later a 17-unit "home for new citizens." Only seven units remain, these now comprising a California history museum circa the 1840s. Restored rooms illustrate how Native American, Californio, and Irish American families once lived. Call for current information about guided tours and "living history" demonstrations (usually offered on Sundays, the latter just in March). School groups are welcome on Thursdays and Fridays—by advance reservation only. Plan a picnic here anytime (bring your own water). The park is open Thursday through Sunday 10 A.M. to 4 P.M. A small admission fee is charged.

Mission Santa Cruz

Nearby, at 126 High St., is what's left of the original mission: just a memory, really. The original site of the **Misión de Exaltacion de la Santa Cruz** was at High and Emmet Streets, too close to the San Lorenzo River, as it turned out. The move to higher ground left only the garden at the lower level. The original Santa Cruz mission complex was finished in 1794 but was completely destroyed by earthquakes in the mid-19th century. The replica church, scaled down by half and built in 1931 on the upper level, seems to have lost more than just stature. It's open Tuesday through Saturday 10 A.M. to 4 P.M., Sunday 10 A.M. to 2 P.M.; call 831/426-5686 for more information.

MELISSA SHEROWSKI

Mission Santa Cruz

Santa Cruz City Museum of Natural History

At least for now, the city's natural history museum is at home in Tyrell Park above Seabright/Castle Beach, east of the Boardwalk at 1305 East Cliff Drive. The onetime 1915 Carnegie Library that anchors the park's southern edge, overlooking Monterey Bay, features exhibits and displays on the Santa Cruz area's natural and cultural history. There's a Tidepool Touch Tank and a Fossil Sand Dollar Dig—and the kids also dig that big cement gray whale on the lawn. The museum is open Tuesday through Sunday 10 A.M. to 5 P.M. A small admission fee is charged. The museum also sponsors a year-round schedule of classes and events. For more information, call 831/420-6115 or see website: www.santacruzmuseums.org.

Santa Cruz Harley-Davidson Museum

The local Harley-Davidson shop, 1148 Soquel Ave., 831/421-9600, website: www.santacruzharley.com, is something of a "destination dealership." Among the exquisitely restored Harleys on display are an H-D bicycle, first introduced in 1917, a 1929 JDH two-cam twin, and a stylish 1930 VL. Historical photos, posters, and memorabilia round out the collection, which is available for public viewing Tuesday through Sunday.

Santa Cruz Mystery Spot

The much bumper-sticker–ballyhooed Mystery Spot is a place where "every law of gravitation has gone haywire." Or has it? Trees, people, even the Spot's rustic shack and furnishings seem spellbound by "the force"—though people wearing slick-soled shoes seem to have the hardest time staying with the mysterious program. Hard-core tourists tend to love this place— Mom, Dad, and the kids can *literally* climb the walls—but others leave wondering why they spent the $5 to get in.

The Mystery Spot is located at 465 Mystery

SANTA CRUZ

Spot Rd., 831/423-8897, website: www
.mysteryspot.com. To get there, follow Market
Street north from Water Street for a few miles.
Market becomes Branciforte; Mystery Spot
Road branches left off Branciforte—you can't
miss it. Open daily 9 A.M. to 7 P.M. (last tour at
7) in summer, 9 A.M. to 4:30 P.M. (last tour at
4:20) the rest of the year.

Santa Cruz Surfing Museum

Cowabunga! Instead of cutting a ribbon, they
snipped a hot pink surfer's leash when they
opened the world's first surfing museum here
in May 1986. This historical exhibit reaches
back to the 1930s, with displays on the evolution
of surfboards and equipment—including the
Model T of boards, a 15-foot redwood plank
weighing 100 pounds, and an experimental Jack
O'Neill wetsuit made of nylon and foam, the
forerunner to the Neoprene "short john." Some
say two Polynesian princes introduced surfing to
Santa Cruz in 1885. True or not, by 1912 local
posters announced the surfing exploits of
Olympic swimmer and "Father of Surfing" Duke
Kahanamoku.

The museum's location on the ground floor of
the brick lighthouse on West Cliff Drive, north-

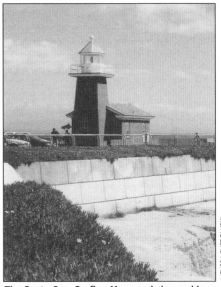

MELISSA SHEROWSKI

The Santa Cruz Surfing Museum is housed in
the Mark Abbott Memorial Lighthouse.

west of town near Steamer's Lane—prime surf
turf—seems the most fitting place for official
homage to life in pursuit of the perfect wave.

SANTA CRUZ WINERIES

The coastal mountains near Santa Cruz are well
known for their redwoods. But since the late
1800s, they have also been known for their vineyards. Regional winemaking is back, helped along
since 1981 by the official federal recognition of
the Santa Cruz Mountain appellation for wine
grapes grown in the region defined by Half Moon
Bay in the north and Mount Madonna in the
south. More than 40 wineries now produce Santa
Cruz Mountain wines.

The eclectic **Bonny Doon Vineyard,** north of
Santa Cruz at 10 Pine Flat Rd., tel. 831/425-4518,
www.bonnydoonvineyard.com, specializes in
RhÙne and Italian varietals, though wine lovers
and critics are also smitten with the winery's worldly, witty, and wildly footnoted newsletter (also
available online). Open 11 a.m.-5 p.m. daily for
tastings, except major holidays.

Nearby in Felton is the award-winning and historic **Hallcrest Vineyards,** 379 Felton Empire Rd.
(call for directions), tel. 831/335-4441, noted for its
cabernet sauvignon, chardonnay, merlot, and zinfandel. Hallcrest is also home to **The Organic
Wine Works,** producing the nation's first certified organic wines. Made from certified organi-
cally grown grapes, the winemaking process is also
organic, without the use of sulfites. Open daily 11
a.m.-5:30 p.m. Also in Felton and open only by appointment is the small **Zayante Vineyards,** 420
Old Mount Rd., tel. 831/335-7992.

For more information about Santa Cruz area
wineries, including a current wineries map, contact: **Santa Cruz Mountains Winegrowers Association,** 7605 Old Dominion Ct., Ste. A,
Aptos, CA 95003, tel. 831/479-9463, www
.wines.com/santa_cruz_mountains.

SANTA CRUZ

The lighthouse was built by the family of Mark Abbott, a surfer killed nearby. The museum is open noon to 4 P.M. Wednesday through Monday in summer, Thursday through Monday in winter; admission is free. For more information, call 831/420-6289.

Spiritual/Supernatural Attractions

Perhaps more interesting even than the Mystery Spot are two other oddball attractions, located at the **Santa Cruz Memorial Park & Funeral Home,** 3301 Paul Sweet Rd., 831/426-1601. Here you'll find a wax interpretation of *The Last Supper,* plus displays attempting to rekindle the controversy over the **Shroud of Turin**—that renowned piece of linen purported to show Christ's after-death visage—by challenging the conclusions of carbon tests declaring the shroud a fake.

An interpretation of Da Vinci's famous painting in life-sized wax figures, *The Last Supper* is the original work of two Katherine Struberghs (mother and daughter) from Los Angeles. The women spared themselves no trial or trouble in this endeavor. (Each hair on every wax head was implanted by hand—that task alone requiring eight months.) But after some 40 years' residence at the Santa Cruz Art League, Jesus and his disciples were in a sad state of disrepair. That was before the funeral home and local Oddfellows Lodge took on the task of financing something of a resurrection. The job involved patching the cracks in the figures' heads, washing and setting their hair and beards, replacing fingers (and fingernails and toenails), and polishing their glass eyeballs.

Visitors can see both attractions Monday through Friday by appointment. Contributions are appreciated.

UC Santa Cruz

When the doors of UC Santa Cruz opened in the 1960s, few California students could gain admission to the close-knit, redwood-cloistered campus on the hill. The selection process (complete with essay) was weighted in favor of students with unusual abilities, aptitudes, and attitudes—those not likely to thrive within the traditional university structure. So many children of movie stars and other members of Cali-

---

ALL HAIL THE SANTA CRUZ SLUGS

Refreshingly out of step with the period's college careerism, the UC Santa Cruz student body convinced then-Chancellor Robert Sinsheimer in 1986 to declare the noble banana slug—a common on-campus companion—their school mascot (instead of the more acceptable sea lion) after a hard-fought, five-year campaign. When the chancellor declared the Santa Cruz Sea Lions the official choice in 1981, students protested that the banana slug would more appropriately be "a statement about the ideology of Santa Cruz," a philosophy with no room for football teams, cheerleaders, fraternities, and sororities.

Finally acceding to the students' preference for a slimy, spineless, sluggish, yellow gastropod—defended as "flexible, golden, and deliberate" by one professor—Sinsheimer said that students should have a school mascot "with which they can empathize." He also proposed genetic engineering research on slugs to "improve the breed" because "the potential seems endless."

---

fornia's moneyed upper classes have attended UC Santa Cruz that it has been playfully dubbed "California's public finishing school." The university's student body has so far remained relatively small (more than 12,000 currently), though growth is on the agenda. A sign that the times they are a-changin' at Santa Cruz came in February 2000, when the faculty voted overwhelmingly to eliminate the university's founding "no required grading" policy.

The University of California regents set about transforming the redwood-forested rangeland here, once the Henry Cowell Ranch, into California's educational Camelot in 1961. They hired some of the state's finest architects, whose designs ranged from modern Mediterranean to "Italian hill village" (Kresge College). The official explanation for the Santa Cruz "college cluster" concept was to avoid the depersonalization common to large UC campuses, but another reason was alluded to when then-Governor Ronald Reagan declared the campus "riot-proof."

To truly appreciate this place, wander the campus hiking trails and paths (but not alone). Some of the old converted ranch buildings are worth noting: the lime kilns, blacksmith's shop, cookhouse, horse barn, bull barn, slaughterhouse, cookhouse, workers' cabins, and cooperage. On a clear day, the view of Monterey Bay (and of whales passing offshore in winter and spring) from the top of the hill on the 2,000-acre campus is marvelous. For information and guided campus tours, stop by the wood-and-stone Cook House near the entrance. You can also contact UCSC Admissions Office, Cook House, Santa Cruz, CA 95064, 831/459-4008, email: slugvisits@cats.ucsc.edu.

Long Marine Laboratory

Well worth a stop for nature lovers, the Joseph M. Long Marine Laboratory is just off Delaware Avenue near Natural Bridges State Beach on the western edge of town. A university research and education facility, the lab is affiliated with the on-campus Institute of Marine Sciences, established in 1972. Research conducted here ranges from marine biology and marine geophysics to paleooceanography and coastal processes—from plankton to blue whales, from cold water ecology to tropical coral reefs. Associated facilities include an 18,000-square-foot California Department of Fish and Game Marine Wildlife Veterinary Care and Research Center, the nation's largest and most advanced, and a state-of-the-art National Marine Fisheries Service laboratory, which conducts fisheries research and houses the nation's first National Science Center for Marine Protected Areas. Under construction, at last report: the UC Santa Cruz Center for Ocean Health and a seabird/raptor facility.

To help interpret the lab's work and to educate future generations of marine biologists, the new **Seymour Marine Discovery Center** is open to the public Tuesday through Saturday 10 A.M. to 5 P.M., Sunday noon to 5 P.M. Admission is $5 adults; $3 students, seniors, and youths 6 to 16; free for children 5 and under. Docent-led tours of the lab's other marine research facilities are available. For information contact 831/459-3800 or www2.ucsc.edu/seymourcenter. For additional information about Long Marine Lab programs and facilities, see website: www.natsci.ucsc.edu.

blue whale skeleton at Long Marine Laboratory

MELISSA SHEROWSKI

MELISSA SHEROWSKI

Natural Bridges State Beach

To get here from Santa Cruz, take Highway 1 (Mission Street) north, turn left on Swift Street, then right on Delaware Avenue. Continue on Delaware to the Long Marine Lab entrance at the end of the road.

AT THE BEACH

Beaches in Town

Most of the outdoor action in Santa Cruz proper happens at local beaches; swimming, surfing, and fishing are all big, as are tamer pastimes like beachcombing, sandcastle building, and sunbathing. The in-town **Santa Cruz Beach** at the Boardwalk, with fine white sand and towel-to-towel baking bodies in summer, is "the scene"—especially for outsiders from San Jose, locals say. For more privacy, head east to the mouth of the San Lorenzo River. Southwest of the pier, **Cowell Beach** is a surfing beach, where Huey Lewis and the News filmed one of their music videos. Just before **Lighthouse Field State Beach** on West Cliff is the Santa Cruz Surfing Museum, an eclectic lighthouse collection of surf's-up memorabilia keeping watch over the hotdoggers in churning Steamer Lane.

Natural Bridges State Beach

Located farther southwest, at the end of West Cliff Drive, Natural Bridges attracts the mythic monarch butterflies each year from October to May. Though Pacific Grove near Monterey proudly proclaims itself the destination of choice for these regal insects, Santa Cruz claims to get the most monarchs. This is the only state-owned monarch butterfly preserve in California. One of the sandstone "natural bridges" here collapsed in 1980, under assault from a winter storm. The other still stands, though. To the north are some great tidepools, available for exploration (don't touch) at low tide. Leathery green fields of Brussels sprouts fringe the fragile sandy cliffs.

Monarch butterfly tours (wheelchair accessible) are offered on weekends from mid-October through February. For information on guided butterfly walks and tidepool tours, stop by the visitors center or call 831/423-4609. Come in October for **Welcome Back Monarchs Day** and again in February for the annual **Migration Festival** sendoff, a park fundraiser cosponsored by Friends of Santa Cruz State Parks. (The monarchs may be leaving, but the gray whales offshore are just

WILDER RANCH STATE PARK

Open to the public since mid-1989, Wilder Ranch State Park is best summed up as "a California coastal dairy-farm museum," a remnant of the days when dairies were more important to the local economy than tourists. Before it was a dairy farm, this was the main rancho supplying Mission Santa Cruz. Though damaged by the 1989 earthquake, the old Victorian ranch house is open again, decked out in period furnishings. The grounds also include an elaborate 1890s stable, a dairy barn, and a bunkhouse-workshop with water-driven machinery. Seasoned vehicles and farm equipment, from a 1916 Dodge touring sedan to seed spreaders and road graders, are scattered throughout the grounds.

Almost more appealing, though, are the park's miles of coastline and thousands of acres of forest, creeks, and canyons. To help visitors take in the landscape, 4,505-acre Wilder Ranch features 34 miles of hiking, biking, and equestrian trails. Restoration of these coastal wetlands is ongoing.

General ranch tours, led by docents dressed in period attire, are offered every Saturday and Sunday, usually at 1 P.M. Historical games are played on the lawn—hoop 'n' stick, bubbles, stilts—on weekends as well. A variety of other history- and natural history-oriented events are sponsored throughout the year, from demonstrations on making corn-husk dolls or quilts to mastering cowboy-style roping, plus guided hikes and bird walks. Usually on the first Saturday in May is the park's annual open house, a full day of old-fashioned family fun (and fundraising, for future park restoration work).

Wilder Ranch is two miles north of Santa Cruz on the west side of Hwy. 1 (1401 Coast Rd., about a mile past the stoplight at Western Dr.), 831/423-9703 or 831/426-0505, and is open for day-use only ($3 per car). To get here by bus, take Santa Cruz Metro No. 40 and ask the driver to drop you at the ranch.

arriving in February; migrants come and go all year.) The parking fee at Natural Bridges is $3 per car; walk-ins and bike-ins are free. Natural Bridges is open daily 8 A.M. to sunset.

Locals' Beaches

Along East Cliff Drive are **Tyrell Park** and more inaccessible sandy beaches. **Twin Lakes Beach,** near the Santa Cruz Yacht Harbor on the eastern extension of East Cliff before it becomes Portolá, is a popular locals' beach, usually quite warm. Beyond the Santa Cruz Yacht Harbor, various small, locally popular beaches line East Cliff Drive. The unofficially named **26th Street Beach** (at the end of 26th Street, naturally enough) is probably tops among them. Hot for local surfing is the **Pleasure Point,** East Cliff at Pleasure Point Drive.

Beaches North of Town

Davenport Beach, at Davenport Landing up the coast toward Año Nuevo, is a hot spot for sailboarders and is often relatively uncrowded. **Red White and Blue Beach,** 5021 Coast Rd., just south of Davenport, 831/423-6332, is a popular, privately operated nude beach (too popular, some say; women shouldn't go alone). It costs $5 per day for an all-over tan. Camping is also available. Nearby is **Bonny Doon Beach,** up the coast from Santa Cruz at the intersection of Highway 1 and Bonny Doon Road south of Davenport. It's free, and even wilder for sunbathing sans swimsuit. It's also popular with surfers.

Beaches East and South of Town

About six miles down the coast from Santa Cruz City Beach and just south of the Capitola suburbs is **New Brighton State Beach,** 1500 Park Ave., 831/464-6330. Its 65 often-sunny acres are protected by wooded headlands that offer nature trails, good bird-watching, and a dazzling nighttime view of Monterey Bay. The day use fee is $3.

Several miles farther south, two-mile-long **Seacliff State Beach,** on Park Drive in Aptos, 831/685-6500, 831/685-6442 (recorded information), or 831/685-6444 (visitors center), is so popular you may not be able to stop. It's nice for hiking, pelican-watching, fossil spotting, swimming, and sunbathing. The wheelchair-accessible pier reaches out to the pink concrete carcass of the doomed World War I–vintage *Palo Alto,* sunk here after seeing no wartime action and now a long-abandoned amusement pier (not open to the public). Birds live in the prow these days. People enjoy the pier's more mundane pleasures: people-watching, fishing (no license required), and strolling. Guided walks are occasionally offered; call the visitors center for schedules and reservations. The day use fee is $3.

As the name suggests, **Rio del Mar** beach is where Aptos Creek meets the sea. Here you'll find restrooms, miles of sand, and limited parking. It's free.

For beaches farther south, see Watsonville and Vicinity.

OUT ON THE WATER
Sailing Santa Cruz and the Bay

For an unusual view of the Boardwalk and the bay, take a boat ride. One of the best going—definitely not just any boat—is the *Chardonnay II,* a 70-foot ultralight sailing yacht offering special-emphasis cruises. Choose from astronomy, fireworks, "gourmet on the bay," marine ecology, wine-tasting, and whale-watching (winter and spring) cruises. There's even a Wednesday night Boat Race Cruise in the company of almost every other boat from the Santa Cruz Yacht Harbor. At last report, per-person fare for most scheduled trips was $43.50. This sleek albino seal of a sailboat can hold up to 49 passengers and features every imaginable amenity, including a CD player, a TV/VCR, cellular phones, a built-in bar, and plenty of below-deck space, making it fun as a private group charter for personally designed adventures. There's a two-hour minimum rental for departures from Santa Cruz, a three-hour minimum from Monterey. Private charter rates are $550–800 per hour. For more information and to make reservations (required), call **Chardonnay Sailing Charters** at 831/423-1213 or inquire online at website: www.chardonnay.com.

Other boat and charter companies at or near the city's yacht harbor include **Pacific Yachting,** 790 Mariner Park Way, 831/423-7245 or toll-free 800/374-2626, website: www.pacificsail.com, which offers similar boat rides on smaller yachts as well as sailing lessons and a six-day seagoing instruction vacation. Probably the best deal going, though, is through the University of California at Santa Cruz Boating Club. In summer, UCSC sailing and boating courses are open to the public. For information, call 831/425-1164, email: ucscboat@cats.ucsc.edu,

© ROBERT HOLMES/CALTOUR

Santa Cruz is one of the most popular surfing spots in Northern California.

or see website: www.ucsc.edu/opers/boating. If you qualify for membership—as a student or alumnus—you can use the boats all year. The local **Coast Guard Auxiliary,** 432 Oxford Way, 831/423-7119, also offers sailing, boating skills, seamanship, and coastal navigation courses.

Other Ocean Adventures

For more traditional boat tours, whale-watching trips, and fishing charters, contact **Stagnaro's Fishing Trips** at the municipal wharf, 831/427-2334, or **Scurfield's Landing/Shamrock Charters** at the yacht harbor, 831/476-2648.

Kayaking is great sport in these parts. **Venture Quest,** 125 Beach St., 831/427-2267, and at the municipal wharf, 831/425-8445, website: www.kayaksantacruz.com, sells kayaks and accessories and offers lessons and guided tours. **Kayak Connection** at the Santa Cruz Yacht Harbor, 413 Lake Ave., 831/479-1121, website: www.kayakconnection.com, also rents and sells equipment, in addition to offering guided bird-watching, fishing, and moonlight tours.

Several full-service dive shops in town can provide complete information on local diving conditions, as well as instruction, rentals, and sales. Try **Aqua Safaris Scuba Center,** 6896-A Soquel Ave., 831/420-5270, website: www .aquasafaris.com, or **Adventure Sports Unlimited,** 303 Potrero St., 831/458-3648, website: www.asudoit.com.

Club Ed, on Cowell Beach (on the right side of Santa Cruz Wharf, in front of the WestCoast Santa Cruz Hotel), 831/459-9283 or toll-free 800/287-7873, rents surfboards, boogie boards, skim boards, and sailboards, and offers lessons in riding all of the above. Find out more about their surf camps on the web at www.club-ed.com.

EVENTFUL SANTA CRUZ

For an up-to-date quarterly calendar of city and county events, contact the local visitors council (see Santa Cruz Information and Services, below). Bike races have prominent local appeal, and professional volleyball competitions are also held year-round. Whale-watching in winter is another popular draw.

For wine lovers, mid-January features the countywide **Wineries Passport Program,** offering tours, tastings, and open houses at Santa Cruz Mountains wineries (also held in mid-April, mid-July, and mid-November). Mid-month, Santa Cruz celebrates its **Fungus Fair,** always fun for mushroom lovers.

Cold and very cool in February is the **O'Neill Cold Water Classic** surfing competition, sponsored by Santa Cruz–based O'Neill, Inc. and its legendary founder, Jack O'Neill, inventor of the wetsuit. Also in February, the **Migration Festival** at Natural Bridges State Beach celebrates many migrants, from monarch butterflies and the gray whale to salmon, salamanders, elephant seals, and shorebirds. The decades-long tradition of the **Santa Cruz Baroque Festival** starts in February and continues until May, offering concerts of early music masterworks. For information, call 831/457-9693 or see website: www.scbaroque.org. Head for the Boardwalk in late February for the annual **Clam Chowder Cook-Off.**

Come in March for the free annual **Jazz on the Wharf** festival, which serenades Monterey Bay from the Santa Cruz Municipal Wharf and its restaurants, and for the **Santa Cruz Kayak Surf Festival,** the world's largest. In mid- to late March, Felton holds its **Great Train Robberies** festival, followed by the **Amazing Egg Hunt** in April (usually). Memorial Day weekend brings the annual **Civil War Reenactment** at Roaring Camp.

May is big for art, wine, and music, starting with **Celebrate Santa Cruz Art, Wine & Jazz** in downtown Santa Cruz and continuing with the **Boulder Creek Art, Wine & Music Festival.** Come in mid-May for the popular **Industrial Hemp Expo,** a celebration of hemp products from soaps to backpacks and hammocks. A fashion show is included. Also fun in May: **Bug Day** at Henry Cowell Redwoods State Park in Felton. Come in June for the **We Carnival Street Parade and World Music Festival.** Come in July 4 for Aptos's **World's Shortest Parade.**

The acclaimed and innovative **Shakespeare Santa Cruz** festival runs mid-July through August in an outdoor theater in the redwoods at UCSC. For information call 831/459-2121, for

MELISSA SHEROWSKI

Del Mar Theater, downtown Santa Cruz

tickets 831/459-2159, or see website: www .shakespearesantacruz.org. The very fast **Santa Cruz to Capitola Wharf-to-Wharf Race** in late July is a major event for runners, with more than half the applicants turned away due to the event's immense popularity—a popularity fueled by the $12,000 total prize purse. For information, call the race hotline, 831/475-2196.

After 20-some years, the famed August **Cabrillo Music Festival** (described by *The New Yorker* as one of the most adventurous and attractive in America) is still going strong, with performances at UC Santa Cruz, Mission San Juan Bautista, and Watsonville. For information—and do make your plans well in advance—contact the Cabrillo Music Festival, 831/426-6966, website: www.cabrillomusic.org. To reserve tickets, call 831/420-5260, beginning in late June.

The first couple of weeks in September, Capitola's **Begonia Festival** includes several big events, including a sandcastle contest and nautical parade. It's followed (and nearly overshad-

owed) in mid-September by the city's annual **Art & Wine Festival,** which has become incredibly popular. The second and third weekends in October, come for the countywide artists' **Open Studios,** with open-house art shows held everywhere, from private homes and studios to galleries and museums. It's wonderful exposure for artists and great pleasure for aficionados.

In late November, look for Felton's **Mountain Man Rendezvous** and the **Christmas Craft and Gift Festival** at the Boardwalk's Cocoanut Grove. In December, Felton sponsors its **Holiday Lights Train** Christmas festivities.

For more information on many of the above festivals, contact **Santa Cruz County Conference and Visitors Council,** downtown at 1211 Ocean St., 831/425-1234 or 800/833-3494, website: www.santacruzca.org.

ARTFUL, ENTERTAINING SANTA CRUZ

For an introduction to local galleries, at the visitors council request the self-guided **Gallery Walk** tour map of downtown Santa Cruz, which will also guide you to coffeehouses and unusual shops. Santa Cruz has more than its fair share of good movie theaters and film series. To get an idea of what's playing where, scan local entertainment papers and/or pick up a current copy of the free bimonthly *Santa Cruz Movie Times*.

Santa Cruz Clubs

If you're into big-band swing, check out **Cocoanut Grove** dances (call 408/423-5590 for information); tickets run $15 and up. **The Kuumbwa Jazz Center,** 320-2 Cedar St. #2, 831/427-2227, website: www.kuumbwajazz.com, is a no-booze, no-cigarettes, under-21-welcome place with great jazz (often big names), and it's rarely packed. Most shows are Monday and Friday at 8 P.M.; ticket prices vary and are often low. The **Catalyst,** 1011 Pacific Ave., 831/423-1336, is legendary for its Friday afternoon happy hour in the Atrium—seems like *everybody's* here from 5 to 7 P.M., drinking beer, making the scene, and sometimes tapping their toes to the house band:

SANTA CRUZ

MELISSA SHEROWSKI

the performing arts complex at UC Santa Cruz

Wally's Swing World. The 700-seat theater (massive dance floor) hosts good local bands or national acts nightly (cover charge). Local coffeehouses from Santa Cruz to Capitola also offer casual, relaxed, and sometimes highbrow entertainment (like poetry readings).

Santa Cruz Area Performing Arts

On a smaller scale, local performing arts are al-ways an adventure. The **Santa Cruz Chamber Players** specialize in both traditional and modern chamber music, with an emphasis on the unusual. For a performance schedule, call 831/425-3149. The **Santa Cruz County Symphony,** 200 Seventh Ave. #225, 831/462-0553, schedules performances year-round at both the Santa Cruz Civic Auditorium and Watsonville's Mello Center.

The noted **Tandy Beal & Company** dance troupe, 740 Front St. #300B, 831/429-1324, performs locally when not touring internationally. The **Santa Cruz Ballet Theatre,** 2800 S. Rodeo Gulch Rd., Soquel, 831/479-1600, is a good bet for a year-end production of *The Nutcracker.* **Actors' Theatre,** 1001 Center St., 831/425-1003 (administration) or 831/425-7529 (tickets and reservations), schedules live stage productions year-round. In Capitola, the Quonset hut–housed Capitola Theater is now the **Bay Shore Lyric Opera Company and Theater for the Performing Arts,** 831/462-3131.

On-Campus Performances

For information on what's going on at UCSC, pick up a copy of the quarterly **UCSC Performing Arts Calendar,** available around town, or call 831/459-ARTS. (Other useful campus numbers include Arts and Lectures, 831/459-2826; Theatre Arts, 831/459-2974; and the Music Department, 831/459-2292). To order tickets by phone ($2 service charge), call the UCSC Ticket Office at 831/459-2159.

SANTA CRUZ

Practical Santa Cruz

SANTA CRUZ AREA CAMPING

Camping at the Beach

Best for nearby tent camping is **New Brighton State Beach,** 1500 Park Ave. in Capitola, 831/464-6330. "New Bright" features 115 developed campsites (especially nice ones on the cliffs), some sheltered picnic tables, and a small beach. It's a good base camp for the entire Santa Cruz area. You can get here via local bus—take number 58 or the Park Avenue route. This area was once called China Beach or China Cove, after the Chinese fishermen who built a village here in the 1870s. Developed family campsites cost $12. The campground is popular, so reserve for summer at least six months ahead.

Near Aptos, **Seacliff State Beach,** 831/685-6500 or 831/685-6444, has a better beach than New Brighton, but camping is a disappointment. Strictly an RV setup, the park has 26 sites (with hookups) that cost $18; $12 for overflow campsites.

For more information about the area's beach parks, contact the state parks office in Santa Cruz, 600 Ocean St., 831/429-2850. For state campground reservations, contact Reserve America at 800/444-7275 or website: www.reserveamerica.com.

Camping in the Redwoods

Big Basin Redwoods State Park, 21600 Big Basin Hwy., Boulder Creek, 831/338-8860, website: www.bigbasin.org, offers family campsites, group camps, and horse camps. Family campsites cost $12. Tents-only trail campsites are $5; hiker/biker campsites $1. The park also boasts 41 year-round "tent cabins," each with two double beds, a camp lamp, and a woodstove. Tent cabins sleep four comfortably but can house up to eight. Rates are $39–49. (Add $10 for linen and blanket rental in lieu of sleeping bags.) You can also arrange "hassle-free" tent camping—all you have to pack is kids and clothes. For cabin reservations, call 800/874-

MELISSA SHEROWSKI

Camping is available at New Brighton State Beach.

8368. To reserve trail camps, call Big Basin headquarters, 831/338-8860.

Henry Cowell Redwoods State Park, just north of the UC campus on Highway 9 in Felton, 831/335-4598 (administration) or 831/438-2396 (campground), offers 150 sites, 105 of them developed ($7–12). Sites in the developed areas are quite civilized, with amenities including hot showers, flush toilets, tables, barbecues, and cupboards.

Family and group campsites at both Big Basin and Henry Cowell Redwoods State Park are sometimes available at the last minute, even in summer and on warm-season weekends. But make reservations—up to seven months in advance—to guarantee a space. Reserve through ReserveAmerica, 800/444-7275, website: www.reserveamerica.com.

Camping Elsewhere

Private campgrounds and trailer parks are always a possibility; a complete current listing is available at the local chamber of commerce. Possibilities include **Cotillion Gardens,** 300 Old Big Trees Rd., Felton, CA 95018, 831/335-7669; **Carbonero Creek,** 917 Disc Dr., Scotts Valley, CA 95066, 831/438-1288; and the **Santa Cruz KOA,** 1186 San Andreas Rd., Watsonville, CA 95076, 831/722-0551 or 831/722-2377.

STAYING IN SANTA CRUZ
HI-AYH Santa Cruz Hostel

The Santa Cruz Hostel, 321 Main St., 831/423-8304, website: www.hi-santacruz.org, occupies the historic 1870s Carmelita Cottages downtown. The hostel is open year-round, is wheelchair accessible, and features an on-site cyclery, fireplace, barbecue, lockers, and rose and herb gardens. Family rooms and limited parking available (extra fee for both). Reservations strongly suggested. Under $50.

Santa Cruz Motels and Hotels

As a general rule, motels closer to the freeway are cheaper, while those on the river are seedier. There are some fairly inexpensive motels near the beach (some with kitchens, Jacuzzis, pools, cable TV, etc.). Off-season rates in Santa Cruz are

usually quite reasonable, but prices can sometimes mysteriously increase in summer and on weekends and holidays—so verify prices before you sign in.

$50–100: The **Beachview Inn,** less than a block from the beach at 50 Front St., 831/426-3575 or 800/946-0614, features all the essentials plus air-conditioning and direct-dial phones, with rooms $65 and up in the high season. The **Econo Lodge Santa Cruz,** just a block from the Boardwalk and the Wharf at 550 Second St., 831/426-3626 or 800/553-2666, offers rooms for $75 and up. Close to downtown, **Travelodge Santa Cruz,** 525 Ocean St., 831/426-2300 or 800/578-7878, offers rooms for $79 and up.

$100–150: Endlessly convenient for Boardwalkers is the Boardwalk's own **Carousel Motel,** 110 Riverside Ave., 831/425-7090 or 800/214-7400, website: www.santacruzmotels.com. Also a best bet is the attractive **Best Inn & Suites,** 600 Riverside Ave., 831/458-9660 or 800/527-3833, where standard rooms include two queen beds. Other options are available—including two-story suites and "evergreen" rooms with air, water, and shower filtration. The inn also features a heated pool and hot tubs, a pleasant garden courtyard, and a picnic area with barbecues, plus complimentary expanded continental breakfast. The appealing **Comfort Inn Beach Boardwalk,** 314 Riverside Ave., 831/471-9999 or 800/228-5150, offers 28 rooms with color TV and cable, a complimentary breakfast bar, and a heated pool and hot tub. Suites are available. Though they can range higher in the high season, reasonably priced rooms can also be found at the **Best Western Inn,** 126 Plymouth St., 831/425-4717 or 800/528-1234, and the **Best Western All Suites Inn,** 500 Ocean St., 831/458-9898 or 800/528-1234, an all-suites setup that offers rooms with whirlpool tubs and microwaves, plus some with gas fireplaces. Other amenities include a heated pool, lap pool, and sauna. Some rooms at the pleasant **Sunset Inn,** close to UC Santa Cruz and Natural Bridges at 2424 Mission St., 831/423-7500, also fit this price category. Amenities include microwaves, refrigerators, some in-room Jacuzzis, free local phone calls, breakfast, a hot tub, and a sauna.

$150–250: Close to the wharf and overlooking the bay is the Boardwalk's small **Sea & Sand Inn,** 201 W. Cliff Dr., 831/427-3400, website: www.santacruzmotels.com. All 20 rooms boast an ocean view; suites have abundant amenities.

$250 and Up: Adjacent to the wharf and across from the Santa Cruz Beach Boardwalk, the imposing **WestCoast Santa Cruz Hotel,** 175 W. Cliff Dr., 831/426-4330 or 800/325-4000, website: www.westcoasthotels.com, is right on the beach (the only beachfront hotel in Santa Cruz), not far from the lighthouse. It features 163 rooms and suites with balconies and patios, in-room coffeemakers, modern amenities, satellite TV, a heated pool, and a whirlpool.

For value and views, nothing beats **Chaminade at Santa Cruz,** up on the hill and overlooking Monterey Bay at 1 Chaminade Lane (just off Paul Sweet Rd.), 831/475-5600 or 800/283-6569, website: www.chaminade.com. Occupying the old Chaminade Brothers Seminary and Monastery, this quiet resort and conference center offers a wealth of business amenities—but also personal perks such as a health club (with massage and men's and women's therapy pools), jogging track, heated pool, saunas, and whirlpools. There are lighted tennis courts, too. Rooms and suites are scattered around the 80-acre grounds in 11 "villas" that include shared parlors with refrigerators, wet bars, and conference tables. Rooms feature king or queen beds, in-room coffeemakers, irons and ironing boards, and two direct-line phones. Valet parking and airport transportation are available. Chaminade also boasts two good restaurants and a bar (with meal service), all open to the general public.

Santa Cruz Bed-and-Breakfasts

One of the loveliest newer B&Bs in Santa Cruz is actually the nation's first "BB&B"—Bed, Bud, and Breakfast. The **Compassion Flower Inn,** 216 Laurel St., Santa Cruz, CA 95060, 831/466-0420, website: www.compassionflowerinn.com, opened in March 2000 with the express purpose of being a hemp- and medical marijuana–friendly bed-and-breakfast. The establishment is "named for both the beauty of the passion flower and the compassion of the medical marijuana movement"

to which the owners have dedicated themselves. If you come, don't expect to find some tie-dyed, weed-happy scene reminiscent of San Francisco's Haight-Ashbury district during the Summer of Love. The proprietors have impeccably restored this gothic revival Victorian, at a cost of a half-million dollars. Tastefully and creatively decorated with antiques, hand-painted furniture, and custom tilework, the Compassion Flower Inn instead harks back to its historical roots as the onetime home of Judge Edgar Spalsbury, who made regular trips to a pharmacy downtown to buy opium as a pain medication for his tuberculosis. Rooms range from the fairly simple **Hemp Room** and **Passionflower Room,** "twin" accommodations tucked under the eaves (these two share a bath), to the first-floor, fully wheelchair accessible **Canabliss Room** and the elegant **Lovers' Suite.** Particularly striking in the suite is its bathroom, where exquisite tiled hemp designs wrap the two-person sunken tub. Rates, $100–250, include full organic breakfast, with fresh-baked bread (two-night minimum stay).

Quite inviting and a perfect stay downtown is **The Adobe on Green Street,** 103 Green St., 831/469-9866 or 888/878-2789, website: www.adobeongreen.com. This historic yet unfrilly adobe features four uniquely decorated guest rooms—Adobe, Courtyard, Mission, and Ohlone—that marry elements of Native American, Mexican, and Arts and Crafts style. Amenities include private baths, in-room Jacuzzis, cable TV, and VCRs. Rates run $150–250.

Other Santa Cruz inns tend to cluster near the ocean. Tastefully decorated is the **Cliff Crest Bed and Breakfast Inn,** just blocks from both downtown and Main Beach at 407 Cliff St., 831/427-2609, website: www.cliffcrestinn.com, a Queen Anne by the beach and Boardwalk. Full breakfast is served in the solarium. Rates fall in the $150–250 range, starting at $220. The **Chateau Victorian,** 118 First St., 831/458-9458, website: www.chateauvictorian.com, offers seven rooms a bit more on the frilly side, with queen-sized beds, private tiled bathrooms, and woodburning fireplaces. Local Santa Cruz Mountains wines are served, as are generous continental breakfasts. Rates run $100–150.

For something more formal, the 1910 **Darling House** seaside mansion at 314 W. Cliff Dr., 831/458-1958 or 800/458-1988, website: www.darlinghouse.com, is an elegant 1910 Spanish Revival mansion designed by architect William Weeks. In addition to spectacular ocean views, Darling House offers eight rooms (two with private baths, two with fireplaces), telephones, and TV on request. There's a hot tub in the backyard; robes are provided. If you loved *The Ghost and Mrs. Muir,* you'll particularly enjoy the Pacific Ocean Room here—complete with telescope. Rates, including breakfast and evening beverages, are $100–250.

Legendary is the been-there-forever local landmark, the **Babbling Brook Inn,** 1025 Laurel St., 831/427-2437 or 800/866-1131, website: www.cacoastalinns.com. Once a log cabin, this place was added to and otherwise spruced up by the Countess Florenzo de Chandler. All 13 rooms and suites are quite romantic, with private bathrooms, phones, and TVs. Most are decorated to suggest the works of Old World artists and poets, from Cézanne and Monet to Tennyson. Most also feature a fireplace, private deck, and outside entrance. Two have whirlpool bathtubs. Full breakfast and afternoon wine and cheese (or tea and cookies) are included. Also here: a babbling brook, waterfalls, and a garden gazebo. Rates run $150–250.

For more bed-and-breakfast choices in the greater Santa Cruz area, see the listings below.

STAYING NEAR SANTA CRUZ

Staying in Regional Hostels

In additional to the HI-AYH hostel in downtown Santa Cruz (see above), the region boasts other exceptional budget choices—including the **Pigeon Point** and **Point Montara Lighthouse Hostels** up the coast toward San Francisco, both unique and incredibly cheap for on-the-beach lodgings—if you don't mind bunk beds or spartan couples' rooms. Or try the **Sanborn Park** hostel just over the hills in Saratoga, 408/741-0166 or 408/741-9555, website: www.sanbornparkhostel.org. If you're heading south, another best bet is the new **Carpenter's Hall Hostel** in

Monterey, at 778 Hawthorne St. (see Monterey Camping and Area Hostels). Rates at all are under $50.

Staying in New Davenport

If you're heading up the coast from Santa Cruz, consider a meal stop or a stay at the **Davenport Bed and Breakfast Inn,** 31 Davenport Ave. (Hwy. 1), 831/425-1818 or 800/870-1817, website: www.davenportinn.com. The 12 comfortable rooms are upstairs, above the New Davenport Cash Store and Restaurant, where the food is very good at breakfast, lunch, and dinner. Rates, including full breakfast, are $100–150. Some of the pastries served here are made just up the road at **Whale City Bakery Bar & Grill,** 831/423-9803 or 831/429-6209, where the wide variety of homemade treats and very good coffee are always worth a stop.

Staying in Ben Lomond and Felton

Nothing fancy, but fine for pine-paneled cabin ambience just five miles north of Santa Cruz, the **Fern River Resort Motel,** 5250 Hwy. 9, Felton, 831/335-4412, website: www.fernriver.com, offers 14 cabins with kitchens or kitchenettes, fireplaces, cable TV, and a private beach on the river. Rates are $50–150.

For a bed-and-breakfast stay in Ben Lomond, consider the lovely and woodsy **Fairview Manor,** 245 Fairview Ave., 831/336-3355 or 800/553-8840, website: www.fairviewmanor.com, which features five rooms with private baths as well as a big deck overlooking the San Lorenzo River. Rates run $100–150. For a super-stylish (and expensive) stay, there's the elegant **Inn at Felton Crest,** 780 El Solyo Heights Dr., Felton, 831/335-4011 (also fax) or 800/474-4011, website: www.feltoncrest.com, featuring just four guest rooms—each on a separate floor—with in-room Jacuzzis, cable TV and VCRs, and private baths. Rates: $250 and up.

Staying in Soquel and Capitola

The **Blue Spruce Inn,** 2815 S. Main St. in Soquel, 831/464-1137 or 800/559-1137, website: www.bluespruce.com, is a romantic 1875 Victorian farmhouse just a few miles from downtown Santa Cruz. Its six rooms—three in the house, three garden rooms—all feature private baths and entrances, queen-sized featherbeds, and unique antique decor color-keyed to handmade Lancaster County quilts. Five rooms have private spas; two have gas fireplaces. Great breakfasts. Rates start at $100.

A long-standing Capitola jewel is the **Capitola Venetian Hotel,** 1500 Wharf Rd., 831/476-6471 or 800/332-2780, website: www.capitolavenetian.com, California's first condominium complex, built in the 1920s. These clustered, Mediterranean-style stucco apartments are relaxed and relaxing, and close to the beach. In various combinations, rooms have kitchens with stoves and refrigerators, in-room coffeemakers, color TV with cable, and telephones with voicemail and data ports; some have separate living rooms, balconies, ocean views, and fireplaces. Rates are $150–250, with real deals available in the off-season.

Almost legendary almost overnight, Capitola's **Inn at Depot Hill,** 250 Monterey Ave., 831/462-3376 or 800/572-2632, website: www.cacoastalinns.com, is a luxurious bed-and-breakfast (essentially a small luxury hotel) housed in the one-time railroad depot. Each of the eight rooms features its own unique design motif, inspired by international themes (the Delft Room, Stratford-on-Avon, the Paris Room, and Portofino, for example), as well as a private garden and entrance, fireplace, telephone with modem/fax capability, and state-of-the-art TV/VCR and stereo system. The private white-marble bathrooms feature bathrobes, hair dryers, and other little luxuries. Bathrooms have double showers, so two isn't necessarily a crowd. The pure linen bed sheets are hand washed and hand ironed daily. Rates include full breakfast, afternoon tea or wine, and after-dinner dessert. Off-street parking is provided. Rates are $150 and up, though ask about winter specials (up to 40 percent off rack rates) and off-season packages.

Staying in Aptos

The apartment-style **Rio Sands Motel,** 116 Aptos Beach Dr., 831/688-3207 or 800/826-2077, website: www.riosands.com, has a heated pool, spa, and decent rooms not far from the beach. The "kitchen suites" feature full kitchens and a separate sitting room and sleep up to four. "Super rooms"

MELISSA SHEROWSKI

Capitola, California's first seaside resort

FOREST OF NISENE MARKS STATE PARK

Forest of Nisene Marks is definitely a hiker's park. Named for the Danish immigrant who hiked here until the age of 96 and whose family donated the land for public use, Nisene Marks is an oasis of solitude. (This was also the epicenter of the 1989 earthquake that brought down much of Santa Cruz.) You'll have lots to see here but little more than birdsong, rustling leaves, and babbling brooks to listen to. The park encompasses 10,000 acres of hefty second-growth redwoods on the steep southern range of the Santa Cruz Mountains, six creeks, lovely Maple Falls, alders, maples, and more rugged trails than anyone can hike in a day. Also here are an old mill site, abandoned trestles and railroad tracks, and logging cabins.

To get here from the coast, take the Aptos-Seacliff exit north from Hwy. 1 and turn right on Soquel Drive. At the first left after the stop sign, drive north on Aptos Creek Rd. and across the railroad tracks. (Bring water and food for day trips. No fires allowed.) The park is open daily 6 A.M.–sunset. For information and a trail map, contact: Forest of Nisene Marks State Park, Aptos Creek Rd., Aptos, CA 95003, 831/763-7062. Call for information about the trailside campsites—a six-mile one-way hike, just six sites, primitive, first-come, first camped, $3 per night.

sleep up to six and include a refrigerator and microwave. All rooms have two TVs. Extras include the large heated pool, spa, picnic area with barbecue pits, and expanded continental breakfast. Peak-season rates are $150–250, with real deals ($100–150) available in winter.

Also a pleasant surprise is the **Best Western Seacliff Inn,** just off the highway at 7500 Old Dominion Court, 831/688-7300 or 800/367-2003. It's a cut or two above the usual motel and an easy stroll to the beach. The rooms are large and comfortable, with private balconies. They cluster village-style around a large outdoor pool and Jacuzzi area. Suites have in-room spas. But the best surprise of all is the restaurant, **Severino's,** 831/688-8987, which serves good food both inside the dining room and outside by the koi pond. Great "sunset dinner" specials are served Sunday through Thursday 5 to 6:30 P.M. Rates are $150–250.

On the coast just north of Manresa State Beach is the condo-style **Seascape Resort Monterey Bay,** 1 Seascape Resort Dr., 831/688-6800 or 800/929-7727, website: www.seascaperesort.com. Choices here include tasteful studios and one- and two-bedroom villas. You'll also find a restaurant, golf course, tennis courts, and on-site fitness and spa facilities. Two-night minimum stay, late May through September. Rates are expensive, $250 and up.

For a bed-and-breakfast stay, the historic **Sand Rock Farm** at 6901 Freedom Blvd., 831/688-8005, website: www.sandrockfarm.com, offers a huge, exquisitely restored, turn-of-the-20th-century Craftsman-style home—complete with original push-button light switches. The 10-acre setting includes country gardens, walking trails, and the ruins of the old Liliencrantz family winery. Open since fall 2000, Sand Rock features five guest rooms and suites with in-room Jacuzzis, cable TV, VCRs, and private baths, plus a lounge, fireplace, hot tub, and room service. Well-informed foodies will make a beeline to Sand Rock strictly for the wondrous breakfasts created by famed Chef Lynn Sheehan. Rates are $150–250.

Historic Victoriana in Aptos includes the **Apple Lane Inn,** 6265 Soquel Dr., 831/475-6868 or 800/649-8988, website: www.applelaneinn.com. Rates are $100–250. Also quite nice, and near Forest of Nisene Marks State Park, is the newly restored and redecorated **Bayview Hotel Bed and Breakfast Inn,** 8041 Soquel Dr., 831/688-8654 or 800/422-9843, website: www.bayviewhotel.com, an 1878 Italianate Victorian hotel with new owners and 12 elegant guest rooms, all with private baths and some with fireplaces and two-person tubs. Rooms also feature TVs, telephones, and modem hookups. Rates are $100–150.

Another possibility is the **Aptos Beach Inn,** once known as the Inn at Manresa Beach, 1258 San Andreas Rd. in La Selva Beach, 831/728-1000 or 888/523-2244, website: www.aptos beachinn.com, built in 1897 as a replica of Abraham Lincoln's home in Springfield, Illinois. One grass and two clay courts are available for tennis, and guests can also play badminton, croquet, or volleyball on the lawn. The eight rooms and suites here feature king or queen beds, fireplaces, private bathrooms (most with two-person spa tubs), two-line phones, cable TV, VCRs, and stereos. From here amid the strawberry and calla lily fields, it's an easy walk to both Manresa and Sand Dollar State Beaches. Rates are $150–250.

EATING IN SANTA CRUZ

Farm Trails and Farmers' Markets

To do Santa Cruz area farm trails, pick up a copy of the *Country Crossroads* map and brochure, a joint venture with Santa Clara County row-crop farmers and orchardists. It's the essential guide for hunting down strawberries, raspberries, apples, and homegrown veggies of all kinds. Or head for the local farmers' markets. The **Santa Cruz Community Certified Farmers' Market,** 831/335-7443, is held downtown at Lincoln and Cedar every Wednesday from 2:30 to 6:30 P.M. There are many other markets in the area; inquire at the visitors center for a current listing.

Near the Beach in Santa Cruz

Unforgettable for breakfast or lunch is funky **Aldo's,** 616 Atlantic Ave. (at the west end of the yacht harbor), 831/426-3736. The breakfast menu features various egg and omelette combinations. Best of all, though, is the raisin toast, made with Aldo's homemade focaccia bread. Eat outdoors on the old picnic tables covered with checkered plastic tablecloths and enjoy the sun, sea air, and seagulls. At lunch and dinner, look for homemade pastas and fresh fish.

The Boardwalk alone features about 20 restaurants and food stands. The best Sunday brunch experience around is also here, at the historic **Cocoanut Grove,** 400 Beach, 831/423-2053, a veritable feast for the eyes as well as the stomach. In good weather, you'll enjoy the sunny atmosphere created by the sunroof. Nearby, along streets near the beach and Boardwalk, are a variety of restaurants, everything from authentic and casual ethnic eateries to sit-down dining establishments. Head to the municipal wharf to see what's new in the fresh-off-the-boat seafood department.

For romantic California-style and continental cuisine, the place is **Casablanca Restaurant,** 101 Main St. (at Beach), 831/426-9063, open for dinner nightly and brunch on Sunday. Lively for worldly American—and a surprising selection of vegetarian—options is **Blacks Beach Café,** E. Cliff at 15th, 831/475-2233, open Tuesday through Sunday for dinner, on weekends for brunch.

Veggie Fare and Other Cheap Eats

The Crepe Place, 1134 Soquel Ave., 831/429-6994, offers inexpensive breakfasts, dessert crêpes (and every other kind), good but unpretentious lunches, and dinners into the wee hours—a great place for late-night dining. Open daily for lunch and dinner, on weekends for brunch. The **Saturn Cafe,** downtown at 145 Laurel St., 831/429-8505, has inexpensive ($8 or less) and wonderful vegetarian meals for lunch, dinner, and beyond. Open daily for lunch and dinner, until late for desserts and coffee (Sunday through Thursday 11:30 A.M.–3:00 A.M., Friday and Saturday 11:30 A.M.–4 A.M.). Theme days here can be a scream. During Monday Madness, Chocolate Madness sells at two for the price of one. Random Tuesdays, on random Tuesdays, feature local live music. On Wig-Out Wednesday, just wear a wig and you'll get 20 percent off your tab. Such a deal.

A vegetarian visit to Santa Cruz wouldn't be complete without feasting at the **Whole Earth Restaurant** on the UC Santa Cruz campus (Redwood Blvd. next to the library), 831/426-8255. A quiet, comfortable place, this very fine organic eatery was the inspiration and training ground for Sharon Cadwallader's well-known *Whole Earth Cookbook* and its sequel. After all these years, the food is still good and still reasonable. For "natural fast foods," don't miss **Dharma's**

Natural Foods Restaurant, in Capitola at 4250 Capitola Rd., 831/462-1717, where you can savor a Brahma Burger, Dharma Dog, or Nuclear Sub sandwich (baked tofu, guacamole, cheese, lettuce, olives, pickle, and secret sauce on a roll).

The **Seabright Brewery** brewpub, 519 Seabright Ave., Ste. 107, 831/426-2739, is popular for its Seabright Amber and Pelican Pale—not to mention casual dining out on the patio. If you're heading toward Boulder Creek, beer fans, stop by the **Boulder Creek Brewery and Cafe,** 13040 Hwy. 9, 831/338-7882.

The Santa Cruz Coffee Roasting Company at the Palomar Inn, 1330 Pacific Ave., 831/459-0100, serves excellent coffee and a bistro-style café lunch. Not far away and absolutely wonderful is **Zoccoli's Delicatessen,** 1534 Pacific Ave., 831/423-1711, where it's common to see people lining up for sandwiches, salads, fresh homemade pastas, and genuine "good deal" lunch specials, usually under $5. Open Monday through Saturday 9 A.M. to 5:30 P.M.

MELISSA SHEROWSKI

Zoccoli's sidewalk seating

Best Bets Downtown

Downtown Santa Cruz is getting pretty uptown these days. A case in point: Eccentric India Joze, 1001 Center St., serving up affordable Southeast Asian and Middle Eastern food since 1971—and responsible for launching the famed Santa Cruz **International Calamari Festival**—has been replaced by the relaxed yet sophisticated San Francisco-style Mediterranean **Restaurant Azur,** 831/427-3554, which opened in late 2000. Enjoy such things as seafood gazpacho, pizzas, and spit-roasted chicken at lunch, similar fare plus braised salmon, roast leg of lamb, pork rib chops, and New York steak at dinner (veggie selections always available). There's a tasting menu, too, and a nice patio. Naturally raised meat and organic local produce are served at Azur, along with wines by the glass; $10 corkage fee. Open Tuesday through Friday noon to 10 or 11 P.M., Saturday from 4:30 P.M., Sunday 11 A.M. to 3 P.M. for brunch and 3 to 9 P.M. for dinner.

El Palomar at the Pacific Garden Mall, 1336 Pacific Ave., 831/425-7575, is a winner for relaxed Mexican meals—especially seafood. For about a decade now, it's been just about everybody's top choice for south-of-the-border fare. Open daily for breakfast, lunch, and dinner. Full bar. (At the yacht harbor, you'll find **Café El Palomar,** 2222 E. Cliff Dr., 831/462-4248, open 7 A.M. to 5 P.M. daily.)

Quite fashionable yet eclectic for ethnic fare is the fairly affordable **Pearl Alley Bistro & Café,** 110 Pearl Alley (at Cedar), 831/429-8070, open daily for lunch (until 5 P.M.) and dinner. Full bar.

Chaminade

The old Chaminade Brothers Seminary and Monastery, 1 Chaminade Lane (just off Paul Sweet Rd.), 831/475-5600, fell into the hands of developers and is now Chaminade Executive Conference Center and Resort. As part of the deal, the new owners had to include a public restaurant in their development plans. The **Sunset Dining Room at Chaminade** is the place to come on Friday nights for no doubt the best seafood buffet in Santa Cruz County—15 types of fish and seafood, an outdoor grill, and a spectac-

NEWMAN'S OWN SANTA CRUZ

Not Paul Newman, but the other one—Nell Newman, Cool Hand Luke's daughter—is the farm-loving Santa Cruz resident posing with the actor on all those tongue-in-cheek, stylized *American Gothic* Newman's Own Organics product labels.

Formerly a biologist with the Ventana Wilderness Sanctuary Research and Education Center down the coast in Big Sur, Nell Newman is an accomplished cook who in 1993 was inspired by the Santa Cruz area's love affair with whole food to add an organics division to her father's popular company, Newman's Own.

The point of Newman's Own Organics is producing "good tasting food that just happens to be organic." So far the brand has focused on what might be considered the inessentials—snack foods including chocolate bars, tortilla chips, pretzels, Pop's Corn, and several cookie varieties, from Fig Newmans to Oreo-like Newman-O's.

Like the first generation of Newman's Own, Newman's Own Organics—the second generation—donates 100 percent of after-tax profits to charitable causes. To date these have included the University of California Santa Cruz Farm and Garden Project, the Organic Farming Research Foundation, the Henry A. Wallace Institute for Alternative Agriculture, and the Western Environmental Law Center in Taos, New Mexico. For more information, see www.newmans ownorganics.com.

ular view of Monterey Bay. It's worth every penny of the (fairly high) price. The Sunset Room also serves appetizing breakfast, lunch, and dinner buffets and a popular Sunday brunch. Outdoor dining is available, weather permitting. Open daily; reservations advised. You can also sign on for a stay here (see Staying in Santa Cruz, above).

EATING NEAR SANTA CRUZ
Eating in Soquel
The **Little Tampico,** 2605 Main St., 831/475-4700, isn't exactly inexpensive. A real bargain, though, is the specialty Otila's Plate: a mini-taco, enchilada, tostada, and taquito, plus rice and beans. Another good choice: nachos with everything. (Various Tampico restaurant relatives dot the county.) Another popular Mexican restaurant is **Tortilla Flats,** 4616 Soquel Dr., 831/476-1754. Open daily for lunch, dinner, and Sunday brunch.

Eating in Capitola
Dharma's Natural Foods Restaurant, a Santa Cruz institution at 4250 Capitola Rd., 831/462-1717, is purported to be the oldest completely vegetarian restaurant in the country. Open daily

for breakfast, lunch, and dinner. Also classic in Capitola is **Mr. Toots Coffeehouse,** upstairs at 221-A Esplanade, 831/475-3679, where you can get a cup of joe until late, and **Pizza-My-Heart,** 209-A Esplanade, 831/475-5714.

Casual, in more upscale style, and unbeatable for pastries and decadent desserts is **Gayle's Bakery and Rosticceria,** 504 Bay Ave., 831/462-1200. The rosticceria has a wonderful selection of salads and homemade pastas, soups, sandwiches, pizza, spit-roasted meats—even dinners-to-go and heat-and-serve casseroles. But the aromas drifting in from Gayle's Bakery are the real draw. The bakery's breakfast pastries include various cheese Danishes, croissants, chocolatine, lemon tea bread, muffins, pecan rolls, apple nut turnovers, and such specialties as a schnecken ring smothered in walnuts. The apple crumb and ollalieberry pies are unforgettable, not to mention the praline cheesecake and the two dozen other cakes—chocolate mousse, hasselnuss, raspberry, poppy seed, mocha. . . (All pies and cakes are also served by the slice.) For decadence-to-go, try Grand Marnier truffles, florentines, éclairs, or Napoleons. Gayle's also sells more than two dozen types of fresh-baked bread. The Capitola sourdough bread and sour baguette would be good for picnics, as would the two-pound loaf of the excellent Pain de Compagne. Gayle's is open daily 7 A.M. to 7 P.M. (If you're heading toward the bay or San Jose the back way via Corralitos, stop by the **Corralitos Market and Sausage Co.**, 569 Corralitos Rd. Watsonville, 831/722-2633, for homemade sausages, smoke-cured ham and turkey breast, or other specialty meats—all great with Gayle's breads.)

Near the beach, on or near the Esplanade, you'll find an endless variety of eateries. **Margaritaville**, 221 Esplanade, 831/476-2263, serves appetizers and sandwiches along with its margaritas. Open for lunch and dinner daily and for brunch on weekends. The **Paradise Beach Grill**, 215 Esplanade, 831/476-4900, offers California cuisine as well as a variety of international dishes. Great views. Open for lunch and dinner daily. Also serving California cuisine is **Zelda's on the Beach,** 203 Esplanade, 831/475-4900, which features an affordable lobster special on Thursday night.

The most famous restaurant in Capitola is the **Shadowbrook Restaurant,** 1750 Wharf Rd. (at Capitola Rd.), 831/475-1511, known for its romantic garden setting—ferns, roses, ivy outside, a Monterey pine and plants inside—and the tram ride down the hill to Soquel Creek. The Shadowbrook is open for "continental-flavored American" dinners nightly. The wine list is extensive. Brunch, with choices like apple and cheddar omelettes, is served on weekends. Reservations recommended.

Eating in Aptos

The **Bittersweet Bistro,** 787 Rio Del Mar Blvd., 831/662-9799, offers Mediterranean-inspired bistro fare featuring fresh local and organic produce—everything from Greek pizzettas and seafood puttanesca to garlic chicken and grilled Monterey Bay king salmon. Open Tuesday through Sunday for "bistro hour" (3 to 6 P.M.)—half-priced pizzettas and drink specials—and for dinner. The best place around for Thai food, locals say, is **Bangkok West**, 2505 Cabrillo College Dr., 831/479-8297, open daily for lunch and dinner. For stylish and fresh Mexican food, the place is **Palapas** at Seascape Village on Seascape

Boulevard, 831/662-9000, open daily for lunch and dinner, brunch on Sunday.

For a romantic dinner, splurge at the **Cafe Sparrow,** 8042 Soquel Dr., 831/688-6238, which serves pricey but excellent country French cuisine at lunch and dinner daily. Family friendly. Open Monday through Saturday for lunch, daily for dinner. Extensive wine list.

SHOPPING SANTA CRUZ

Clothing shops abound along Pacific Avenue, places such as **The Vault** at 1339 Pacific Ave., 831/426-3349, noted for unique jewelry and clothing, and **Eco Goods** at 1130 Pacific Ave., 831/429-5758, "an alternative general store offering organic, recycled, and non-toxic products at affordable prices"—everything from organic cotton underwear and hemp backpacks to handcrafted maple bedroom sets. **Madame Sidecar** at 907 Cedar St., 831/458-1606, offers distinctive style in quality women's clothing, lingerie, jewelry, and accessories—inspired by flattering 1930s and 1940s fashions.

Downtown also boasts thrift and vintage clothing shops. **Ample Annies,** 717 Pacific Ave., 831/425-3838, is the vintage destination for larger sizes. **Cognito,** 821 Pacific, 831/426-5414, offers such things as swing dance fashions, two-toned panel shirts, and Hawaiian shirts. Other best bets include **Moon Zoom Endangered Clothing,** 813 Pacific, 831/423-8500; **Volume!,** 803 Pacific, 831/457-9262; and **The Wardrobe,** 113 Locust St., 831/429-6363.

There are plenty of bookstores, too, including the classic **Bookshop Santa Cruz,** 1520 Pacific Ave., 831/423-0900, a community institution that offers a full calendar of author and reader events. Downtown also draws music fans, to **Rhythm Fusion,** 1541 Pacific, 831/423-2048, and **Union Grove Music,** 1003 Pacific, 831/427-0670.

Santa Cruz County is marvelous for locally made wares—some almost affordable. Barbra Streisand and Oprah Winfrey are among the national fans of Santa Cruz's **Annieglass,** which has a shop downtown at 109 Cooper St., 831/427-4260. Translucent sculptural glass dinnerware with fused metal rims, Annieglass comes in various styles, including Roman antique gold or platinum. Also check out **Strini Art Glass** at the Pacific Garden Mall, 103 Locust, 831/462-4240. **Artisans Gallery,** 1368 Pacific Ave., 831/423-8183, features handcrafted leather, wood, pottery, and other wares, with an emphasis on local craftspeople. For a large selection of strictly local wares, head for the Santa Cruz Wharf and **Made in Santa Cruz,** 831/426-2257 or toll-free 800/982-2367, website: www.madeinsantacruz.com, where you'll find everything from art glass, ceramics, and sculpture—check out the struttin' teapots—to soap, salsa, and jewelry.

For a truly unique housewarming gift, head for **West Coast Weather Vanes** in Bonny Doon, 831/425-5505 or toll-free (U.S.) 800/762-8736, a company whose artisans carefully craft—without molds—copper and brass weather vanes in the Victorian tradition. Visitors are welcome by appointment.

For more shopping ideas, contact the **Downtown Association of Santa Cruz,** 831/429-1512, website: www.downtownsantacruz.com, and the **Santa Cruz County Conference & Visitors Council,** 831/425-1234 or 800/833-3494, website: www.santacruzca.org.

SANTA CRUZ INFORMATION AND SERVICES

Santa Cruz Visitor Information

The best all-around source for city and county information is the **Santa Cruz County Conference and Visitors Council,** downtown at 1211 Ocean St., 831/425-1234 or 800/833-3494, website: www.santacruzca.org, open Monday through Saturday 9 A.M. to 5 P.M., Sunday 10 A.M. to 4 P.M. Definitely request the current accommodations, dining, and visitor guides. If you've got time to roam farther afield, also pick up a current copy of the *County Crossroads* farm trails map and ask about area wineries. Cyclists, request the *Santa Cruz County Bikeway Map.* Antiquers, ask for the current *Antiques, Arts, & Collectibles* directory for Santa Cruz and Monterey Counties, published every June—

not a complete listing, by far, but certainly a good start. If you once were familiar with Santa Cruz and—post-1989 earthquake—now find yourself lost, pick up the *Downtown Santa Cruz Directory* brochure.

Useful Publications

A valuable source of performing arts information, focused on the university, is the *UCSC Performing Arts Calendar,* published quarterly and available all around town. The excellent UC Santa Cruz paper, *City on a Hill,* is published only during the regular school year. *Santa Cruz Good Times* is a good, long-running free weekly with an entertainment guide and sometimes entertaining political features. The free *Student Guide* comes out seasonally, offering lots of ads and some entertaining reading about Santa Cruz.

The *Santa Cruz County Sentinel* and the *Watsonville Register-Pajaronian* are the traditional area papers. The **Santa Cruz Parks and Recreation Department** at Harvey West Park, 307 Church St., 831/429-3663, open weekdays 8 A.M. to noon and 1 to 5 P.M., usually publishes a *Summer Activity Guide* (especially useful for advance planning).

Santa Cruz Services

The Santa Cruz post office is at 850 Front St., 831/426-5200, and is open weekdays 8 A.M. to 5 P.M. The **Santa Cruz Public Library** is at 224 Church St., 831/420-5700. (If you want to hobnob with the people on the hill, visit the **Dean McHenry Library** on campus, 831/459-4000.) For senior information, stop by the **Senior Center,** 222 Market, 831/423-6640, or 1777 Capitola Rd., 831/462-1433.

SANTA CRUZ TRANSPORTATION

Getting Here

If you're driving from the San Francisco Bay Area, the preferred local route to Santa Cruz (and the only main alternative to Highway 1) is I-280 or 880 south to San Jose, then hop over the hills on the congested and treacherously twisting Highway 17.

The **Greyhound** bus terminal is at 425 Front St., 831/423-1800, open weekdays 7:30 A.M. to 8 P.M. Greyhound provides service from San Francisco to Santa Cruz, Fort Ord, and Monterey, as well as connections south to L.A. via Salinas or San Jose. From the East Bay and South Bay, take Amtrak (see below), now also offering bus connections from Salinas. You can get *close* to Santa Cruz by plane. The **San Jose International Airport,** 408/501-7600, website: www.sjc.org, the closest major airport in the north and not far from Santa Cruz, is served by commuter and major airlines. Or fly into Monterey (see Monterey Transportation).

Getting Around

Bicyclists will be in hog heaven here, with everything from excellent bike lanes to locking bike racks at bus stops. But drivers be warned: Parking can be impossible, especially in summer, especially at the beach. There's a charge for parking at the Boardwalk (in lots with attendants) and metered parking elsewhere. Best bet: Park elsewhere and take the shuttle. Second best: Drive to the beach, unload passengers and beach paraphernalia, then park a mile or so away. By the time you walk back, your companions should be done battling for beach towel space.

You can usually find free parking on weekends in the public garage at the county government center at 701 Ocean Street, conveniently also a stop for the **Santa Cruz Beach Shuttle** on summer weekends. The shuttle—a great way to avoid parking nightmares—provides regular service between the county government center, downtown, and the wharf area, weekends only Memorial Day through Labor Day. The fare is $1.

The **Santa Cruz Metro,** 230 Walnut Ave., 831/425-8600, website: www.scmtd.com, provides superb public transit throughout the northern Monterey Bay area. The Metro has a "bike and ride" service for bicyclists who want to hitch a bus ride partway (bike racks onboard). Call for current route information or pick up a free copy of the excellent *Headways* (which includes Spanish translations). Buses will get you anywhere you want to go in town and considerably beyond for $1 ($3 for an all-day pass)—exact change only.

THE ROARING CAMP AND BIG TREES RAILROAD

F♦ Norman Clark, the self-described "professional at oddities" who also owns the narrow-gauge railroad in Felton, bought the Southern Pacific rails connecting Santa Cruz and nearby Olympia, to make it possible for visitors to get to Henry Cowell Redwoods State Park and Felton (*almost* to Big Basin) by train. During logging's commercial heyday here in the 1900s, 20 or more trains passed over these tracks every day.

Today you can still visit Roaring Camp and ride the rails on one of two different trips. Hop aboard a 100-year-old steam engine and make an hour-and-fifteen-minute loop around a virgin redwood forest ($15 general, $10 kids 3–12), or take a 1940s-vintage passenger train from Felton down to Santa Cruz (roundtrip fare $16.50 general, $11.50 kids 3–12). The year-round calendar of special events includes October's **Harvest Faire** and the **Halloween Ghost Train,** the **Mountain Man Rendezvous** living history encampment in November, and December's **Pioneer Christmas.**

The railroad offers daily runs (usually just one train a day on nonsummer weekdays) from spring through November and operates only on weekends and major holidays in winter. For more information, contact: Roaring Camp and Big Trees Narrow-Gauge Railroad, 831/335-4484, fax 831/335-3509, www.roaringcamp.com.

You can rent a car from **Enterprise Rent-A-Car,** 1025-B Water St., 831/426-7799 or 800/325-8007; **Avis,** 630 Ocean St., 831/423-1244 or 800/831-2847; or **Budget,** 919 Ocean St., 831/425-1808 or 800/527-0700. **Yellow Cab** is at 131 Front St., 831/423-1234, also home to the **Santa Cruz Airporter,** 831/423-1214 or toll-free in California 800/223-4142, which provides shuttle van service to both the San Francisco and San Jose Airports, as well as to *Caltrain* and the Amtrak station in San Jose (see also Getting Away, below).

For some guided assistance in seeing the sights, contact **Earth, Sea and Sky Tours,** P.O. Box 1630, Aptos, CA 95001, 831/688-5544.

Getting Away

Metro buses can get you to Boulder Creek, Big Basin State Park, Ben Lomond, Felton, north coast beaches, *almost* all the way to Año Nuevo State Reserve just across the San Mateo County line, and to south coast beaches and towns. (**Monterey-Salinas Transit** from Watsonville provides good service in Monterey County.) For ridesharing out of town, check the ride board at UC Santa Cruz and local classifieds.

Another way to get out of town is via Santa Cruz Metro's **Caltrain Connector** buses to the San Jose train station—more than 10 trips daily on weekdays (fewer on weekends and holidays)—which directly connect with **Caltrain** (to San Francisco) and **Amtrak** (to Oakland, Berkeley, and Sacramento). The fare is just $6. For information on the Connector, call 831/425-8600. For Caltrain fares and schedules, call 650/508-6200 or 800/660-4287 (in the service area). For Amtrak, contact 800/872-7245 or website: www.amtrak.com.

North of Santa Cruz

Travelers heading north toward San Francisco via Highway 1 will discover Año Nuevo State Reserve, breeding ground for the northern elephant seal—quite popular, so don't expect to just drop by—and two delightful hostels housed in former lighthouses. Not far from Año Nuevo, as the crow flies, is spectacular Big Basin Redwoods State Park, California's first state park, and other spectacular redwood parks.

AÑO NUEVO STATE RESERVE

About 20 miles north of Santa Cruz and just across the county line is the 4,000-acre Año Nuevo State Reserve, breeding ground and rookery for sea lions and seals—particularly the unusual (and once nearly extinct) northern elephant seal. The pendulous proboscis of a "smiling" two- to three-ton alpha bull dangles down like a fire hose, so the name is apt.

At first glance, the windswept and cold seaward stretch of Año Nuevo seems almost desolate, inhospitable to life. This is far from the truth, however. Año Nuevo is the only place in the world where people can get off their bikes or the bus or get out of their cars and walk out among aggressive, wild northern elephant seals in their natural habitat. Especially impressive is that first glimpse of hundreds of these huge seals nestled like World War II torpedoes among the sand dunes. A large number of other animal and plant species also consider this area home; to better appreciate the ecologically fascinating animal and plant life of the entire area, read *The Natural History of Año Nuevo,* by Burney J. Le Boeuf and Stephanie Kaza.

California poppies explode in bloom on the hillsides of Año Nuevo State Reserve.

SANTA CRUZ

MELISSA SHEROWSKI

the visitors center at Año Nuevo State Reserve

Survival of the Northern Elephant Seal

Hunted almost to extinction for their oil-rich blubber, northern elephant seals numbered only 20 to 100 at the turn of the 20th century. All these survivors lived on Isla de Guadalupe off the west coast of Baja California. Their descendants eventually began migrating north to California. In the 1950s, a few arrived at Año Nuevo Island, attracted to its rocky safety. The first pup was born on the island in the 1960s. By 1975 the mainland dunes had been colonized by seals crowded off the island rookery, and the first pup was born onshore. By 1988, 800 northern elephant seals were born on the mainland, part of a total known population of more than 80,000 and an apparent ecological success story. (Only time will tell, though, since the species' genetic diversity has been eliminated by the swim at the brink of extinction.) Though Año Nuevo was the first northern elephant seal rookery established on the California mainland, northern elephant seals are now establishing colonies elsewhere along the state coastline.

The Año Nuevo Mating Season

Male northern elephant seals start arriving in December. Who arrives first and who remains dominant among the males during the long mating season is important because the alpha bull gets to breed with most of the females. Since the males are biologically committed to conserving their energy for sex, they spend much of their time lying about as if dead, in or out of the water, often not even breathing for stretches of up to a half hour. Not too exciting for spectators. But when two males battle each other for the "alpha" title, the loud, often bloody nose-to-nose battles are something to see. Arching up with heads back and canine teeth ready to tear flesh, the males bellow and bark and bang their chests together.

In January the females start to arrive, ready to bear offspring conceived the previous year. They give birth to their pups within the first few days of their arrival. The males continue to wage war, the successful alpha bull now frantically trying to protect his harem of 50 or so females from marauders. For every two pounds in body weight a pup gains, its mother loses a pound. Within

28 days, she loses about half her weight, then, almost shriveled, she leaves. Her pup, about 60 pounds at birth, weighs 300 to 500 pounds a month later. Although inseminated by the bull before leaving the rookery, the emaciated female is in no condition for another pregnancy, so conception is delayed for several months, allowing the female to feed and regain her strength. Then, after an eight-month gestation period, the cycle starts all over again.

Año Nuevo Etiquette

The Marine Mammal Act of 1972 prohibits people from harassing or otherwise disturbing these magnificent sea mammals, so be respectful. While walking among the elephant seals, remember that the seemingly sluglike creatures *are* wild beasts and can move as fast as any human across the sand, though for shorter distances. For this reason, keeping a 20-foot minimum distance between you and the seals (especially during the macho mating season) is important. No food or drinks are allowed on the reserve, and nothing in the reserve may be disturbed. The first males often begin to arrive in November, before the official docent-led tours begin, so it's possible to tour the area unsupervised. Visit the dunes without a tour guide in spring and summer also, when many elephant seals return here to molt.

The reserve's "equal access boardwalk" across the sand makes it possible for physically challenged individuals to see the seals.

Information and Tours

Official 2.5-hour guided tours of Año Nuevo begin in December and continue through March, rain or shine, though January and February are the prime months, and reservations are necessary. The reserve is open 8 A.M. to sunset; the day-use parking fee is $5 (hike-ins and bike-ins are free, but you still must pick up a free day-use permit). Tour tickets ($4 plus surcharge for credit card reservations) are available only through ReserveAmerica's Año Nuevo and Hearst Castle reservations line, 800/444-4445. For international reservations, call 916/414-8400, ext. 4100. Reservations cannot be made before November 1. To take a chance on no-shows, arrive at Año Nuevo before scheduled tours and get on the waiting list. For wheelchair access reservations, December 1 through March 15, call 650/879-2033, 1 to 4 P.M. only on Monday, Wednesday, and Friday.

Organized bus excursions, which include walking tour tickets, are available through **San Mateo Transit,** 945 California Dr., Burlingame, CA 94010, 800/660-4287 or 650/508-6441 (call after November 1 for reservations), and **Santa Cruz Metro** (see Santa Cruz Transportation—Getting Around). The AYH Pigeon Point Hostel, near Año Nuevo, sometimes has extra tickets for hostelers. For more information, contact Año Nuevo State Reserve, New Year's Creek Rd., Pescadero, CA 94060, 650/879-2027 (recorded information) or 650/879-2025, website: www.anonuevo.org.

BIG BASIN REDWOODS STATE PARK

California's first state park was established here, about 24 miles up canyon from Santa Cruz on Highway 9. To save Big Basin's towering *Sequoia sempervirens* coast redwoods from loggers, 60-some conservationists led by Andrew P. Hill camped at the base of Slippery Rock on May 15, 1900, and formed the Sempervirens Club. Just two years later, in September 1902, 3,800 acres of primeval forest were deeded to the state, the beginning of California's state park system.

Big Basin Flora and Fauna

Today, Big Basin Redwoods State Park includes more than 18,000 acres on the ocean-facing slopes of the Santa Cruz Mountains, and efforts to protect (and expand) the park still continue under the auspices of the Sempervirens Fund and the Save-the-Redwoods League. (Donations are always welcome.) Tall coast redwoods and Douglas fir predominate. Wild ginger, violets, and milkmaids are common in spring, also a few rare orchids grow here. Native azaleas bloom in early summer, and by late summer huckleberries are ready for picking. In the fall and winter rainy season, mushrooms and other forest fungi "blossom."

At one time, the coast grizzly (one of seven bear species that roamed the state's lower regions) thrived between San Francisco and San Luis Obispo. The last grizzly was spotted here in 1878. Common are black-tailed deer, raccoons, skunks, and gray squirrels. Rare are mountain lions, bobcats, coyotes, foxes, and opossums. Among the fascinating reptiles in Big Basin is the endangered western skink. Predictably, rattlers are fairly common in chaparral areas, but other snakes are shy. Squawking Steller's jays are ever-present, and acorn woodpeckers, dark-eyed juncos, owls, and hummingbirds—altogether about 250 bird species—also haunt Big Basin. Spotting marbled murrelets (shorebirds that nest 200 feet up in the redwoods) is a birding challenge.

Seeing and Doing Big Basin

The best time to be in Big Basin is in the fall, when the weather is perfect and most tourists have gone home. Winter and spring are also prime times, though usually rainier. Road cuts into the park offer a peek into local geology—tilted, folded, twisted layers of thick marine sediments. Big Basin's **Nature Lodge** museum features good natural history exhibits and many fine books, including *Short Historic Tours of Big Basin* by Jennie and Denzil Verado. The carved-log seating and the covered stage at the amphitheater attract impromptu human performances (harmonica concerts, freestyle soft-shoe, joke routines) when no park campfires or other official events are scheduled.

Also here: more than 80 miles of hiking trails. (Get oriented in the Sempervirens Room adjacent to park headquarters.) Take the half-mile **Redwood Trail** loop to stretch your legs and to see one of the park's most impressive stands of virgin redwoods. Or hike the more ambitious **Skyline-to-the-Sea** trail, at least an overnight trip. It's 11 miles from the basin rim to the seabird haven of Waddell Beach and adjacent **Theodore J. Hoover Natural Preserve,** a freshwater marsh. There are trail camps along the way (camping and fires allowed only in designated areas). Hikers, bring food and water, as Waddell Creek flows with reclaimed wastewater. Another popular route is the **Pine Mountain Trail.** Thanks to recent land acquisitions along the coast north of Santa Cruz, the new 1.5-mile **Whitehouse Ridge Trail** now joins Big Basin with Año Nuevo State Reserve; call ahead or inquire at either park for directions.

the Highway 1 entrance to Big Basin Redwoods State Park

MELISSA SHEROWSKI

Most dramatic in Big Basin are the waterfalls. **Berry Creek Falls** is a particularly pleasant destination, with rushing water, redwood mists, and glistening rocks fringed with delicate ferns. Nearby are both **Silver Falls** and the **Golden Falls Cascade.**

Practical Big Basin

For park information, contact Big Basin Redwoods State Park, 21600 Big Basin Way, Boulder Creek, CA 95006, 831/338-8860. Big Basin has family campsites ($12) plus five group camps. Reserve all campsites through ReserveAmerica, 800/444-7275, website: www.reserveamerica .com, up to seven months in advance. An unusual "outdoor" option: the park's tent cabins. For more information, see Santa Cruz Camping. To reserve backpacker campsites at the park's six trail camps ($5), contact park headquarters. Big Basin's day-use fee is $3 per vehicle (walk-ins and bike-ins are free), and a small fee is charged for the map/brochure showing all trails and major park features. To get oriented to the town, pick up a copy of the Boulder Creek Historical Walking Tour, available at most area merchants and at the **San Lorenzo Valley Historical Museum,** now at home in a onetime church built with

local old-growth redwood at 12547 Hwy. 9, 831/338-8382, at last report open on Wednesday, Saturday, and Sunday afternoons. Call for current details.

OTHER PARKS NEAR BIG BASIN

Henry Cowell Redwoods State Park

The Redwood Grove in the dark San Lorenzo Canyon here is the park's hub and one of the most impressive redwood groves along the central coast, with the Neckbreaker, the Giant, and the Fremont Tree all standouts. You can camp at Graham Hill, picnic near the grove, or head out on the 15-mile web of hiking and horseback trails. New in the summer of 1999 was the **U-Con Trail** connecting Henry Cowell to Wilder Ranch State Park on the coast—making it possible to hike, bike, or horseback ride from the redwoods to the ocean on an established trail. For information about Henry Cowell Redwoods State Park, off Highway 9 in Felton, call 831/335-4598 or 831/438-2396 (campground). Henry Cowell has 150 campsites; reserve through ReserveAmerica, 800/444-7275 or website: www .reserveamerica.com.

Other Parks off Highway 9

Between Big Basin and Saratoga is **Castle Rock State Park,** 15300 Skyline Blvd., Los Gatos, 408/867-2952, an essentially undeveloped park and a hiker's paradise. Ask at Big Basin for current trail information. Primitive campsites are $7 per night. **Highlands County Park,** 8500 Hwy. 9 in Ben Lomond, is open daily 9 A.M. to dusk. This old estate, transformed into a park with picnic tables and nature trails, also has a sandy beach along the river. Another swimming spot is at **Ben Lomond County Park** on Mill Street, which also offers shaded picnic tables and barbecue facilities. Free, open daily in summer. Closer to Big Basin is **Boulder Creek Park** on Middleton Avenue east of Highway 9 in Boulder Creek; also free. The swimming hole here has both shallows and deeps, plus there's a sandy beach. Other facilities include shaded picnic tables and barbecue pits.

UNIQUE STAYS NORTH OF SANTA CRUZ

Unusual in the nature getaway category is **Costanoa Coastal Lodge and Camp** on the coast near Pescadero. In addition to its sophisticated 40-room lodge, deluxe traditional cabins, luxurious "camp bathroom" comfort stations, and gourmet-grub General Store, Costanoa also offers the nation's first "boutique camping resort." Though some RV and pitch-your-own-tent campsites are available, most of the camping provided is tent camping—in 1930s-style canvas "safari tents," complete with skylights, that range from economy to luxury. Deluxe canvas cabins feature queen-size beds, heated mattress pads, nightstands with reading lamps, and Adirondack chairs for taking in the great outdoors. And nature *is* the main attraction. Costanoa itself, near Año Nuevo State Reserve, is linked to four nearby state parks—30,000 acres of hiking trails. Other possible adventures here include mountain biking, sea kayaking, tidepooling, whale-watching, elephant seal observation, and bird-watching. For more information, contact: Costanoa, P.O. Box 842, 2001 Rossi Rd. (at Hwy. 1), Pescadero, CA 94060, 650/879-1100 or toll-free 800/738-7477 for reservations, fax 650/879-2275, website: www.costanoa.com. Pitch-your-own-tent camping is Under $50. RV camping and most canvas cabins: $50–100. Deluxe canvas cabins: $100–150. Regular cabins and lodge rooms: $150–250.

Considerably more affordable—and quite appealing in a back-to-basics style—are the two lighthouse hostels offered in California by Hostelling International-American Youth Hostels (HI-AYH), both located on the coast north of Santa Cruz.

Closest to Santa Cruz is the **Pigeon Point Lighthouse Hostel,** 210 Pigeon Point Rd. (at Hwy. 1) in Pescadero, 650/879-0633 (for phone-tree reservations, call toll-free 800/909-4776 #73), website: www.pigeonpointlighthouse.org— *the* inexpensive place to stay while visiting the elephant seals. Named after the clipper ship *Carrier Pigeon,* one of many notorious shipwrecks off the coastal shoals here, the 1872 lighthouse is now automated but still impressive with its Fresnel lens and distinctive 10-second flash pattern. Lighthouse tours (40 minutes) are offered by state park staff every weekend year-round, and also on Fridays in summer; rain cancels. Small fee. For tour reservations, call 650/879-2120.

The hostel itself is made up of four former family residences for the U.S. Coast Guard—basic male or female bunkrooms, plus some spartan couples' and family rooms. The old Fog Signal Building is now a rec room; there's also a hot tub perched on rocky cliffs above surging surf. Fabulous sunset views, wonderful tidepools. Rates: Under $50. Extra charge for couples'/family rooms and for linen rental (if you don't bring your own sleep sack or sleeping bag). Get groceries in Pescadero and prepare meals in the well-equipped communal kitchens, or ask for local restaurant suggestions. For information and/or to check in, the hostel office is open 7:30–9:30 A.M. and 4:30–9:30 P.M. only. Very popular, so reserve well in advance.

Farther north, beyond Half Moon Bay between Montara and Moss Beach, is picturesque **Point Montara Lighthouse Hostel,** 16th St. at Hwy. 1 in Montara, 650/728-7177 (for phone-tree reservations, call toll-free 800/909-4776 #64), website: www.norcalhostels.org. Point Montara is popular with bicyclists, and it's also accessible via bus from the Bay Area. The 1875 lighthouse itself is no longer in operation, and the Fog Signal Building here is now a roomy woodstove-heated community room. Hostel facilities include kitchens, dining rooms, laundry, bunkrooms, and couples' and family quarters. Volleyball court, outdoor hot tub, and bicycle rentals are also available. Open to travelers of all ages. Popular, so reserve in advance. Under $50. Ask at the office for restaurant recommendations.

Resources

Suggested Reading

The virtual "publisher of record" for all things Californian is the **University of California Press,** 2120 Berkeley Way, Berkeley, CA 94720, 510/642-4247 or toll-free 800/777-4726 and fax 800/999-1958 for orders, website: www.ucpress.edu, which publishes hundreds of titles on the subject—all excellent. Stanford University's **Stanford University Press,** 521 Lomita Mall, Stanford, CA 94305, 650/723-9434, fax 650/725-3457, website: www.sup.org, also offers some books of particular interest to Californiacs—especially under the subject categories of American Literature, California History, and Natural History—though in general these are books of academic interest.

Other publishers offering California titles, particularly general interest, history, hiking, and regional travel titles, include **Chronicle Books,** Division of Chronicle Publishing Co., 85 Second St., Sixth Floor, San Francisco, CA 94105, 415/537-3730 or toll-free 800/722-6657, website: www.chronbooks.com, and **Heyday Books,** 2054 University Ave., Ste. 400, P.O. Box 9145, Berkeley, CA 94709, 510/549-3564, fax 510/549-1889. **Foghorn Outdoors,** Avalon Travel Publishing, 1400 65th Street, Suite 250, Emeryville, CA 94608, 510/595-3664, fax 510/595-4228, website: www.foghorn.com, publishes a generous list of unusual, and unusually thorough, California outdoor guides, including Tom Stienstra's camping, fishing, and "getaways" guides.

Contact these and other publishers, mentioned below, for a complete list of current titles relating to California.

The following book listings represent a fairly basic introduction to relevant books about history, natural history, literature, recreation, and travel. The interested reader can find many other titles by visiting good local bookstores and/or state and national park visitor centers. As always, the author would appreciate suggestions about other books that should be included. Send the names of new candidates—or actual books, if you're either a publisher or an unusually generous person—for *Moon Handbooks: Monterey Bay*'s booklist, not to mention possible text additions, corrections, and suggestions, to: Kim Weir, c/o *Moon Handbooks: Monterey & Carmel,* Avalon Travel Publishing, 1400 65th Street, Suite 250, Emeryville, CA 94608.

Companion Reading, General Travel

Baldy, Marian. *The University Wine Course.* San Francisco: The Wine Appreciation Guild, 1992. Destined to be a classic and designed for both instructional and personal use, this friendly book offers a comprehensive education about wine. *The University Wine Course* explains it all, from viticulture to varietals. And the lips-on lab exercises and chapter-by-chapter examinations help even the hopelessly déclassé develop the subtle sensory awareness necessary for any deeper appreciation of the winemaker's art. Special sections and appendixes on reading (and understanding) wine labels, combining wine and food, and understanding wine terminology make it a lifelong personal library reference. Definitely "do" this book before doing the California wine country. For college wine appreciation instructors and winery personnel, the companion *Teacher's Manual for The University Wine Course* (1993) may also come in handy.

Bierce, Ambrose Gwinnet, wickedly illustrated by Gahan Wilson. *The Devil's Dictionary.* New York: Oxford University Press, 1998. According to *The Devil's Dictionary,* a saint is a "dead sinner revised and edited," and a bore is a "person who talks when you wish him to listen." The satiric aphorisms included herein earned Ambrose Bierce the nicknames Bitter Bierce and the Wickedest Man in San

Francisco, though—considering his talent for heaving his witty pitchfork at any and all he happened to encounter in life—it's clear that Bierce was born way too soon. He would have a field day in contemporary California. Bierce also spent time in Carmel and environs.

Brautigan, Richard. *A Confederate General from Big Sur, Dreaming of Babylon, and the Hawk-line Monster.* New York: Mariner Books, reissue edition, 1991. Did you miss the sixties? If so, you probably also missed Richard Brautigan, whose literary star ascended then flamed out too quickly.

Bright, William O. *1,500 California Place Names: Their Origin and Meaning.* A revised version of the classic *1,000 California Place Names* by Erwin G. Gudde, first published in 1949. University of California Press, 1998. Though you can also get the revised edition of Gudde's original masterpiece (see below), this convenient, alphabetically arranged pocketbook—now in an expanded and updated edition—is perfect for travelers, explaining the names of mountains, rivers, and towns throughout California.

Cain, Pamela, and Larry Ulrich. *Big Sur to Big Basin: California's Dramatic Central Coast.* San Francisco: Chronicle Books, 1998. Here it is, a celebration of the greater Monterey Bay area—from the redwoods and fog of Big Basin to the stony drama of Big Sur—by photographer Larry Ulrich and writer Pamela Cain.

Cameron, Robert (photographer), with text by Harold Gilliam, long-time San Francisco newspaper columnist. *Above Carmel, Monterey and the Big Sur.* San Francisco: Cameron & Co., 1994. Here it is, aerial photo fans— the spectacular seagull's-eye-view of Monterey Bay and Big Sur.

Clark, Donald Thomas. *Monterey County Place Names: A Geographical Dictionary.* Carmel Valley, CA: Kestrel Press, 1991. This marvelous resource, meticulously researched and guaranteed to enlighten all who dip into it, is a gift from the UC Santa Cruz University Librarian, Emeritus. Also well worth searching for, though out of print at last report, is the author's *Santa Cruz County Place Names* (1986).

De La Pérouse, Jean François, with commentary by Malcolm Margolin. *Monterey in 1786: The Journals of Jean François de La Pérouse.* Berkeley: Heyday Books, 1989. On September 14, 1786, two ships sailed out of the fog and into Monterey Bay. The ships were French, *L'Astrolabe* and *La Boussole,* the first foreign vessels to visit the Spanish colonies in California. Onboard, as Malcolm Margolin tells us in his introduction, "was a party of eminent scientists, navigators, cartographers, illustrators, and physicians" sent by King Louis XVI to explore the western coast of North America, look for sea otters (for the fur trade), and report on Spain's colonies. Leader of the expedition was Jean François de La Pérouse, whose journal describes the presidio at Monterey, the mission at Carmel, Indian customs, and the land and its abundant plant and animal life. Reading his journals, as Margolin points out, allows to unfold before us "not a tale of a distant fantasy land, but the far more gripping story of our place, of our times, the story of 'us.'" The journals are greatly enhanced by Margolin's historical introduction and his careful annotations.

Gilbar, Steven. *Natural State: A Literary Anthology of California Nature Writing.* Berkeley: University of California Press, 1998. This hefty and dazzling collection includes many of the writers you'd expect—Gretel Ehrlich, M.F.K. Fisher, John McPhee, John Muir, Gary Snyder, and Robert Louis Stevenson—but also a few surprises, including Joan Didion, Jack Kerouac, and Henry Miller. Not specifically a book about greater Monterey Bay but always an enjoyable California companion.

Gudde, Erwin G. Edited by William O. Bright. *California Place Names: The Origin and Etymology of Current Geographical Names.* Berkeley: University of California Press, 1998. Did you know that *Siskiyou* was the Chinook word for "bobtailed horse," as borrowed from the Cree language? More such complex truths await every time you dip into this fascinating volume—the ultimate guide to California place names (and how to pronounce them). A revised and expanded fourth edition, building upon the masterwork of Gudde, who died in 1969.

Hart, James D. *A Companion to California.* Berkeley: University of California Press. Revised and expanded, 1987 (OP). Another very worthy book for Californiacs to collect, if you can find it, with thousands of brief entries on all aspects of California as well as more in-depth pieces on subjects such as literature.

Jeffers, Robinson. *Selected Poems.* New York: Random House, 1965. The poet Robinson Jeffers died in 1961 at the age of 75, on a rare day when it actually snowed in Carmel. One of California's finest poets, classically sophisticated yet accessible, many of his poems pay homage to the beauty of his beloved Big Sur coast. Poems collected here are selections from some of his major works, including *Be Angry at the Sun, The Beginning and the End, Hungerfield,* and *Tamar and Other Poems.*

Jeffers, Robinson, with an introduction by James Karman, photography by Morley Baer. *Stones of the Sur.* Stanford, CA: Stanford University, 2001. A coffeetable book for people who don't even have coffee tables, this stunning work is crafted from the words of the Carmel poet Robinson Jeffers and the brilliant black-and-white photos of Morley Baer. As a general introduction to the significance of Jeffers's work and his connection to Carmel, scholar James Karman's contribution is invaluable.

Kael, Pauline, Herman J. Mankiewicz, and Orson Welles. *The Citizen Kane Book: Raising Kane.* New York: Limelight Editions, 1984 (OP). Includes an excellent essay on the classic American film—which one can't help wanting to see again, following a tour of Hearst's San Simeon palace—plus script and stills.

Karman, James. *Robinson Jeffers: Poet of California.* Ashland, OR: Story Line Press, Inc., revised second ed., 1995. This marvelous critical biography details the life and times of the reticent poet Robinson Jeffers, for whom the Big Sur coast was once named. "It is not possible to be quite sane here," Jeffers wisely observed. Though here Karman also sympathetically introduces us to Jeffers's wife Una, also of interest to Jeffers fans is Story Line's *Of Una Jeffers* by Edith Greenan.

Kerouac, Jack. *Big Sur.* New York: Penguin USA, reprint edition, 1992. Here is Kerouac's hellish Big Sur hike into the dark side of manic depression, paranoia, and alcoholism, as experienced by his alter ego Jack Dulouz, now a writer experiencing fame. Sobering followup to the more optimistic *On The Road* and *The Dharma Bums.*

Michaels, Leonard, David Reid, and Raquel Scherr, eds. *West of the West: Imagining California.* New York: HarperCollins Publishers, 1991. Though any anthology about California is destined to be incomplete, this one is exceptional—offering selections by Maya Angelou, Simone de Beauvoir, Joan Didion, Umberto Eco, Gretel Ehrlich, M.F.K. Fisher, Aldous Huxley, Jack Kerouac, Maxine Hong Kingston, Rudyard Kipling, Henry Miller, Ishmael Reed, Kenneth Rexroth, Richard Rodriguez, Randy Shilts, Gertrude Stein, John Steinbeck, Octavio Paz, Amy Tan, Gore Vidal, Walt Whitman, and Tom Wolfe.

Miller, Henry. *Big Sur and the Oranges of Hieronymus Bosch.* New York: W.W. Norton & Co., 1978. First published in 1958, the famed writer shares his impressions of art and writing along with his view of life as seen from the Big Sur coastline—the center of his personal universe in his later years, and the first real home he had ever found.

Muscatine, Doris. *The University of California/Sotheby Book of California Wine.* Berkeley: University of California Press, 1984. A rather expensive companion but worthwhile for wine lovers.

Paddison, Joshua, ed. *A World Transformed: Firsthand Accounts of California Before the Gold Rush.* Berkeley: Heyday Books, 1999. According to popular California mythology, the Golden State was "born" with the onrushing change that came with the gold rush of 1848. But this collection of earlier California writings gathers together some intriguing earlier observations—from European explorers and visitors, missionaries, and sea captains—that reveal pre-gold rush California.

Stegner, Wallace Earle. Edited and with a preface from the author's son, Page Stegner. *Marking the Sparrow's Fall: Wallace Stegner's American West.* New York: H. Holt, 1998. This brilliant collection of Stegner's conservation writings traces his development as a Westerner—and as a Western writer—starting with his seemingly inauspicious beginnings as an avid reader, hunkered down in small-town libraries in places almost no one's ever heard of. The first collection of Stegner's work since the author's death in 1993, *Marking the Sparrow's Fall* includes 15 essays never before published, his best-known essays on the American West—including *Wilderness Letter*—and a little-known novella.

Stegner, Wallace Earle. *Where the Bluebird Sings to the Lemonade Springs: Living and Writing in the West.* New York: Penguin USA, 1993. Reprint ed. It's certainly understandable that, at the end of his days, Wallace Stegner wasn't entirely optimistic about the future of the West, bedeviled as it is, still, by development

pressures and insane political decisions. In these 16 thoughtful essays, he spells out his concerns—and again pays poetic homage to the West's big sky and bigger landscapes. In the end, he remains hopeful that a new spirit of place is emerging in the West—and that within a generation or two we will "work out some sort of compromise between what must be done to earn a living and what must be done to restore health to the earth, air, and water."

Steinbeck, John. *Cannery Row.* New York: Penguin USA, 1993. Reprint ed. Here it is, a poem, a stink, a grating noise, told in the days when sardines still ruled the boardwalk on Monterey's Cannery Row. Also worth an imaginative sidetrip on a tour of the California coast is Steinbeck's *East of Eden,* first published in 1952, the Salinas Valley version of the Cain and Abel story. Steinbeck's classic California work, though, is still *The Grapes of Wrath.*

Stevenson, Robert Louis. *The Complete Short Stories of Robert Louis Stevenson: With a Selection of the Best Short Novels.* New York: Da Capo Press, 1998. It's hard to know where to start with Stevenson, whose California journeys served to launch his literary career. Da Capo's collection is as good a place as any.

Warshaw, Matt. *Maverick's.* San Francisco: Chronicle Books, 2000. Here it is, a full-color paen to the Santa Cruz area phenomenon known as Maverick's—and big-wave surfing in general.

WPA Guide to California: The Federal Writers Project Guide to 1930s California. New York: Pantheon Press (an imprint of Random House), 1984. The classic travel guide to California, first published during the Depression, is somewhat dated as far as contemporary sights but excellent as a companion volume and background information source.

WPA Guide to the Monterey Peninsula. Introduced by Page Stegner (son of Wallace Stegner). Tucson: University of Arizona Press, 1990. Another Federal Writers Project guide, long out of print in its original version, this more recent paperback version is also OP. Finding a used copy would be well worth it.

History and People

Adams, Ansel, with Mary Alinder. *Ansel Adams: An Autobiography.* Boston: Bulfinch Press, 1990. A compelling, expansive, enlightening sharing of self by the extraordinary photographer—not coincidentally also a generous, extraordinary human being, one who spent many years in Carmel.

Cleland, Robert Glass. *From Wilderness to Empire: A History of California.* New York: Alfred A. Knopf, 1944 (OP).

Gutiérrez, Ramon A., and Richard J. Orsi, eds. *Contested Eden: California Before the Gold Rush.* Berkeley: University of California Press, 1998. In this first volume of a projected four-part series, essays explore California before the gold rush.

Harlow, Neal. *California Conquered: The Annexation of a Mexican Province, 1846–1850.* Berkeley: University of California Press, 1982.

Heizer, Robert F. *The Destruction of the California Indians.* Utah: Gibbs Smith Publishing, 1974.

Heizer, Robert F., and Albert B. Elsasser. *The Natural World of the California Indians.* Berkeley: University of California Press, 1980. As an adjunct to the rest of Heizer's work, this fact-packed volume provides the setting—the natural environment, the village environment—for California's native peoples.

Heizer, Robert F., and M.A. Whipple. *The California Indians.* Berkeley: University of California Press, 1971. A worthwhile collection of essays about California's native peoples, covering general, regional, and specific topics—a good supplement to the work of A.L. Kroeber (who also contributed to this volume).

Hine, Robert V. *California's Utopian Colonies.* Berkeley: University of California Press, 1983.

Holiday, James. *The World Rushed In: The California Gold Rush Experience: An Eyewitness Account of a Nation Heading West.* New York: Simon and Schuster, 1981. Reprint of a classic history, made while new Californians were busy making up the myth.

Kroeber, Alfred L. *Handbook of the Indians of California.* New York: Dover Publications, 1976 (unabridged facsimile version of the original work, *Bulletin 78* of the Bureau of American Ethnology of the Smithsonian Institution, published by the U.S. Government Printing Office). The classic compendium of observed facts about California's native peoples by the noted UC Berkeley anthropologist who befriended Ishi—but also betrayed him, posthumously, by allowing his body to be autopsied (in violation of Ishi's beliefs) then shipping his brain to the Smithsonian Institution.

Margolin, Malcolm. *The Way We Lived.* Berkeley: Heyday Books, 1981. A wonderful collection of California native peoples' reminiscences, stories, and songs. Also by Margolin: *The Ohlone Way,* about the life of California's first residents of the San Francisco–Monterey Bay Area.

McCaffery, Jerry. *Lighthouse: Point Pinos.* Pacific Grove, CA: Jerry McCaffery, 2001. This gem of a book tells the story of the lighthouse at Point Pinos, starting in 1855 and continuing into the present. The story is particularly strong on Emily Fish, principal keeper from 1893 to 1914, sometimes known as the "socialite lightkeeper." Yet Emily, in the author's view, was the lighthouse's hero—"not a heroine in the fainting but persistent Scarlett O'Hara fashion" but a straight-on heroine who battled on behalf of the lighthouse for 21 years. Great black and white photos, lighthouse plans, timeline, and map of nearby shipwreck locations are included, along with select lightkeeper log entries.

McDonald, Linda, and Carol Cullen. *California Historical Landmarks.* Sacramento, CA: California Department of Parks and Recreation, 1997. Revised ed. Originally compiled in response to the National Historic Preservation Act of 1966, directing all states to identify all properties "possessing historical, architectural, archaeological, and cultural value," this updated edition covers more than 1,000 California Registered Historical Landmarks, organized by category—sites of aboriginal, economic, or government interest, for example—and indexed by county.

McWilliams, Carey, with a foreword by Lewis H. Lapham. *California, the Great Exception.* Berkeley: University of California Press, 1999. Historian, journalist, and lawyer Carey McWilliams, editor of *The Nation* from 1955 to 1975, stepped back from his other tasks in 1949 to assess the state of the Golden State at the end of its first 100 years. And while he acknowledged the state's prodigious productivity even then, he also noted the brutality with which the great nation-state of California dealt with "the Indian problem," the water problem, and the agricultural labor problem—all issues of continuing relevance to California today. McWilliams' classic work on the essence of California, reprinted with a new foreword by the editor of *Harper's* magazine, is a must-read for all Californians.

Milosz, Czeslaw. *Visions from San Francisco Bay.* New York: Farrar, Straus & Giroux, 1982. Essays on emigration from the Nobel Prize winner in literature. Originally published in Polish, 1969.

Monroy, Douglas. *Thrown Among Strangers: The Making of Mexican Culture in Frontier California.* Berkeley: University of California Press, 1990.

Nasaw, David. *The Chief: The Life of William Randolph Hearst.* New York: Mariner Books, 2001. A hot seller these days and named one of the best books of the year by the New York Times, the Los Angeles Times, the Washington Post, Business Week, and GQ, *The Chief* draws on papers and interviews that were previously unavailable, as well as on newly released documentation of interactions with such figures as Hitler, Mussolini, Churchill, every president from Grover Cleveland to Franklin Roosevelt, and movie giants Louis B. Mayer, Jack Warner, and Irving Thalberg. David Nasaw completes the picture of this colossal American "engagingly, lucidly and fair-mindedly," according to Arthur Schlesinger, Jr.

Pitt, Leonard. *Decline of the Californios: A Social History of the Spanish-Speaking Californians, 1846–1890.* Berkeley: University of California Press, 1966.

Powers, Stephen. *Tribes of California.* Berkeley: University of California Press, 1977.

Robinson, W.W. *Land in California: The Story of Mission Lands, Ranchos, Squatters, Mining Claims, Railroad Grants, Land Scrip, Homesteads.* Berkeley: University of California Press, 1979.

Rowland, Leon. *Santa Cruz the Early Years.* Santa Cruz, CA: Otter B Books, OP. A great little history if you can find it, originally privately published as four separate tracts in the 1940s by Santa Cruz newspaper reporter Leon Rowland.

Royce, Josiah. *California from the Conquest in 1846 to the Second Vigilance Committee in San Francisco 1856.* New York: AMS Press. Originally published in Boston, 1886.

St. Pierre, Brian. *John Steinbeck: The California Years.* San Francisco: Chronicle Books, 1983 (OP).

Saunders, Richard. *Ambrose Bierce: The Making of a Misanthrope.* San Francisco: Chronicle Books, 1984 (OP).

Starr, Kevin. *Americans and the California Dream: 1850–1915.* New York: Oxford University Press, 1973. A cultural history, written by a native San Franciscan, former newspaper columnist, onetime head of the city's library system, professor and historian, and current California State Librarian. The focus on Northern California taps an impressively varied body of sources as it seeks to "suggest the poetry and the moral drama of social experience" from California's first days of statehood through the Panama-Pacific Exposition of 1915 when, in the author's opinion, "California came of age."

Starr, Kevin. *The Dream Endures: California Enters the 1940s.* New York: Oxford University Press, 1997. This, the fifth volume in Kevin Starr's impressive California history series, traces the history of the California good life— in architecture, fiction, film, and leisure pursuits—and how it came to define American culture and society. Chosen Outstanding Academic Book of 1997 by *Choice,* and one of the best 100 books of 1997 by the *Los Angeles Times Book Review.*

Starr, Kevin. *Endangered Dreams: The Great Depression in California.* New York: Oxford University Press, 1996. "California," Wallace Stegner has noted, "is like the rest of the United States, only more so." And so begins the fourth volume of Starr's imaginative and immense California history, in which the author delves into the Golden State's dark past—a period in which strikes and unions were forcibly suppressed, soup kitchens became social institutions, and both socialism and fascism had their day.

Stevenson, Robert Louis. *From Scotland to Silverado.* Cambridge, MA: The Belknap Press of Harvard University Press, 1966. An annotated collection of the sickly and lovelorn young Stevenson's travel essays, including his first impressions of Monterey and San Francisco, and the works that have come to be known as *The Silverado Squatters.* Contains considerable text—marked therein—that the author's family and friends had removed from previous editions. A useful introduction by James D. Hart details the journeys and relationships behind the essays.

Stone, Irving. *Men to Match My Mountains.* New York: Berkeley Publishers, 1987. A classic California history, originally published in 1956.

Nature and Natural History

Alden, Peter. *National Audubon Society Field Guide to California.* New York: Alfred A. Knopf, 1998. A wonderful field guide to some 1,000 of the state's native inhabitants, from the world's smallest butterfly—the Western Pygmy Blue—to its oldest, largest, and tallest trees. Well illustrated with striking color photography.

Alt, David, and Donald Hyndman. *Roadside Geology of Northern & Central California.* Missoula, MT: Mountain Press, 1999. Second edition. The classic glovebox companion guide to the northstate landscape is now revised— and expanded to include central regions.

Bakker, Elna. *An Island Called California: An Ecological Introduction to Its Natural Communities.* Berkeley: University of California Press, 1985. Expanded revised ed. An excellent, time-honored introduction to the characteristics of, and relationships between, California's natural communities.

Balls, Edward K. *Early Uses of California Plants.* Berkeley: University of California Press, 1962.

Barbour, Michael, Bruce Pavlik, Susan Lindstrom, and Frank Drysdale, with a foreword by Pulitzer Prize-winning California poet Gary Snyder. *California's Changing Landscapes: Diversity and Conservation of California Vegetation.* Sacramento: California Native Plant Society Press, 1993. Finalist for the Publishers Marketing Association's 1994 Benjamin Franklin Award in the Nature category, this well-illustrated, well-indexed lay guide to California's astonishing botanical variety is an excellent introduction. For more in-depth personal study, the society also publishes some excellent regional floras and plant keys.

California Coastal Commission, State of California. *California Coastal Resource Guide.* Berkeley: University of California Press, 1997. This is the revised and expanded fifth edition of the California coast lover's bible, the indispensable guide to the Pacific coast and its wonders—the land, marine geology, biology—as well as parks, landmarks, and amusements. But for practical travel purposes, get the commission's *The California Coastal Access Guide,* listed under Enjoying the Outdoors below.

Clarke, Charlotte Bringle. *Edible and Useful Plants of California.* Berkeley: University of California Press, 1977. With this book in hand, almost anyone can manage to make a meal in the wilderness—or whip up a spring salad from the vacant lot next door.

Cogswell, Howard. *Water Birds of California.* Berkeley: University of California Press, 1977.

Collier, Michael. *A Land in Motion: California's San Andreas Fault.* Berkeley: University of California Press, 1999. An intriguing geologic tour of the world's most famous fault, which runs the entire length of western California—and right through the San Francisco Bay Area. Wonderful photographs.

Crampton, Beecher. *Grasses in California.* Berkeley: University of California Press, 1974.

Dawson, E. Yale, and Michael Foster. *Seashore Plants of California.* Berkeley: University of California Press, 1982.

Duremberger, Robert. *Elements of California Geography.* Out of print but worth searching for. This is the classic work on California geography.

Farrand, John Jr. *Western Birds: An Audubon Handbook.* New York: McGraw-Hill Book Co., 1988. This birding guide includes color photographs instead of artwork for illustrations; conveniently included with descriptive listings. Though the book contains no range maps, the "Similar Species" listing helps eliminate birds with similar features.

Fitch, John. *Tidepool and Nearshore Fishes of California.* Berkeley: University of California Press, 1975.

Fitch, John E., and Robert J. Lavenberg. *California Marine Food and Game Fishes.* Berkeley: University of California Press, 1971.

Fix, David, and Andy Bezener. *Birds of Northern California.* Renton, WA: Lone Pine Publishing, 2000. This great new birding guide includes detailed, full-color illustrations of 328 birds found in Northern California along with other visual identification aids; range maps; complete bird descriptions; and lesser-known facts about each bird.

Fradkin, Philip L. *The Seven States of California: A Natural and Human History.* New York: Henry Holt & Co., 1995; subsequently published in paperback by the University of California Press. Both personal and historical exploration of California.

Fuller, Thomas C., and Elizabeth McClintock. *Poisonous Plants of California.* Berkeley: University of California Press, 1987.

Suggested Reading

Garth, John S., and J.W. Tilden. *California Butterflies*. Berkeley: University of California Press, 1986. At long last, the definitive field guide and key to California butterflies (in both the larval and adult stages) is available, and in paperback; compact and fairly convenient to tote around.

Grillos, Steve. *Fern and Fern Allies of California*. Berkeley: University of California Press, 1966.

Hale, Mason, and Mariette Cole. *Lichens of California*. Berkeley: University of California Press, 1988.

Hedgpeth, Joel W. *Introduction to Seashore Life of the San Francisco Bay Region and the Coast of Northern California*. Berkeley: University of California Press, 1969.

Henson, Paul, Donald J. Usner, and Valerie Kells (illustrator). *The Natural History of Big Sur*. Berkeley: University of California Press, 1996. Both useful guide to Big Sur's public lands and a fascinating natural—geology, climate, flora, and fauna—and human history, this user-friendly book includes color photographs, drawings, maps, species lists, and a bibliography.

Hickman, Jim, ed. *The Jepson Manual: Higher Plants of California*. Berkeley: University of California Press (with cooperation and support from the California Native Plant Society and the Jepson Herbarium), 1993. Hot off the presses nearly 10 years ago but at least 10 years in the making, *The Jepson Manual* is the bible of California botany. The brainchild of both Jim Hickman and Larry Heckard, curator of the Jepson Herbarium, this book is a cumulative picture of the extraordinary flora of California, and the first comprehensive attempt to fit it all into one volume since the Munz *A California Flora* was published in 1959. The best work of almost 200 botanist-authors has been collected here, along with exceptional line drawings and illustrations (absent from the Munz flora) that make it easier to identify and compare plant species. This book is the botanical reference book for a California lifetime—a hefty investment for a hefty tome, especially essential for serious ecologists and botanists, amateur and otherwise.

Hill, Mary. *California Landscape: Origin and Evolution*. Berkeley: University of California Press, 1984. An emphasis on the most recent history of California landforms.

Houk, Walter, Sue Irwin, and Richard A. Lovett. *A Visitor's Guide to California's State Parks*, Sacramento, CA: California Department of Parks and Recreation, 1990. This large-format, very pretty book includes abundant full-color photography and brief, accessible basic information about the features and facilities of the state's parks and recreation areas. *A Visitor's Guide* is available at retail and online bookstores and at the state parks themselves.

Kaufman, Kenn. *Lives of North American Birds*. New York: Houghton Mifflin Co., 1997. Sponsored by the Roger Tory Peterson Institute. A bit bulky for a field guide but already considered a classic, this 674-page hardbound tome focuses less on identifying features and names and more on observing and understanding birds within the contexts of their own lives. Now, there's a concept.

Klauber, Laurence. *Rattlesnakes*. Berkeley: University of California Press, 1982.

Leatherwood, Stephen, and Randall Reeves. *The Sierra Club Handbook of Whales and Dolphins*. San Francisco: Sierra Club Books, 1983.

Le Boeuf, Burney J., and Stephanie Kaza. *The Natural History of Año Nuevo*. Santa Cruz, CA: Otter B Books, 1985. Reprint ed. An excellent, very comprehensive guide to the natural features of the Año Nuevo area just north of Santa Cruz.

Lederer, Roger. *Pacific Coast Bird Finder.* Berkeley: Nature Study Guild, 1977. A handy, hippocket-sized guide to birding for beginners. Also available: *Pacific Coast Tree Finder* by Tom Watts, among similar titles. All "Finder" titles are now available through Wilderness Press.

McCauley, Jane, and the National Geographic Society staff. *National Geographic Society Field Guide to the Birds of North America.* Washington, D.C.: National Geographic Society, 1993. One of the best guides to bird identification available.

McConnaughey, Bayard H., and Evelyn McConnaughey. *Pacific Coast.* New York: Alfred A. Knopf, 1986. One of the Audubon Society Nature Guides. More than 600 color plates, keyed to region and habitat type, make it easy to identify marine mammals, shorebirds, seashells, and other inhabitants and features of the West Coast, from Alaska to California.

McGinnis, Samuel. *Freshwater Fishes of California.* Berkeley: University of California Press, 1985. Including a simple but effective method of identifying fish, this guide also offers fisherfolk help in developing better angling strategies, since it indicates when and where a species feeds and what its food preferences are.

McMinn, Howard. *An Illustrated Manual of California Shrubs.* Berkeley: University of California Press, 1939. Reprint ed. An aid in getting to know about 800 California shrubs, this classic manual includes keys, descriptions of flowering, elevations, and geographic distributions. For the serious amateur botanist, another title for the permanent library.

Miller, Crane S., and Richard S. Hyslop. *California: The Geography of Diversity.* Palo Alto, CA: Mayfield Publishing Company, 1999. Second ed.

Munz, Phillip A., and David D. Keck. *A California Flora and Supplement.* Berkeley: University of California Press, 1968. Until fairly recently this was it, the California botanist's bible—a complete descriptive "key" to every plant known to grow in California—but quite hefty to tote around on pleasure trips. More useful for amateur botanists are Munz's *California Shore Wildflowers* and other illustrated plant guides published by UC Press.

Ornduff, Robert. *Introduction to California Plant Life.* Berkeley: University of California Press, 1974. An essential for native plant libraries, this classic offers a marvelous introduction to California's botanical abundance.

Orr, Robert T., and Roger Helm. *Marine Mammals of California.* Berkeley: University of California Press, 1989. Revised ed. A handy guide for identifying marine mammals along the California coast—with practical tips on the best places to observe them.

Orr, R.T., and D.B. Orr. *Mushrooms of Western North America.* Berkeley: University of California Press, 1979.

Pavlik, Bruce, Pamela Muick, Sharon Johnson, and Marjorie Popper. *Oaks of California.* Santa Barbara: Cachuma Press, 1991. In ancient European times, oaks were considered spiritual beings, the sacred inspiration of artists, healers, and writers since these particular trees were thought to court the lightning flash. Time spent with this stunning book will soon convince anyone that this truth lives on. Packed with photos and lovely watercolor illustrations, maps, even an oak lover's travel guide, this book celebrates the many species of California oaks.

Peterson, Roger Tory. *A Field Guide to Western Birds.* Boston: Houghton Mifflin Co., 1990. The third edition of this birding classic has striking new features, including full-color illustrations (including juveniles, females, and in-flight birds) facing the written descriptions. The only thing you'll have to flip around for are the range maps, tucked away in the back. Among other intriguing titles in the Peterson Field Guide series: *A Field Guide to Western Birds' Nests* by Hal Harrison.

Powell, Jerry. *California Insects.* Berkeley: University of California Press, 1980.

Raven, Peter H. *Native Shrubs of California.* Berkeley: University of California Press, 1966.

Raven, Peter H., and Daniel Axelrod. *Origin and Relationships of the California Flora.* Sacramento: California Native Plant Society Press, 1995. Reprint of the 1978 original, another title most appropriate for serious students of botany.

Rigsby, Michael A. (editor), and Lawrence Ormsby (illustrator). *The Natural History of Monterey Bay.* Boulder, CO: Roberts Rinehart Publishers, 1997. Here's a look-see beneath the waters of the nation's largest marine sanctuary, the first complete natural history of one of the most popular dive and tourist meccas in this country.

Robbins, Chandler, et al. *Birds of North America.* New York: Golden Books Publishing Co., 1983. A good field guide for California birdwatching.

Roos-Collins, Margit. *The Flavors of Home: A Guide to the Wild Edible Plants of the San Francisco Bay Area.* Berkeley: Heyday Books, 1990. Just the thing to help you whip up a fresh trailside salad, a botanical essay, field guide, and cookbook all in one.

Schmitz, Marjorie. *Growing California Native Plants.* Berkeley: University of California Press, 1980. A handy guide for those interested in planting, growing, and otherwise supporting the success of California's beleaguered native plants.

Schoenherr, Allan A. *A Natural History of California.* Berkeley: University of California Press,

1992. With introductory chapters on ecology and geology, *A Natural History* covers California's climate, geology, soil, plant life, and animals based on distinct bioregions, with almost 300 photographs and numerous illustrations and tables. An exceptionally readable and well-illustrated introduction to California's astounding natural diversity and drama written by an ecology professor from CSU Fullerton, this 700-some page reference belongs on any Californiac's library shelf.

Schoenherr, Allan A. and C. Robert Feldmeth. *A Natural History of the Islands of California.* Berkeley: University of California Press, 1999. A comprehensive introduction to California's Año Nuevo Island, Channel Islands, Farallon Islands, and the islands of San Francisco Bay—living evolutionary laboratories with unique species and ecological niches.

Starker, Leopold A. *The California Quail.* Berkeley: University of California Press, 1985. This is the definitive book on the California quail, its history and biology.

Stebbins, Robert. *California Amphibians and Reptiles.* Berkeley: University of California Press, 1972.

Wiltens, James. *Thistle Greens and Mistletoe: Edible and Poisonous Plants of Northern California.* Berkeley: Wilderness Press, 1988 (OP). How to eat cactus and pine cones and make gourmet weed salads are just a few of the fascinating and practical facts shared here about common northstate plants.

Enjoying the Outdoors: Recreation, Tours, Travel

California Coastal Commission, State of California. *The California Coastal Access Guide.* Berkeley: University of California Press, 1997. Fifth revised ed. According to the *Oakland Tribune,* this is "no doubt the most comprehensive look at California's coastline published to date."

Clark, Jeanne L. *California Wildlife Viewing Guide*. Helena, MT: Falcon Press, 1996. Second ed. This revised and expanded guide tells you where to go for a good look at native wildlife, and what to do once you're there. Color photos, overview maps.

Culliney, John, and Edward Crockett. *Exploring Underwater*. San Francisco: Sierra Club Books, 1980.

Jeneid, Michael. *Adventure Kayaking: Trips from the Russian River to Monterey*. Berkeley: Wilderness Press, 1998. Tired of fighting that freeway traffic around the Bay Area? Try a kayak. Under decent weather conditions—and with an experienced kayaker to clue you in—you can get just about everywhere. If you'll be shoving off a bit farther south, try *Adventure Kayaking: Trips from Big Sur to San Diego*, by Robert Mohle (1998).

Kirkendall, Tom, and Vicky Springs. *Bicycling the Pacific Coast*. Seattle: The Mountaineers, 1998. Third edition. A very good, very practical mile-by-mile guide to the tricky business of cycling along the California coast (and north).

Lorentzen, Bob, and Richard Nichols. *Hiking the California Coastal Trail, Volume One: Oregon to Monterey*. Mendocino, CA: Bored Feet Publications, 1998. The first comprehensive guide to the work-in-progress California Coastal Trail, America's newest and most diverse long-distance trail. Published in conjunction with Coastwalk—which receives a hefty percentage of the proceeds, to support its efforts to complete the trail—this accessible guide describes 85 sections of the California Coastal Trail's northern reach. Keep an eye out, too, for *Hiking the California Coastal Trail, Volume Two: Monterey to Mexico*.

McKinney, John. *Coast Walks: 150 Adventures Along the California Coast*. Santa Barbara: Olympus Press, 1999. The new edition of McKinney's coast hiking classic contains plenty of new adventures, from Border Field State Park at the Mexican Border north to Damnation Creek and Pelican Bay. Along the way, you'll also learn about local lore, history, and natural history—a bargain no matter how you hike it. Maps and illustrations.

McKinney, John. *Day Hiker's Guide to California State Parks*. Santa Barbara: Olympus Press, 2000. All you need to know to stretch your legs *and* see the sights in the Golden State's hikable parks and recreation areas.

Mitchell, Linda, and Allen Mitchell. *California Parks Access*. Berkeley: Cougar Pass Publications, 1992 (distributed by Wilderness Press). A very useful guide to national and state parks in California for visitors with limited mobility. Both challenges and wheelchair-accessible features are listed. Informationally accessible appendixes are helpful, too.

National Register of Historic Places, *Early History of the California Coast*. Washington, D.C.: National Conference of State Historic Preservation Officers, 1997. Map. This fold-out introduction to the California coast serves as a travel itinerary with 45 stops illustrating the coast's earliest settlement and culture.

Niesen, Thomas M. *Beachcomber's Guide to California Marine Life*. Houston: Gulf Publishing Co, 1994.

Perry, John, and Jane Greverus Perry. *The Sierra Club Guide to the Natural Areas of California*. San Francisco: Sierra Club Books, 1997. Second ed. A just-the-facts yet very useful guide to California's public lands and parks—a book to tuck into the glovebox. Organized by regions, also indexed for easy access.

Schaffer, Jeffrey. *Hiking the Big Sur Country: The Ventana Wilderness*. Berkeley: Wilderness Press, 1988. Other good hiking and backpacking guides by this prolific pathfinder include: *The Carson-Iceberg Wilderness; Desolation Wilderness and the South Lake Tahoe Basin; Lassen Volcanic National Park; The Pacific Crest Trail Volume 1: California; The Tahoe Sierra;* and *Yosemite National Park.*

Soares, Marc J. *Best Coast Hikes of Northern California: A Guide to the Top Trails from Big Sur to the Oregon Border.* San Francisco: Sierra Club Books, 1998. There's something for everyone here—75 scenic trails, organized north to south, suited for all skill levels (including mention of those that allow dogs). Also well worth it from Soares: *75 Year-Round Hikes in Northern California* and *100 Classic Hikes in Northern California,* the latter coauthored with John R. Soares.

Stevens, Barbara, and Nancy Conner. *Where on Earth: A Guide to Specialty Nurseries and Other Resources for California Gardeners.* Berkeley: Heyday Books, 1999. Fourth edition. Ever wondered where to get that unusual color of iris or that exotic azalea, or where to find the state's best native plant nurseries? Wonder no more. California gardeners won't be able to live for long without *this* essential resource.

Stienstra, Tom. *Foghorn Outdoors: California Camping—The Complete Guide to More Than 1,500 Campgrounds in The Golden State.* Emeryville, CA: Avalon Travel Publishing, 2001. Twelfth edition. This is undoubtedly the ultimate reference to California camping and campgrounds, public and private. Every single one is in here. Also included here are Stienstra's "Secret Campgrounds," an invaluable list when the aim is to truly get away from it all. In addition to a thorough practical introduction to the basics of California camping—and reviews of the latest high-tech gear, for hiking and camping comfort and safety—this guidebook is meticulously organized by

area, starting with the general subdivisions of Northern, Central, and Southern California. Even accidental outdoorspeople should carry this one along at all times.

Stienstra, Tom. *Foghorn Outdoors: California Fishing—The Complete Guide to More than 1,200 Fishing Spots.* Emeryville, CA: Avalon Travel Publishing, 2001. Sixth edition. This is it, *the* guide for people who think finding God has something to do with strapping on rubber waders or climbing into a tiny boat; making educated fish-eyed guesses about lures, ripples, or lake depths; and generally observing a strict code of silence in the outdoors. As besieged as California's fisheries have been by the state's 30 million-plus population and the attendant devastations and distractions of modern times, fisherfolk can still enjoy some world-class sport in California. This tome contains just about everything novices and masters need to know to figure out what to do as well as where and when to do it.

Taber, Tom. *The Santa Cruz Mountains Trail Book.* San Mateo, CA: Oak Valley Press, 1998. Eighth edition. Hey, trail lovers—beachcombers, off-road bicyclists, equestrians, and hikers—this book will keep you busy, with more than 1,000 miles of trails weaving through some 153,000 acres of mountains, forests, and coastline. The most popular coastal access guide to the Santa Cruz County coast and area parks and trails.

Thomas Bros., eds. *Thomas Guide, Metropolitan Monterey Bay: Including Monterey, Santa Cruz & San Benito Counties (Metropolitan Monterey Bay Street Guide).* Irvine, CA: Thomas Bros. Maps. Issued annually. This is it, the definitive spiral-bound map book to the area—probably essential only if you plan to stay awhile.

Index

Marine Reserves and Research Centers

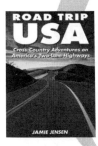

U.S.~Metric Conversion

1 inch	=	2.54 centimeters (cm)
1 foot	=	.304 meters (m)
1 yard	=	0.914 meters
1 mile	=	1.6093 kilometers (km)
1 km	=	.6214 miles
1 fathom	=	1.8288 m
1 chain	=	20.1168 m
1 furlong	=	201.168 m
1 acre	=	.4047 hectares
1 sq km	=	100 hectares
1 sq mile	=	2.59 square km
1 ounce	=	28.35 grams
1 pound	=	.4536 kilograms
1 short ton	=	.90718 metric ton
1 short ton	=	2000 pounds
1 long ton	=	1.016 metric tons
1 long ton	=	2240 pounds
1 metric ton	=	1000 kilograms
1 quart	=	.94635 liters
1 US gallon	=	3.7854 liters
1 Imperial gallon	=	4.5459 liters
1 nautical mile	=	1.852 km

To compute celsius temperatures, subtract 32 from Fahrenheit and divide by 1.8. To go the other way, multiply celsius by 1.8 and add 32.

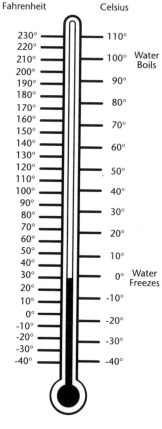

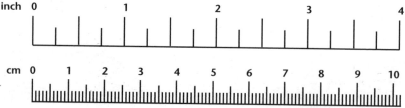